ADDITIONAL COOKBOOKS AND DVD SETS AVAILABLE FROM THE PUBLISHERS OF *COOK'S COUNTRY* INCLUDE:

The *America's Test Kitchen* Library Series

The *America's Test Kitchen* Do-It-Yourself Cookbook
Slow Cooker Revolution
The Best Simple Recipes
The *Cook's Country* Cookbook
Cook's Country Blue Ribbon Desserts
From Our Grandmothers' Kitchens
Cook's Country Best Potluck Recipes
Cook's Country Best Grilling Recipes
Cook's Country Annual Editions
from each year of publication (2005–2012)

From the Editors of *Cook's Illustrated*

The Science of Good Cooking
Cook's Illustrated Cookbook
The Best One-Dish Suppers
The *America's Test Kitchen* Menu Cookbook
Soups, Stews & Chilis
The New Best Recipe
The Best Skillet Recipes
The Best Slow and Easy Recipes
The Best Chicken Recipes
The Best International Recipe
The Best Make-Ahead Recipe
The Best 30-Minute Recipe
The Best Light Recipe
The *Cook's Illustrated* Guide to
Grilling and Barbecue
Best American Side Dishes
Cover & Bake
Steaks, Chops, Roasts, and Ribs
Baking Illustrated
Perfect Vegetables
Italian Classics
The Best American Classics
1993–2012 *Cook's Illustrated* Master Index
Cook's Illustrated Annual Editions
from each year of publication (1993–2012)

America's Test Kitchen

The Best of *America's Test Kitchen* (2007–2013 Editions)
Light & Healthy (2010–2012 Editions)
Cooking for Two (2009–2012 Editions)
The *America's Test Kitchen* Family Baking Book
The *America's Test Kitchen* Family Cookbook
The *America's Test Kitchen* Healthy Family Cookbook
The *America's Test Kitchen* Quick Family Cookbook

The *America's Test Kitchen* Series Companion Cookbooks

America's Test Kitchen: The TV Companion Cookbook (2013)
America's Test Kitchen: The TV Companion Cookbook (2012)
America's Test Kitchen: The TV Companion Cookbook (2011)
The Complete *America's Test Kitchen* TV Show Cookbook (2010)
America's Test Kitchen: The TV Companion Cookbook (2009)
Behind the Scenes with *America's Test Kitchen* (2008)
Test Kitchen Favorites (2007)
Cooking at Home with *America's Test Kitchen* (2006)
America's Test Kitchen Live! (2005)
Inside *America's Test Kitchen* (2004)
Here in *America's Test Kitchen* (2003)
The *America's Test Kitchen* Cookbook (2002)

The *America's Test Kitchen* Series DVD Sets
(featuring each season's episodes from our hit
public television series)

The *America's Test Kitchen* 4-DVD Set (2002–2012 Seasons)
The *America's Test Kitchen* 2-DVD Set (2001 Season)

The *Cook's Country* TV Series Cookbooks and DVD Sets
(featuring each season's episodes from our hit
public television series)

The Complete *Cook's Country* TV Show Cookbook
The *Cook's Country* 2-DVD Set (Seasons 1–5)

Visit our online bookstore at CooksCountry.com to order any of our cookbooks and DVDs listed above. You can also order subscriptions, gift subscriptions, and any of our cookbooks and DVDs by calling 800-611-0759 inside the U.S., or 515-246-6911 if calling from outside the U.S.

$35.00

Copyright © 2012 by The Editors of *Cook's Country*
All rights reserved, including the right of reproduction in whole or in part in any form.
Published by America's Test Kitchen, 17 Station Street, Brookline, MA 02445
ISBN-13: 978-1-936493-34-0 ISSN: 1552-1990

To get home delivery of *Cook's Country,* call 800-526-8447 inside the U.S., or 515-247-7571 if calling from outside the U.S.,
or subscribe online at CooksCountry.com.

2012 Recipe Index

Cook's Country

Dear Country Cook,

Irma Rombauer's Joy of Cooking was perhaps the best-named cookbook of all time, more inspirational than The Virginia Housewife, The Boston Cooking School Cook Book, or even Mastering The Art of French Cooking. In the 80-plus years since its publication, nutritionists, weight watchers, food scientists, quick-cooking promoters, and food safety experts have been working full time to scare us about what we eat or to help us cook less to enjoy life more. One is compelled to ask how we might use our time better than to stand in front of the stove preparing dinner.

Memory distills what is important. I remember the sights and smells of work, not play. Green hay. Sweat on a horse's flank. The wooden heft of whippletrees and the tangled weight of a working team's harness. The ripe scent of yeast and molasses in the front parlor as bread baked in the Kalamazoo cookstove. The froth of just-pumped milk. The scorching heat of a freshly baked potato.

Children understand this instinctively. Good cooks allow the senses to take over: chocolate faces, hands frescoed with sticky dough, waves of garlic or cumin or baking apples streaming airborne. Noses, tongues, and fingers come alive in the kitchen, where they become enthroned, crushing the mathematics of daily life.

When we step into the kitchen, we let go of ourselves and become children with sticky faces. Lick your lips and enjoy the mess.

Christopher Kimball
Founder and Editor, Cook's Country

Cook's Country

Founder and Editor Christopher Kimball
Editorial Director Jack Bishop
Executive Editor, Magazines John Willoughby
Executive Editor Peggy Grodinsky
Managing Editor Scott Kathan
Senior Editors Lisa McManus, Cali Rich, Bryan Roof, Diane Unger
Test Kitchen Director Erin McMurrer
Associate Editors Amy Graves, Sarah Wilson
Test Cooks Sarah Gabriel, Rebeccah Marsters, Kelly Price
Assistant Editors Hannah Crowley, Chris Dudley, Shannon Friedmann Hatch, Taizeth Sierra
Assistant Test Cooks Nick Iverson, Carolynn Purpura MacKay
Copy Editors Nell Beram, Megan Chromik
Executive Assistant Christine Gordon
Assistant Test Kitchen Director Gina Nistico
Senior Kitchen Assistants Meryl MacCormack, Leah Rovner
Kitchen Assistants Maria Elena Delgado, Andrew Straaberg Finfrock, Ena Gudiel
Executive Producer Melissa Baldino
Associate Producer Stephanie Stender

Contributing Editors Erika Bruce, Eva Katz, Jeremy Sauer
Consulting Editors Anne Mendelson, Meg Ragland
Science Editor Guy Crosby, Ph.D.
Executive Food Editor, TV, Radio & Media Bridget Lancaster

Online Managing Editor David Tytell
Online Editor Kate Mason
Online Assistant Editors Eric Grzymkowski, Mari Levine
Associate Editor/Camera Operator Nick Dakoulas

Design Director Amy Klee
Art Director, Magazines Julie Cote
Deputy Art Director Susan Levin
Designer Lindsey Timko
Staff Photographer Daniel J. van Ackere
Color Food Photography Keller + Keller
Styling Catrine Kelty
Associate Art Director, Marketing/Web Erica Lee
Designers, Marketing/Web Elaina Natario, Mariah Tarvainen
Online Photo Editor Steve Klise

Vice President, Marketing David Mack
Circulation Director Doug Wicinski
Circulation & Fulfillment Manager Carrie Fethe
Partnership Marketing Manager Pamela Putprush
Marketing Assistant Lauren Perkins
Customer Service Manager Jacqueline Valerio
Customer Service Representatives Jessica Amato, Morgan Ryan

Retail Sales & Marketing Manager Emily Logan
Client Service Manager, Sponsorship Bailey Snyder

Production Director Guy Rochford
Senior Project Manager Alice Carpenter
Production & Traffic Coordinator Kate Hux
Asset & Workflow Manager Andrew Mannone
Production & Imaging Specialists Judy Blomquist, Heather Dube, Lauren Pettapiece

Technology Director Rocco Lombardo
Systems Administrator Marcus Walser
Software Architect Robert Martinez
Software Project Manager Michelle Rushin
Senior Business Analyst Wendy Tseng
Web Developers Chris Candelora, Cameron MacKenzie

VP New Media Product Development Barry Kelly
Social Media Manager Steph Yiu

Chief Financial Officer Sharyn Chabot
Human Resources Manager Adele Shapiro
Publicity Deborah Broide
ON THE COVER:
Black and White Cookies, Keller + Keller, Catrine Kelty
ILLUSTRATION: Greg Stevenson

CORRECTION: December/January 2012 issue, Styling for the Color Food Photography by Catrine Kelty

Cook's Country magazine (ISSN 1552-1990), number 43, is published bimonthly by Boston Common Press Limited Partnership, 17 Station Street, Brookline, MA 02445. Copyright 2012 Boston Common Press Limited Partnership. Periodicals Postage paid at Boston, Mass., and additional mailing offices. Publications Mail Agreement No. 40020778. Return undeliverable Canadian addresses to P.O. Box 875, Station A, Windsor, Ontario N9A 6P2. POSTMASTER: Send address changes to Cook's Country, P.O. Box 8382, Red Oak, IA 51591-1382. Customer Service: It's easy to subscribe, give a gift subscription, change your address, and manage your subscription online. Visit www.AmericasTestKitchen.com/customerservice for all of your customer service needs or write to us at Cook's Country, P.O. Box 8382, Red Oak, IA 51591-1382. PRINTED IN THE USA

Contents

CORNED BEEF AND CABBAGE, 10

SOUR CREAM BISCUITS, 9

GRANDMA PIZZA, 12

Features

In Every Issue

Watch Us on Television

Watch the folks behind our recipes test equipment, taste ingredients, perfect classic American recipes, and stroll through food history. Find out when *Cook's Country from America's Test Kitchen* airs on public television in your area at **CooksCountryTV.com**.

Ask Cook's Country

BY SARAH GABRIEL

Can I substitute yogurt for buttermilk in recipes for pancakes and biscuits?

Alexis Garland Waller, Virginia Beach, Va.

To answer your question, we tested yogurt against buttermilk in a few of our favorite recipes: buttermilk biscuits, buttermilk pancakes, and lemon buttermilk sheet cake. Supermarket buttermilk is typically low fat, so for a fair comparison, we used low-fat yogurt. We made each recipe three times—once with buttermilk as usual, once with yogurt in place of the buttermilk, and once with a mixture of half yogurt and half low-fat milk (to thin the yogurt to the same consistency as buttermilk).

All three batches of biscuits and lemon-buttermilk sheet cakes turned out well. In our buttermilk pancakes, a one-for-one substitution of yogurt for buttermilk didn't turn out so well. The batter was too thick, in turn making too thick pancakes that didn't cook all the way through until the exteriors were too dark. The thinned yogurt performed well here, though. (You can also thin the yogurt with water to similar effect.)

THE BOTTOM LINE: When making cakes or biscuits, you can substitute low-fat yogurt for buttermilk. For pancakes, however, first thin the yogurt with an equal amount of low-fat milk or water.

When I finish a jar of store-bought pickles, there's always so much brine left over. Can I use that brine to make more pickles?

John Flajnik, Northampton, Mass.

To test this premise, we chopped up all kinds of vegetables—cucumbers, radishes, carrots, and celery—and put them in jars of leftover dill pickle brine. (No need to heat the brine, as is often done when pickling, since the salt was already dissolved and the spices already infused.) After four days, the vegetables had picked up a pleasant pickle-y flavor. But none was quite as acidic or salty as the original pickles. The reason? The cucumbers from the original pickles had released moisture into the brine, diluting it. Because the brine that's left over from a jar of pickles is thus less concentrated than fresh brine, the second round of vegetables is probably not truly pickled.

THE BOTTOM LINE: Use leftover pickle brine for quick refrigerator pickles, but never use it for canning, which requires a set level of acid for safe eating. Refrigerator pickles made with leftover pickle brine will not keep as long as those made with fresh brine; we suggest storing them (covered and refrigerated) for no longer than a week.

What's a quick way to turn the box of powdered mustard sitting in my cupboard into prepared mustard?

Jerome Coe, New Orleans, La.

Recipes for homemade, whole-grain mustard start with seeds, which require days of soaking. After that, the mustard itself needs weeks of ripening so the flavor can mellow and deepen. You want something homemade yet less of a commitment. We can understand that. So we started with the instructions on the side of the mustard box, which call for mixing equal parts water and dry mustard (sometimes called "mustard flour"). "It tastes like pain," reported one disgruntled taster. Increasing the water until we could taste the mustard without flinching, we ended up with ¼ cup of water to 1 tablespoon of dry mustard. Once the heat level was right, we balanced the flavor with a few ingredients common in prepared mustards: vinegar, sugar, and salt. Now it tasted right but it was too watery to spread on a hot dog or sandwich. Microwaving the mixture with 1½ teaspoons of cornstarch thickened it to condiment consistency.

A CLEVER CONDIMENT

EASY HOMEMADE MUSTARD
Makes about ½ cup mustard

- ¼ cup water
- 1 tablespoon dry mustard powder
- 1 tablespoon white wine vinegar
- 2 teaspoons packed light brown sugar
- 1½ teaspoons cornstarch
- ½ teaspoon salt

Whisk water, dry mustard, vinegar, brown sugar, cornstarch, and salt in 2-cup liquid measuring cup until combined. Microwave in 10-second intervals, whisking between intervals, until thickened (about 40–50 seconds of total microwaving).

I opened a bottle of vinegar the other day, and it had a strange white film floating on top. Is the vinegar spoiled?

Steve Johnstone-Mosher, Bronx, N.Y.

Actually, the film on top of your vinegar isn't a sign of spoilage. What you noticed is called a "mother." Vinegar mothers are gelatinous amalgamations of plant fiber from the vegetable or grain from which the vinegar was made and the acetic bacteria responsible for turning fruit and grain juices into vinegars. Vinegar needs bacteria and oxygen to form a mother; simply opening the bottle gives it access to both. Vinegar mothers come in a range of colors, from clear to black, and can be thick or thin. While the filmy mass floating on top will not harm the vinegar, it's best to remove it before it sinks, because once at the bottom of the bottle, the mother can die and begin to decay, producing off-flavors and unpleasant aromas.

THE BOTTOM LINE: If you find a filmy mass on top of your vinegar, just strain the vinegar into a clean bottle. If you find the filmy mass at the bottom of the bottle, give the vinegar a thorough sniff and taste it before using it.

Is it better to freeze a loaf of bread sliced or whole? Does sliced translate to more freezer damage?

Mattie Holland, Jamaica Plain, Mass.

Being able to defrost a loaf of bread slice by slice is an attractive option, especially if you can't eat the loaf before it stales or live in a humid climate where bread molds fast.

To find out if slicing before freezing would have any detrimental effects on bread, we baked and cooled two loaves of white bread. We sliced one and then put both in zipper-lock bags and froze them for a week. After thawing them at room temperature for several hours, we tasted the loaves side by side, as-is and toasted, and found them equally acceptable. We got the same results with storebought white bread. To see if the same held true for crustier breads, we repeated the test with baguettes and found that slicing before freezing worked equally well for crusty breads.

THE BOTTOM LINE: Slice loaves of bread before freezing them in heavy-duty zipper-lock bags if you don't plan to use the whole loaf at once. Take out slices as needed, and be sure to press the air out of the bag and reseal it tightly.

I've heard the best way to get neat poached eggs is to put eggs in their shells in the boiling water for one minute, remove them, and then crack them into the water as usual. Does this work?

Marianna Sachse, Philadelphia, Pa.

Who told you that? Don't do it. We cooked eggs in boiling water for one minute, and all it did was cook the outermost portion of the egg white, causing it to stick to the shell. Wondering if a less intense soak in hot tap water would work, we soaked more eggs. No dice. The egg white didn't stick, but the eggs didn't hold together any better than unsoaked eggs. If you want poached eggs without the loose, swirly bits of white, start with the freshest eggs you can get (the whites will be sturdier) and add 2 tablespoons of white vinegar to the water. The vinegar makes the water acidic, which helps set the egg whites quickly, before they get feathery and messy. Once the water (with vinegar) is at a simmer, crack the eggs into small cups with handles; that way, they'll be easy to slide into the water neatly and quickly.

THE BOTTOM LINE: For perfect poached eggs, bring a shallow skillet of salted, vinegar-ed water to a boil. Crack the eggs into small, handled cups. Slide the eggs into the skillet at the same time, turn off the heat, and cover the pan. After three to four minutes, remove the eggs with a slotted spoon.

READY TO POACH
The teacups make for easy, clean, fast handling of the cracked eggs.

To ask us a cooking question: Visit **CooksCountry.com/askcookscountry**. Or write to Ask Cook's Country, P.O. Box 470739, Brookline, MA 02447. Just try to stump us!

Kitchen Shortcuts

COMPILED BY NICK IVERSON

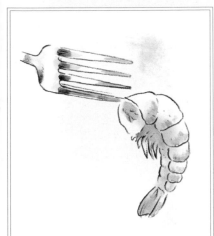

HANDY TIP
Easy Shrimp Shelling
Jen James, Tampa, Fla.

I found an easy way to peel shrimp with an unlikely tool: a fork. Insert one of the end tines into the cut (head) end of the shrimp and, following the curve of the top of the shrimp, pull up. I can then peel the shell and remove the vein (although with this method it often comes right out with the shell). Who says you need fancy gadgets for every kitchen chore?

COOL TRICK
Whip It Good
Molly Hubbard, Logan, Utah

If you've ever tried to whip just a few tablespoons of cream in your KitchenAid mixer, you've found out—like I did—that it doesn't work: The whip attachment doesn't reach deep enough into the bowl to reach the cream. I realized that if I place the whip on but don't lock it into place, it sits slightly lower in the bowl, won't fly off, and makes short work of whipping small amounts of cream.

CLEVER TIP
Ice-Cream Portioning
Gary Stach, Carmel, Ind.

I often make homemade ice-cream sandwiches, but it can be hard to scoop and spread the hard ice cream on fragile cookies. I discovered that I could use my "adjust-a-cup" measuring cup to make easy work of producing perfect ice-cream "disks" for sandwiches. I push the cup into the ice cream until I reach my desired depth, twist, and pull. I reattach the plunger and push the ice cream out onto the cookie.

HANDY TIP
Board Security
Tommy Collins, Portland, Ore.

I used to have problems with my cutting board sliding all over the place when I was using it, which is unsafe, to say the least. To stop the slipping and sliding, I put a small piece of no-skid shelf liner on the counter under the board. It holds the board in place.

NEAT TIP
Icing on the Cake
Danica Hoffman, Wynstone, S.D.

I'm a good baker but not the world's best cake decorator. More than once I've had to scrape the top of a cake clean after messing up the decorative message (I usually run out of space before I finish my message). But I've found a simple solution: I first "mark" the message lightly with a toothpick to make sure it fits and is correct, and then I trace over it with the frosting.

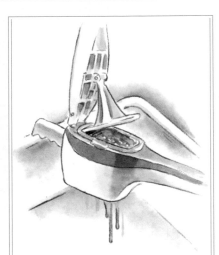

DOUBLE DUTY
Easy Squeeze
Dorothy Gendron, Portland, Maine

We eat a lot of frozen spinach in our house, and I've ruined more than one dish towel wringing the water from the cooked vegetable. Instead of staining more towels, I now use my potato ricer to wring out the spinach. As a bonus, the dried "puck" of spinach is easy to chop.

DOUBLE DUTY
Easy Cheesy
Suzi Hinch, Chicago, Ill.

I've found a cool new use for my waffle iron: I use it to make grilled cheese sandwiches. Prepare the sandwich as usual, butter it up, put it in the hot waffle iron, and close the lid. In about three minutes (no flipping!), you'll have a perfectly crusty, toasty sandwich with plenty of waffled nooks and crannies.

Submit a tip by e-mail at **CooksCountry.com/kitchenshortcuts** or send a letter to Kitchen Shortcuts, *Cook's Country*, P.O. Box 470739, Brookline, MA 02447. Include your name, address, and phone number. If we publish your tip, you will receive a free one-year subscription to *Cook's Country*. Letters may be edited for clarity or length.

Pan-Roasted Chicken and Vegetables

Juicy roast chicken and tender root vegetables complement each other on the plate.
But could they work together in the oven? BY REBECCAH MARSTERS

Roast chicken and vegetables holds the promise of a satisfying, uncomplicated supper that's so easy you hardly need a recipe. But if you casually scatter a few potatoes, onions, and carrots around a whole bird, the vegetables are mushy and scorched by the time the chicken is done an hour later. You could pull the vegetables out early (or start them late), sure, but I wanted everything to go into the oven at the same time, come out at the same time, and still be perfectly cooked. In other words, I wanted roast chicken and vegetables, without the fuss or rigmarole.

Most of the recipes I found featured whole birds and included steps like flipping the chicken over and/or pouring off the fat partway through cooking. To shorten and simplify the cooking, I decided to start with a chicken's worth of pieces (you can, of course, buy a whole chicken and break it down yourself). Then I'd need sturdy vegetables that could absorb the flavorful juices without falling apart to roast alongside the chicken. I settled on skin-on red potatoes, carrots, and Brussels sprouts. To them I added halved shallots and whole garlic cloves, both of which would soften and mellow in the oven. Fresh rosemary and thyme rounded out the flavors.

I cut the vegetables into chunks; tossed them with salt, pepper, rosemary, thyme, and oil; laid them out on a sheet pan; and placed the chicken pieces on top, skin side up so the fat could render and baste both the meat and the vegetables. Since I pictured this as a weeknight dinner, I knew I'd want it fast, so I set the pan in a hot 450-degree oven. A little less than an hour later, the chicken was ready.

The results of this first test were mixed. The vegetables were tender and flavorful (from the drippings), although the Brussels sprouts were charred around the edges. As for the chicken, I ran into a common poultry predicament: By the time the dark meat was cooked, the white meat (which is leaner and cooks to a slightly lower temperature) had dried out. I wondered if I could place the legs and thighs, which can take more heat, on the hotter perimeter of the pan, while leaving the more delicate breasts in the cooler center. This arrangement resulted in moist meat, both dark and light. With this success under my belt, I realized that the problem with the meat was similar to the one with the vegetables. The Brussels sprouts cooked faster than hardier spuds and carrots. Did the sprouts need to be in the "cooler zone," too? For my next test, I treated the vegetables as before but arranged them differently, with the sprouts in the center and the potatoes and carrots huddled around them. My strategy worked.

But despite well-cooked meat and vegetables, the chicken skin remained limp and pale. I increased the temperature to 475 degrees. The hotter oven

▶ To see our testing of instant-read thermometers, search for "inexpensive thermometers" at **CooksCountry.com**.

Another bonus of roasting chicken parts instead of a whole bird? There's no carving to be done.

not only gave the skin better color but also shaved about 15 minutes off the cooking time. Raising the oven rack, which gets the pan into the hottest part of the oven (heat rises), moved me another step closer to crisp, nicely browned chicken. Finally, brushing the raw chicken pieces with melted butter helped the skin crisp more thoroughly and added more savory flavor, too.

As I was testing another batch of chicken, I spied the chopped herbs on my cutting board waiting to get tossed with the vegetables, and I got the idea to mix some of them into the butter for extra flavor. Forty minutes later, the chicken skin was golden brown and the meat—both light and dark—cooked just right. Tossing the chopped vegetables with a little sugar before roasting helped them get nice and brown and caramelized, too.

After several weeks of testing, I'd created a deliciously satisfying one-pan meal. I could put protein, starch, and vegetable out for dinner in one easy go, offering plenty of variety—not to mention extra time for the cook—but few dishes to clean later.

PAN-ROASTED CHICKEN WITH ROOT VEGETABLES
Serves 4
We halve the chicken breasts crosswise for even cooking. Use Brussels sprouts no bigger than golf balls, as larger ones are often tough and woody.

- ¾ **pound Brussels sprouts, trimmed and halved**
- ¾ **pound red potatoes, cut into 1-inch pieces**
- ½ **pound shallots, peeled and halved**
- 4 **carrots, peeled and cut into 2-inch pieces, thick ends halved lengthwise**
- 6 **garlic cloves, peeled**
- 4 **teaspoons minced fresh thyme**
- 1 **tablespoon vegetable oil**
- 2 **teaspoons minced fresh rosemary**
- 1 **teaspoon sugar**
  Salt and pepper
- 2 **tablespoons unsalted butter, melted**
- 3½ **pounds bone-in chicken pieces (2 split breasts cut in half crosswise, 2 drumsticks, and 2 thighs), trimmed**

1. Adjust oven rack to upper-middle position and heat oven to 475 degrees. Toss Brussels sprouts, potatoes, shallots, carrots, garlic, 2 teaspoons thyme, oil, 1 teaspoon rosemary, sugar, ¾ teaspoon salt, and ¼ teaspoon pepper together in bowl. Combine butter, remaining 2 teaspoons thyme, remaining 1 teaspoon rosemary, ¼ teaspoon salt, and ⅛ teaspoon pepper in second bowl; set aside.

2. Pat chicken dry with paper towels and season with salt and pepper. Place vegetables in single layer on rimmed baking sheet, arranging Brussels sprouts

in center. Place chicken, skin side up, on top of vegetables, arranging breast pieces in center and leg and thigh pieces around perimeter of sheet.

3. Brush chicken with herb butter and roast until breasts register 160 degrees and drumsticks/thighs register 175 degrees, 35 to 40 minutes, rotating pan halfway through cooking. Transfer chicken to serving platter, tent loosely with aluminum foil, and let rest for 5 to 10 minutes. Toss vegetables in pan juices and transfer to platter with chicken. Serve.

PAN-ROASTED CHICKEN WITH FENNEL AND PARSNIPS
Replace Brussels sprouts and carrots with 1 fennel bulb, stalks discarded, bulb halved, cored, and sliced into ½-inch wedges, and ½ pound (4 medium) parsnips, peeled and cut into 2-inch pieces.

Quicker Turtle Brownies

BY CAROLYNN PURPURA MACKAY

THE TEST KITCHEN'S Ultimate Turtle Brownies are incredibly delicious, but they call for three different kinds of chocolate plus homemade caramel. Call me lazy, but I hoped to create a similarly tasty recipe with less time and effort.

I started by making two trays of *Cook's Country*'s Basic Brownies, emphasis on "basic," and topping one with jarred caramel sauce and the other with melted caramel candies. The jarred sauce was a goopy mess, and the melted caramels, although tasty, were a little waxy and created a skin that peeled off in a single leathery layer. Worse, the brownies were soggy because the sugar in the caramel added too much moisture. Decreasing the sugar and increasing the flour in the brownie batter seemed to fix the moisture level, but I still had to fix the caramel.

To prevent waxiness in the melted caramels, I melted them with a little cream. But the solidified caramel layer still peeled off. What about putting the caramel layer inside the brownies instead of on top? I poured half of the batter into the pan, layered on the melted caramel, topped it with the rest of the batter, and baked it. The caramel disappeared into the bottom brownie layer.

Ultimately, I found a surprising solution: I parbaked the bottom, only then sprinkled on the nuts and poured on the caramel, and topped it with the remaining batter and more pecans. When the brownies were done, I gave them a finishing drizzle of more caramel.

QUICKER TURTLE BROWNIES
Makes 16 brownies
Hershey's Unsweetened Baking Bar is our taste-test winner. Toast the pecans in a 350-degree oven for 5 to 10 minutes, stirring often, until lightly browned and fragrant.

- ¾ **cup (3 ounces) cake flour**
- ½ **teaspoon baking powder**
- ½ **teaspoon salt**
- 6 **tablespoons unsalted butter, cut into 1-inch pieces**
- 3 **ounces unsweetened chocolate, chopped fine**
- 1 **cup (7 ounces) sugar**
- 2 **large eggs**
- 2¼ **teaspoons vanilla extract**
- 20 **soft caramel candies**
- 3 **tablespoons heavy cream**
- 1¼ **cups (5 ounces) pecans, toasted and chopped**

To get the caramel flavor to really register, we added a layer inside the brownies.

1. Adjust oven rack to middle position and heat oven to 325 degrees. Make foil sling by folding 2 long sheets of aluminum foil so that they are as wide as 8-inch baking pan. Lay sheets of foil in pan perpendicular to each other, with extra foil hanging over edges of pan. Push foil into corners and up sides of pan, smoothing foil flush to pan. Spray with vegetable oil spray.

2. Combine flour, baking powder, and ¼ teaspoon salt in bowl. Microwave butter and chocolate in large bowl, stirring occasionally, until smooth, about 1 minute. Whisk sugar, eggs, and 1½ teaspoons vanilla into chocolate mixture. Add flour mixture in 3 additions, mixing until combined. Scrape ¾ cup batter into prepared pan and spread into even layer. Bake until center is just set, 12 to 14 minutes.

3. Meanwhile, microwave caramels, cream, remaining ¾ teaspoon vanilla, and remaining ¼ teaspoon salt in bowl, stirring occasionally, until smooth, 1 to 2 minutes. Reserve 2 tablespoons caramel mixture for topping. Sprinkle parbaked brownies with half of pecans and pour remaining caramel mixture evenly over pecans. Top with remaining brownie batter and remaining pecans. Bake until toothpick inserted in center comes out with few dry crumbs attached, 25 to 30 minutes.

4. Let brownies cool in pan on wire rack for 1 hour. Reheat reserved caramel mixture in microwave for 30 seconds, drizzle over brownies, and let sit for 30 minutes. Using foil overhang, lift brownies from pan and cut into 16 pieces. Serve. (Brownies can be stored at room temperature for up to 3 days.)

Company's Coming Meatloaf

Stuffing an ordinary meatloaf with ham and cheese turns it into something special—provided you can keep the meat and cheese in place. BY KELLY PRICE

This pleasantly crusty, moist meatloaf has a secret: a ham and cheese filling hiding inside.

KEY STEPS Avoiding a Blowout

1. To make the meatloaf base, spread half of the meat mixture into a 10 by 6-inch rectangle on a rimmed, foil-lined baking sheet.

2. Layer the ham and cheese in the center of the rectangle, leaving a 1-inch border on all sides so the meatloaf can be properly sealed.

3. Form the remaining meatloaf mixture into a 9 by 5-inch rectangle and center it over the filling. Fold the bottom edge up over the top layer and pinch the edges together to seal.

I'VE EATEN IT with vegetables and without, glazed or simply browned, free-form or baked in a loaf pan, with gravy and all by itself. In short, I thought I'd tried all that meatloaf had to offer. Then I got wind of stuffed meatloaf, a simultaneously homey yet dressy dish apparently being eaten (or at least blogged about) from coast to coast. After making a few loaves from several of these online recipes and tasting a crazy array of fillings—lasagna, anyone?—I was sold on a meatloaf stuffed with a particularly satisfying combination of salty, savory ham and oozy, creamy cheese.

It was a promising blend, but there were definitely kinks. The meatloaf itself was bland and wet. Also, something had caused a cheese blowout on one side. Any cheese that hadn't leaked out was broken and greasy. I wanted a neat layer of ham and creamy cheese securely encased in a robust, flavorful meatloaf, and that's not what I was getting.

In the test kitchen, we already have several terrific meatloaf recipes. My favorite is made with equal parts beef and pork, enhanced with Worcestershire sauce, and topped with a ketchup glaze. Why reinvent the wheel? I hoped to take this great basic recipe, make some tweaks, and start stuffing. Taking a cue from many of the blog meatloaves I had tried, I started my testing with sliced deli ham and shredded provolone cheese.

Also following the blogosphere's lead, I tried different stuffing techniques. For one, I pressed the meatloaf mix flat and thin, layered the ham and cheese on top, rolled it up like a pinwheel, and put the whole thing in a loaf pan. This method was laborious, and since the meatloaf cooked in a loaf pan, moisture couldn't evaporate, making the meat soggy. In another test, I rolled the ham and cheese into a tube and built a meatloaf around it. This tubular version had a molten ham and cheese core, so the center bite was fantastic. The outer bites, however, were just plain old meatloaf. For my third attempt, I patted half of the meatloaf mixture into a free-form loaf on a baking sheet, layered the ham and cheese over it, and topped them with the rest of the meatloaf mix. This simple layering technique resulted in better ham and cheese distribution, plus with no loaf pan, the top and sides of the meatloaf developed a nice, brown crust.

With the assembly method settled,

I turned to cheese blowout prevention. Despite my best efforts to seal it in, some of the cheese had oozed out. Making test meatloaf after test meatloaf taught me to leave a 1-inch border around the ham and cheese so that the meatloaf mix met meatloaf mix to form a seal. Second, I learned to pat out the bottom half of the meatloaf slightly bigger than the top. That way, I could wrap the bottom up over the top layer, forming a barrier to escaping cheese.

The filling was finally sealed inside, but that very success created new problems. The cheese was curdled, and the moisture from the contained filling made the interior of the loaf wet. I switched the provolone for Monterey Jack, since it's creamier and less prone to breaking. At the same time, I tossed a tablespoon of cornstarch with the cheese to ensure that it wouldn't curdle. To solve the mushy meat situation, I tried 90 percent lean beef in place of the 85 percent I had been using, hypothesizing that leaner beef would counterbalance the fatty ham and cheese filling. This loaf emerged from the oven juicy and moist, not soggy and mushy.

Tasters loved my classic glaze of ketchup, brown sugar, vinegar, and hot sauce slathered on top. Usually, meatloaf is glazed after it's baked. But the test kitchen has developed a method that reverses the order by browning the meatloaf under the broiler, glazing, briefly broiling again, and then lowering the temperature to cook the meatloaf through. This lets the meatloaf develop a dry crust for the glaze to cling to. All glazed up and ready to go, this was a meatloaf with a delectable secret inside.

HAM-AND-CHEESE-STUFFED MEATLOAF Serves 6 to 8

GLAZE
- 1 cup ketchup
- ¼ cup packed brown sugar
- 2½ tablespoons cider vinegar
- 1 teaspoon hot sauce

MEATLOAF
- 16 saltines
- 1 tablespoon vegetable oil
- 1 onion, chopped fine
- 4 garlic cloves, minced
- 1 pound ground pork
- 1 pound 90 percent lean ground beef

- 2 large eggs, lightly beaten
- 1 tablespoon Worcestershire sauce
- 2 teaspoons dry mustard
  Salt and pepper
- 4 ounces Monterey Jack cheese, shredded (1 cup)
- 1 tablespoon cornstarch
- 3 ounces thinly sliced deli ham

1. FOR THE GLAZE: Whisk ketchup, sugar, vinegar, and hot sauce together in small saucepan until combined; reserve ¼ cup. Bring remaining glaze to simmer over medium heat and cook until slightly thickened, about 5 minutes; set aside.

2. FOR THE MEATLOAF: Adjust oven racks to upper (about 6 inches away from broiler element) and middle positions and heat broiler. Line rimmed baking sheet with aluminum foil and coat lightly with vegetable oil spray. Process saltines in food processor until finely ground, about 30 seconds; transfer to large bowl.

3. Heat oil in 12-inch skillet over medium-high heat until shimmering. Add onion and cook until browned, 6 to 8 minutes. Add garlic and cook until fragrant, about 30 seconds. Transfer to bowl with saltines and let cool to room temperature, about 15 minutes. Add pork, beef, eggs, Worcestershire, mustard, 1 teaspoon salt, and ¾ teaspoon pepper to saltine mixture and knead gently to combine.

4. Combine cheese and cornstarch in medium bowl. Spread half of meat mixture on prepared baking sheet in 10 by 6-inch rectangle. Layer half of ham on meat, leaving 1-inch border on all sides. Sprinkle half of cheese mixture over ham. Repeat with remaining ham and remaining cheese mixture. Form remaining meatloaf mixture into 9 by 5-inch rectangle and place on top of prepared meatloaf bottom, leaving border exposed. Fold bottom edge of meatloaf up over top layer and pinch edges together tightly to seal.

5. Broil meatloaf on upper rack until spotty brown, 6 to 8 minutes. Brush 2 tablespoons uncooked glaze evenly over top and sides of meatloaf and continue to broil until glaze begins to brown, about 1 minute. Move meatloaf to middle rack and brush with remaining 2 tablespoons uncooked glaze. Reduce oven temperature to 350 degrees and bake until meatloaf registers 160 degrees, 30 to 35 minutes. Transfer to carving board, tent with foil, and let rest for 30 minutes. Warm reserved glaze. Slice meatloaf and serve, passing warm glaze at table.

Potatoes Hashed in Cream

From the annals of potato history comes the best potato dish you've never heard of. And a "mistake" made it even better. BY KELLY PRICE

CULINARY INSPIRATION CAN strike in many ways. For me, sometimes all it takes is finding a passing reference to a recipe—in this case, potatoes hashed in cream—in an old cookbook. When I dug a little deeper, I uncovered several recipes, all of which started with leftover boiled potatoes that were cut up, or "hashed." The cooked potato pieces were then either simmered or baked in a thick cream sauce.

These recipes yielded potatoes that were creamy in both flavor and texture but also a little mushy and flat-tasting. For my version, I'd start with raw potatoes to avoid overcooking, and I'd crisp them at the end for a more appealing texture.

Knowing that I'd ultimately need a skillet to do the crisping, I decided to simmer the potatoes in there as well, saving myself a pot. I cut Yukon Gold potatoes (a test kitchen favorite for their medium starch content and creamy texture) into ½-inch cubes and in just six minutes cooked them, covered, to tenderness in water. I then uncovered the pan, let the water boil off, and added cream and butter. The cream reduced and the butter helped the potatoes brown. These potatoes were good but not especially creamy inside or crisp outside.

Maybe I could improve the interior texture (and add flavor) by simmering the potatoes right in the cream instead of in water. Tasters unanimously preferred the potatoes made in cream, and the extra few minutes' cooking time this took was well worth it. After removing the lid and bringing the cream to a boil, I noticed something curious. As the cream reduced, it began to separate, with the milk solids adhering to the potatoes while the fat stayed at the bottom of the pan, where it began to

The naturally creamy texture of Yukon Gold potatoes reinforces the creaminess of this dish.

crisp the potatoes. Usually, when cream separates into its components (water, milk solids, and fat), it's a catastrophe, but in this instance, it was actually helping the potatoes brown. Our science editor explained that, because of its high fat content, cream rarely separates (or "breaks"). But the presence of an acid can trigger breaking, and potatoes, apparently, are just acidic enough.

Hey, if the potatoes could crisp in the fat from the cream, why bother with the butter? In a side-by-side test of potatoes, hashed with butter and without, we found it superfluous. This test also taught me to be miserly with the spoon: If I stirred too much, I agitated the fats away from the bottom of the pan and the potatoes never browned.

Consisting of potatoes, cream, and nothing more—unless you count salt and pepper—this may be the easiest potato dish in my repertoire. But the luscious texture is anything but basic.

KEY TECHNIQUE
Fry in Cream

LOOK, MA, NO BUTTER
After the potatoes have simmered and softened in cream, they crisp in its fat.

POTATOES HASHED IN CREAM
Serves 6

It's essential to use a nonstick skillet here. After removing the lid, stir the potatoes no more than five or six times or they won't brown.

- 2½ pounds Yukon Gold potatoes, peeled and cut into ½-inch pieces
- 1 cup heavy cream
  Salt and pepper

1. Bring potatoes, cream, and 1¼ teaspoons salt to boil in 12-inch nonstick skillet over medium-high heat. Cover, reduce heat to medium-low, and simmer until nearly tender, about 10 minutes.

2. Remove lid, increase heat to medium-high, and cook, stirring occasionally, until liquid evaporates and potatoes are well browned, 15 to 20 minutes. Season with salt and pepper to taste, and serve.

Country-Fried Pork with Gravy

Though nice and tender, this little piggy was too bland.

BY DIANE UNGER

Mild pork tenderloin needs assertive gravy. Ours has garlic, sage, paprika, and Worcestershire.

KEY STEPS To Better Breading

For a craggy, crisp coating that sticks to the pork, follow these steps.

SCORE Use a chef's knife to mark the meat in a crosshatch pattern on both sides. This helps the flour adhere.

FLOUR AND POUND Dredge the scored tenderloin pieces in seasoned flour, wrap in plastic, and pound to ¼ inch.

COAT Dredge the pounded pork in flour again, dip it in the egg mixture, and coat it in the moistened, seasoned flour.

"COUNTRY FRIED" IS a controversial term that means different things in different parts of the country. Call me stubborn, but no matter where I'm hanging my hat, country fried means tender, juicy meat that's shallow fried and firmly encased in a crunchy flour coating. The meat that's most often country fried is beef (as in chicken-fried steak). But I'd seen recipes for country-fried pork, and I wanted to give that a try. I had in mind moist, tender pork with a crisp, bumpy coating—lots of nooks and crannies to capture the flavorful, creamy gravy.

Country-fried meats are always boneless, so I started with boneless pork loin, which I sliced and pounded into thin cutlets before dredging and frying. But tasters found the pounded loin a little chewy. Why not use a cut of pork that is supremely tender to begin with: the tenderloin? A single 1-pound tenderloin is easy to cut into four pieces. Instead of flipping the tenderloin pieces onto their cut sides to pound them out (as other recipes do), I found I got more even pieces if I pounded them without flipping. What's more, pounding them to ¼-inch thick this way resulted in oblong cutlets that easily fit two at a time in the skillet.

Now that I had the right cut of pork, I considered how best to cook it. Several years ago, we developed a recipe for chicken-fried steak. In that case, we'd scored the beef (to help the coating adhere) and then lightly coated it in seasoned flour before pounding it. But this was not your standard seasoned flour. In addition to the usual seasonings, we'd introduced baking powder (for lightness) and cornstarch (to dry the surface and create a super-crisp crust). Finally, to make the coating craggy, we moistened part of the flour mixture with milk and rubbed the mixture until it resembled coarse meal. I wondered if that method would work for pork, too. I adapted the ratios slightly, seasoned heavily, and then followed the procedure, refrigerating the pork for 15 minutes after its final dredging so the coating could set. (Later tests showed that it could hold up to four hours at this stage.) Then I tested the pork in bubbling oil. Happily, this method translated perfectly to pork. Now I had the crisp coating, but

there was still the matter of flavor. To compensate for the tenderloin's blandness, I'd create a super-charged gravy. Most recipes called for making the gravy after frying, but since I didn't want my country-fried pork sitting around getting soggy while awaiting its mate, I'd need to reverse the order. The drawback, though, was that I wouldn't have those browned bits that stuck to the bottom of the pot after cooking the pork, which give the gravy much of its flavor. So I turned to other flavor enhancers. I replaced some of the milk in traditional cream gravy with chicken broth; then added chopped onion along with garlic, lots of dried sage, and paprika; and simmered everything for about 10 minutes to thicken. To finish, I stirred in a generous amount of Worcestershire sauce and took the "more is better" approach with the pepper mill.

The bold gravy lent the lean pork big flavor that one taster described as "the opposite of bland." And that's just what you want out of country-fried pork, no matter where you hang your hat.

COUNTRY-FRIED PORK WITH GRAVY Serves 4

Make the gravy first so the crisp pork doesn't turn soggy waiting for it.

GRAVY

- 3 tablespoons unsalted butter
- ¼ cup finely chopped onion
- 3 tablespoons all-purpose flour
- 1 garlic clove, minced
- 1 teaspoon dried sage leaves
- ½ teaspoon paprika
- 2 cups low-sodium chicken broth
- 1 cup whole milk
- 4 teaspoons Worcestershire sauce
  Salt and pepper

PORK

- 2 cups all-purpose flour
- ½ cup cornstarch
- 2 teaspoons garlic powder
- 2 teaspoons onion powder
  Salt and pepper
- 1½ teaspoons baking powder
- ¼ teaspoon cayenne pepper
- ½ cup whole milk
- 2 large eggs
- 1 (1-pound) pork tenderloin, trimmed, cut crosswise into 4 pieces
- 1 cup peanut or vegetable oil

Sour Cream Biscuits

The sour cream biscuits we tried were either salty, soapy, or tough. We aimed to keep the process simple but fix the taste and texture. BY SARAH GABRIEL

1. FOR THE GRAVY: Melt butter in medium saucepan over medium heat. Add onion and cook until softened, about 5 minutes. Stir in flour, garlic, sage, and paprika and cook, whisking constantly, until golden and fragrant, about 1 minute. Slowly whisk in broth and milk and bring to boil. Reduce heat to medium-low and simmer until thickened, about 10 minutes. Off heat, stir in Worcestershire sauce and season with salt and pepper to taste. Cover and set aside. (Gravy can be refrigerated for up to 2 days.)

2. FOR THE PORK: Meanwhile, combine flour, cornstarch, garlic powder, onion powder, 2 teaspoons pepper, 1 teaspoon salt, baking powder, and cayenne in bowl. Transfer 1 cup seasoned flour to shallow dish. Whisk 6 tablespoons milk and eggs together in second shallow dish. Stir remaining 2 tablespoons milk into remaining seasoned flour, rub with fingers until mixture resembles coarse meal, and transfer to third shallow dish.

3. Pat pork dry with paper towels and season with salt and pepper. Lightly score both uncut sides of pork pieces in ¼-inch crosshatch pattern. Working 1 piece at a time, coat pork lightly in seasoned flour. Place pork between 2 sheets plastic wrap and pound to ¼-inch thickness; remove plastic. Coat pork again with seasoned flour, dip into egg mixture, and dredge in milk and flour mixture, pressing firmly to adhere. Arrange pork on wire rack set inside rimmed baking sheet and refrigerate for 15 minutes or up to 4 hours.

4. Adjust oven rack to middle position and heat oven to 200 degrees. Warm gravy over medium-low heat, stirring occasionally. Heat oil in 12-inch skillet over medium heat until shimmering. Fry 2 pieces pork until deep golden brown and crisp, 2 to 3 minutes per side. Drain on clean wire rack set in rimmed baking sheet and place in oven. Fry remaining pork. Serve with gravy.

> ▶ For more weeknight-friendly recipes, go to CooksCountry.com/recipes.

I LOVE A good biscuit for breakfast as much as anyone. But pulling out the food processor to work the butter and flour into a coarse meal; then mixing in buttermilk; and finally rolling, stamping, and baking is more than I can manage before coffee. Then I came across sour cream biscuits. This, I thought, must be the ultimate easy biscuit recipe. It requires neither cutting the butter into the flour nor (at least for the drop biscuit version) rolling and stamping. It might be the ideal biscuit not just for my own early mornings but also for those folks I know who think biscuits are too much trouble to make from scratch.

Most recipes called for combining sour cream with either self-rising flour or biscuit mix. But tasters complained that these versions tasted either soapy or salty, so they were out of the running. Recipes that used standard flour instead of self-rising or a biscuit mix varied primarily in the ratio of sour cream to flour. Unfortunately, even those that used the highest ratio had none of the characteristic tang of sour cream. And strangely, despite the sour cream, most of my samples came out tough and lean.

Since we had ruled out biscuit mix and self-rising flour, I looked over some of the test kitchen's plain biscuit recipes and decided to follow their lead on the ratios for dry ingredients to make a dozen biscuits. In accordance with the directions, I whisked together all-purpose flour, baking powder, and salt; dumped in as much sour cream as it took to form a cohesive dough; and

---

The Easiest Biscuits Ever

Just stir together the batter and use a greased ¼-cup measure to drop the biscuits onto a baking sheet—what could be easier?

Although sour cream is the star here, they wouldn't be biscuits without butter. We add melted butter to the batter and brush the tops with more butter before baking.

baked a batch of biscuits. "Finally—I can really taste the sour cream," tasters said. Great. But there was something they couldn't taste. Butter.

Easy enough to fix, I thought. I'd just add butter. I hoped to kill two birds with one stone: fix the still lean texture (sour cream has about 20 percent fat to butter's 80 percent) and introduce buttery flavor. The key, obviously, was to get the right balance. At 1 pint of sour cream and one stick of butter (melted to maintain the ease of drop biscuits) to 2 cups of flour, I was making progress, but now the biscuits were too fat: They were greasy and flat. I gradually reduced the butter. At 5 tablespoons, the interior was fluffy, moist, and tender. For more flavor, I brushed the biscuits with more melted butter before baking.

About 30 minutes later, I called my tasters. The brown, light biscuits were tender and buttery, and the flavor perfect. This recipe is so simple—stir, scoop, bake—that no matter how early the hour or bleary-eyed the baker, anyone can throw together a batch.

SOUR CREAM DROP BISCUITS
Makes 12 biscuits

We use vegetable oil spray to grease the ¼ cup measure for portioning.

- 2 cups (10 ounces) all-purpose flour
- 1 tablespoon baking powder
- 1 teaspoon salt
- 1 (16-ounce) container sour cream
- 7 tablespoons unsalted butter, melted and cooled

1. Adjust oven rack to middle position and heat oven to 425 degrees. Line rimmed baking sheet with parchment paper. Combine flour, baking powder, and salt in bowl. Stir in sour cream and 5 tablespoons butter until combined.

2. Scoop and drop generous (slightly heaping) ¼ cup of dough 2 inches apart onto prepared baking sheet using greased ¼-cup measure. Brush with remaining 2 tablespoons butter and bake until golden brown, 20 to 25 minutes, rotating sheet halfway through baking. Let biscuits cool on sheet on wire rack for 15 minutes. Serve warm.

Corned Beef and Cabbage

St. Patrick rid Ireland of snakes. The traditional meal served in his honor seems to have the same effect on guests at the table. Could we revive this Irish classic? BY DIANE UNGER

I love St. Patrick's Day as much as the next person—the bagpipes, the beer, the pinching—but there's one aspect of the celebration that doesn't have my Irish eyes a-smilin': the corned beef. The meat can be as salty as a mouthful of Celtic Sea water, not to mention dry, chewy, and rubbery. And if you rely on supermarket corned beef and the stale, listless seasoning packet that accompanies it, you'll have to turn elsewhere for flavor. Don't look to the vegetables. The classic pairing of cabbage and potatoes is more fat and mush than flavor, glistening with grease from the beef. If ever a meal needed rescuing from its modern incarnation, this was it.

Sure, I could "corn" my own beef, an old term for curing in salt. But to do so, I'd need to salt it, weight it, and then wait seven days before I could even think about cooking it, with the unwieldy brisket hogging valuable refrigerator space all that time. Not going to happen. My idea was to take an ordinary supermarket corned beef, throw away the seasoning packet, and figure out a better way to add flavor. To go with it, I wanted tender, well-seasoned vegetables.

Corned beef and cabbage has a long history. In *The New England Cook Book*, published in 1905, I came across a tip from Marion Harland, a prolific novelist better remembered today for her many best-selling books on homemaking: "Salt meat is much improved by pressing" after cooking, she wrote. Weighting the cooked meat, she explained, gives the brisket a finer texture. Well, either the

We threw out the musty seasoning packet that comes with the corned beef and figured out a better way to add flavor.

brisket of 1905 was much different from the supermarket brisket of today, or Ms. Harland had a few too many pints. After all that soaking and weighting (and waiting), the corned beef was dry.

Returning to the 21st century, I decided to rely instead on the expertise of the test kitchen. Most recipes I'd come across for corned beef boiled the meat on the stovetop (and boiled and boiled). But in the test kitchen, we often prefer the gentle heat of the oven. I ditched the burner for the low,

even temperature of a 300-degree oven. I hoped that this method would keep the meat moist. Made this way, my corned beef showed improvement. I also took a cue from a previous brisket recipe developed in the test kitchen, moistening the cooked meat with a cup of cooking liquid and letting it soak up that liquid as it rested and cooled. Better yet.

That liquid sorely needed help, however. Ever since I'd banished the spice package, I had been cooking the meat in plain water. Now I replaced half of the

water with low-sodium chicken broth. I added carrots, celery, onion, bay leaves, peppercorns, thyme, and allspice to the braising liquid. (I'd discard the spent vegetables after the brisket was done.)

After the meat had cooked for about five hours in the oven, plus a 30-minute rest, I set out my latest version for tasters. While the texture was on target now, there was general agreement that the meat was slightly salty. To fix that, I ran through a battery of tests: soaking the brisket for various intervals before cooking it, bringing it to a boil in water, then discarding the water and beginning again with fresh braising liquid. In the end, though, none of these techniques was necessary (and some actually made the meat tough). To my surprise, the simplest method was best: All I needed to do was rinse the corned beef under running water to remove some salt before I cooked it.

I turned to the vegetables, which I could cook on the stovetop in the brisket's defatted cooking liquid while the beef rested. Cooked quickly, the vegetables wouldn't turn mushy over hours in the oven. I found that I needed to start the potatoes about 10 minutes before the cabbage so they would both be done at the same time. I tossed them into the pot whole—corned beef and cabbage is a rustic dish, after all.

I cut the cabbage into large wedges, being careful to keep the core intact; otherwise, the shreds entwined themselves around the other ingredients like tree-hugging vines. Cooked for just 15 minutes, this cabbage was tender and almost delicate, with not a trace of the old-socks aroma and taste of overcooked cabbage. To give the mix a hint of sweetness I added carrots, and for richness and silkiness a few tablespoons of butter. Half an hour and a little pepper later, the vegetables were done.

I sliced the beef and passed around the vegetables. My tasters praised the corned beef's "good meaty flavor" and moist, tender texture. The vegetables were perfectly cooked, too. Nothing says St. Patrick's Day like corned beef—except, maybe, a pint of Guinness.

TEST KITCHEN DISCOVERY
Divide and Conquer

OVEN BRAISE
We braise the beef for hours in low, even oven heat with chicken broth, spices, and vegetables for flavor.

STOVETOP SIMMER
As the meat rests, we briefly cook fresh vegetables in the braising liquid so they'll retain their flavor and texture.

CORNED BEEF AND CABBAGE
Serves 6 to 8

Use flat-cut corned beef brisket, not point-cut; it's more uniform in shape and thus will cook more evenly. When slicing the cabbage, leave the core intact or the cabbage will fall apart during cooking.

- 1 (4- to 5-pound) corned beef brisket roast, rinsed, fat trimmed to ¼ inch thick
- 4 cups low-sodium chicken broth
- 4 cups water
- 12 carrots, peeled (3 chopped, 9 halved crosswise)
- 2 celery ribs, chopped
- 1 onion, peeled and quartered
- 3 bay leaves
- 1 tablespoon whole black peppercorns
- 1 tablespoon minced fresh thyme
- 1 teaspoon whole allspice
- 3 tablespoons unsalted butter
- 1½ pounds small red potatoes
- 1 head green cabbage (2 pounds), cut into 8 (2-inch) wedges
  Pepper

1. Adjust oven rack to middle position and heat oven to 300 degrees. Combine beef, broth, water, chopped carrots, celery, onion, bay leaves, peppercorns, thyme, and allspice in Dutch oven. Cover and bake until fork slips easily in and out of meat, 4½ to 5 hours.

2. Transfer meat to 13 by 9-inch baking dish. Strain cooking liquid through fine-mesh strainer into large bowl, discard solids, and skim fat from liquid. Pour 1 cup cooking liquid over meat. Cover dish tightly with aluminum foil and let rest for 30 minutes.

3. Meanwhile, return remaining cooking liquid to Dutch oven, add butter, and bring to simmer over medium-high heat. Add potatoes and simmer until they begin to soften, about 10 minutes. Add carrot halves and cabbage, cover, and cook until tender, 10 to 15 minutes. Transfer vegetables to serving platter and season with pepper to taste. (Reserve cooking liquid for making Creamed Chipped Beef using leftover corned beef; recipe at right.)

4. Transfer beef to carving board and slice against grain into ¼-inch-thick slices. Serve with vegetables.

TO MAKE AHEAD
Prepare corned beef through step 2. Refrigerate moistened beef and cooking liquid separately for up to 24 hours. To serve, adjust oven rack to middle position and heat oven to 350 degrees. Transfer meat to carving board and slice against grain into ¼-inch-thick slices and return to baking dish. Cover dish tightly with foil and bake until meat is heated through, about 25 minutes. While meat is heating, proceed with step 3.

WHAT TO DO WITH LEFTOVERS
Creamed Chipped Beef on Toast

Before we sent out the SOS distress call, we tried our best to save this dish. BY DIANE UNGER

MOST OF US know creamed chipped beef by another, less flattering name. Its mere mention can still make my grandfather shudder, bringing back scary memories from his army days of salted, dried beef bound (like cement) in a pasty white sauce and served over soggy toast. One old recipe I found, in a 1910 manual for army cooks, scalded the beef and then made sauce from margarine, flour, evaporated milk, tinned beef stock, and water. Presumably that recipe used jarred or packaged dried beef, too. But I had leftover corned beef, none of the constraints of feeding an army, and a firm conviction that beef suspended in creamy sauce and poured over crisp toast could, should, and would taste delicious. I'd chop (or chip) my corned beef and rescue creamed chipped beef on toast.

I started by building a traditional white sauce with extra flavor: I melted butter, and before adding the flour I stirred in finely chopped onion. Along with the flour, I tossed in dry mustard, thyme, and cayenne pepper, letting them toast briefly to develop their flavor. I tested evaporated milk and found it too sweet. Whole milk was anemic, and heavy cream over the top. But whole milk combined with half-and-half gave the sauce richness, body, and a sense of proportion. To add meaty flavor to the creamy sauce, I tried both chicken and beef broth before realizing I had deeply flavorful cooking liquid left from cooking the corned beef staring me in the face. Out went the canned broth. In came my corned beef cooking liquid, with its traces of spices, herbs, onions, carrots, and more.

I toasted a slice of bread, topped it with a ladleful of creamed chipped beef, and sprinkled on minced fresh chives. Mmm mmm. Maybe the army should try this recipe as a recruitment tool.

Our version gets lots of flavor from leftover corned beef.

CREAMED CHIPPED BEEF
Serves 4 to 6

You can substitute chicken broth for the reserved corned beef cooking liquid.

- 4 tablespoons unsalted butter
- ¼ cup finely chopped onion
- 4 tablespoons all-purpose flour
- 1 teaspoon dry mustard
- 1 teaspoon minced fresh thyme
- ¼ teaspoon cayenne pepper
- 1½ cups half-and-half
- 1½ cups whole milk
- 1 cup reserved corned beef cooking liquid
- 2 cups chopped cooked corned beef
  Pinch nutmeg
  Pepper
- 6 slices hearty white sandwich bread, toasted
- 3 tablespoons minced fresh chives

1. Melt butter in saucepan over medium heat. Add onion and cook until softened, about 1 minute. Stir in flour, mustard, thyme, and cayenne and cook until fragrant, about 1 minute. Slowly whisk in half-and-half, milk, and corned beef cooking liquid. Bring to simmer and cook over low heat, stirring occasionally, until thickened, 6 to 8 minutes.

2. Stir beef and nutmeg into sauce and cook until beef is heated through, about 2 minutes. Season with pepper to taste. Spoon over toast and sprinkle with chives. Serve.

Introducing Grandma Pizza

Grandma pizza is well-known and loved on Long Island, but like some grandmas, it doesn't get out much. We wanted a recipe good enough to introduce to the rest of the country. BY SARAH GABRIEL

Pizza is in New York City's blood. Tourists know they can get a slice on every block, while locals hotly debate the merits of old-school coal-oven pizzerias like Patsy's and Lombardi's versus relative newcomers like Motorino and Forcella. The pizza that rarely gets talked about, however, lives on Long Island. Grandma pizza is a thin-crust, rectangular pan pizza topped in reverse order: first with a modest amount of cheese and then with chunks of tomato. But in order to fully understand this pizza, I'd have to take an eating tour of Long Island pizzerias.

What did I find out on my whirlwind, gut-busting trip? That this is good pizza. Of the dozen or so samples I tried, there was no single version that stood out from the rest, but there were elements of each that I wanted to pull into my recipe. The crusts I liked best were thin and crunchy, like the one I'd sampled at the iconic pizzeria King Umberto. Smaller, more uniformly distributed chunks of tomato were preferable to larger, sporadically placed hunks. And fresh basil was a great complement.

The dough for grandma pizza is stretched and baked on an oiled sheet pan. Starting with a test kitchen recipe for a sheet pan pizza, I mixed all-purpose flour, yeast, salt, sugar, water, and oil in the stand mixer, let it rise in a bowl, stretched it on an oiled pan, and topped it with mozzarella and a can of drained diced tomatoes. My plan was to taste this admittedly crude interpretation and then adjust it to bring it into line with the best of the pizzas I'd eaten on Long Island.

The dough was tender and easy to

Most pizzas are topped with sauce and then cheese. This grandma bucks tradition by laying down the cheese first and then chunks of tomatoes.

stretch, but when baked, it puffed up much thicker and denser than quintessential grandma slices, and it didn't have the crisp-bottomed, chewy crust I was after. Cutting the dough recipe in half still made for a crust that was too thick, but cutting it by two-thirds yielded just enough dough for a properly thin crust. Baking it for 15 minutes at 500 degrees on the lowest rack nicely browned the crust, and sliding the pizza onto a wire rack when it came out of the oven kept the bottom from getting soggy in the

pan. But the crust was still too dense and tender. To add chew, I switched from all-purpose to higher-protein bread flour and increased the kneading time. Ten minutes in the stand mixer gave me the elastic, gluten-rich dough I wanted. But this time, when I stretched the taut dough, it snapped back, refusing to stay in the corners of the pan.

I knew that adding water would make the dough less dense, and I hoped it would also make stretching a bit easier. An extra quarter cup of water fixed the

dense and bready texture. But while it did make stretching the dough a tad easier, I still had to stretch it little by little, letting it rest periodically to allow the dough to slacken. I noticed that just moving it from the rising bowl to the oiled sheet pan was building elasticity. What if I didn't have to move it?

I mixed a batch of dough, this time letting it rise directly on the oiled sheet pan. Not hemmed in by the sides of a bowl, the dough stretched a little itself while rising. When it had

DANISH PUFF PASTRY

Serves 10 to 12

Baking the pastry on two stacked baking sheets prevents it from burning on the bottom. Be sure to cool the pastries completely before glazing. If the glaze is too thick to spread smoothly, whisk in an additional tablespoon of milk.

PASTRY

- **2 cups (10 ounces) all-purpose flour**
- **2 tablespoons granulated sugar**
- **1¾ teaspoons salt**
- **16 tablespoons unsalted butter, cut into ½-inch pieces and chilled**
- **1½ cups cold water**
- **4 large eggs**
- **¾ teaspoon almond extract**

GLAZE

- **1½ cups (6 ounces) confectioners' sugar, sifted**
- **3 tablespoons milk**
- **¼ teaspoon salt**
- **⅛ teaspoon almond extract**
- **3 tablespoons unsalted butter, melted and cooled**
- **⅓ cup sliced almonds, toasted**

1. FOR THE PASTRY: Adjust oven rack to middle position and heat oven to 400 degrees. Line rimmed baking sheet with parchment paper. Pulse flour, sugar, and salt in food processor until combined, about 3 pulses. Add butter and pulse until mixture resembles coarse meal, about 10 pulses. Add ½ cup water and pulse until mixture forms dough, about 10 pulses.

2. Transfer half of dough (11 ounces) to lightly floured counter, knead briefly until dough comes together, and roll into two 12-inch ropes. Transfer ropes to prepared baking sheet. Press ropes with hand into 12 by 3-inch rectangles. Cover with plastic wrap and refrigerate until ready to use.

3. Meanwhile, lightly beat eggs and almond extract in 2-cup liquid measuring cup. Bring remaining 1 cup water to boil in medium saucepan over high heat. Add remaining dough to boiling water and cook, stirring constantly, until ball forms, about 2 minutes. Reduce heat to low and cook, stirring constantly, until mixture is uniformly shiny and pulls away from sides of pan, 3 to 5 minutes.

4. Transfer hot dough to food processor and process for 10 seconds. With processor running, slowly add egg mixture until incorporated, scraping down sides of bowl as needed. Divide warm dough mixture between chilled dough rectangles. Spread evenly.

5. Set baking sheet with pastry inside second rimmed baking sheet. Bake for 15 minutes, then reduce oven temperature to 350 and bake until pastry is puffed and golden brown, about 75 minutes longer. Turn oven off and, using paring knife, make four ½-inch horizontal slits in each long side of both pastries. Prop open oven door with wooden spoon. Leave pastries in turned-off oven for 20 minutes. Remove from oven and let cool completely on baking sheet, about 1 hour.

6. FOR THE GLAZE: Whisk sugar, milk, salt, and almond extract together in bowl until smooth. Slowly whisk in butter until incorporated. Drizzle glaze over each pastry and top with toasted almonds. Serve.

TASTING **Almond Extract**

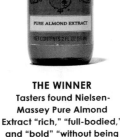

Just ¼ teaspoon of almond extract can perfume entire cakes. Given its potency, will any brand do? To find out, we tasted four nationally distributed supermarket brands (three pure and one imitation) in whipped cream and in almond pound cake.

Pure almond extract is made from three primary ingredients: alcohol, water, and bitter almond oil. The last is extracted from almonds or (more frequently) their kin, drupes, the botanical term for stone fruits such as peaches and apricots. The almond flavor comes from benzaldehyde, a substance in the kernels of drupes. Interestingly, only one of the brands we tasted gets its bitter almond oil even in part from almonds. Imitation almond extract also starts with water and alcohol, but its flavor comes from synthetic benzaldehyde, created in a lab. Our tasters couldn't distinguish the two. In fact, the imitation extract, McCormick, came in second—and ahead of McCormick Pure. Possibly, the imitation contains more benzaldehyde, because the synthetic is cheaper.

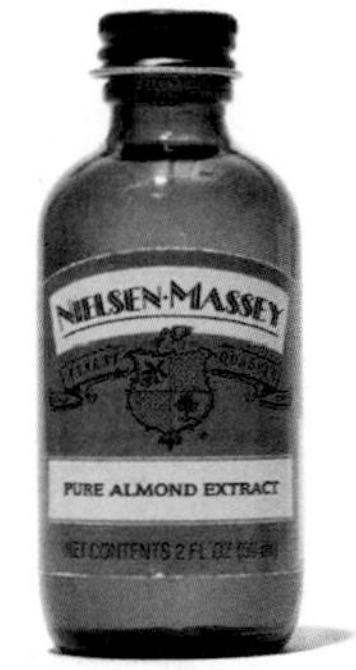

THE WINNER
Tasters found Nielsen-Massey Pure Almond Extract "rich," "full-bodied," and "bold" "without being harsh or artificial." It had a "lovely almond bouquet."

The brand we ranked last (yet would still recommend with reservations) was the only one that derives some of its flavor from actual almonds. Surprisingly, we found it too mild. We preferred "bold" Nielsen-Massey Pure Almond Extract ($10.99 for 4 ounces). It's 90 percent alcohol, by far the highest percentage among the four extracts. The alcohol acts as a solvent to extract flavor. Generally, the higher the percentage the more flavor is extracted, which may account for the "lingering" and "pronounced" taste of our winner. Although it wasn't made from nuts, Nielsen-Massey's extract tasted the "most like actual almonds." –HANNAH CROWLEY

For complete testing results, including full comments, go to **CooksCountry.com** and search for "almond extract."

ecome One Pastry

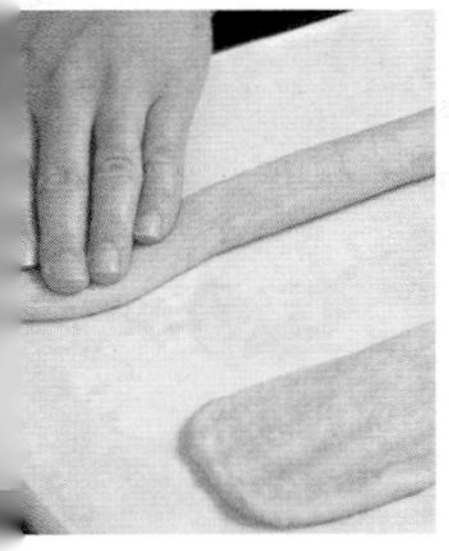

PASTRY BASE
e ropes into 12 by ectangles. Chill the gles in the refrig- while you make the pastry.

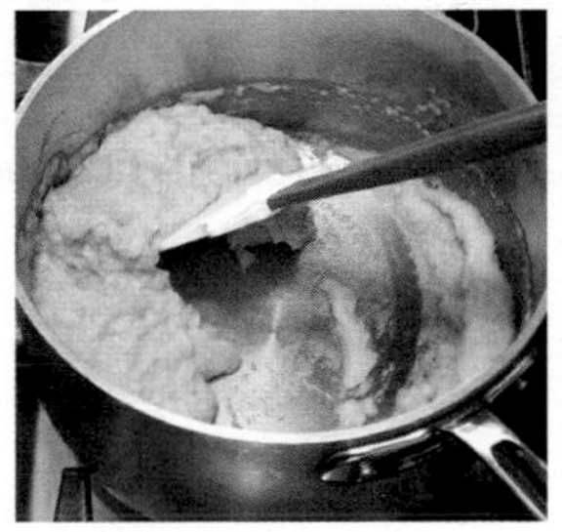

START CHOUX
Combine the reserved pie dough with boiling water in a saucepan and cook, stirring, until the mixture is shiny and pulls away from the pan.

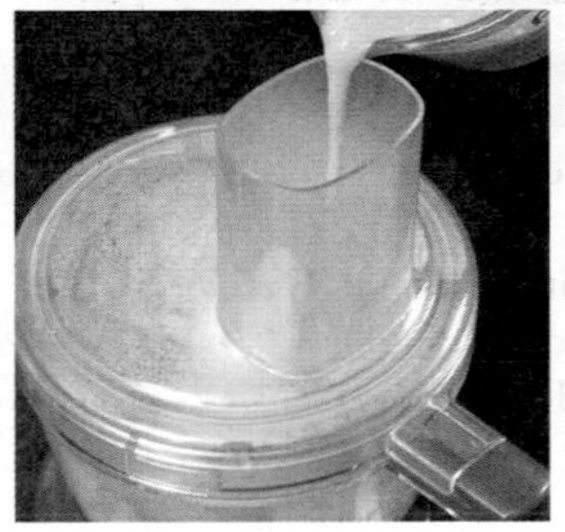

FINISH CHOUX
Move the cooked choux dough into the food processor. Slowly pour in lightly beaten eggs as the processor runs.

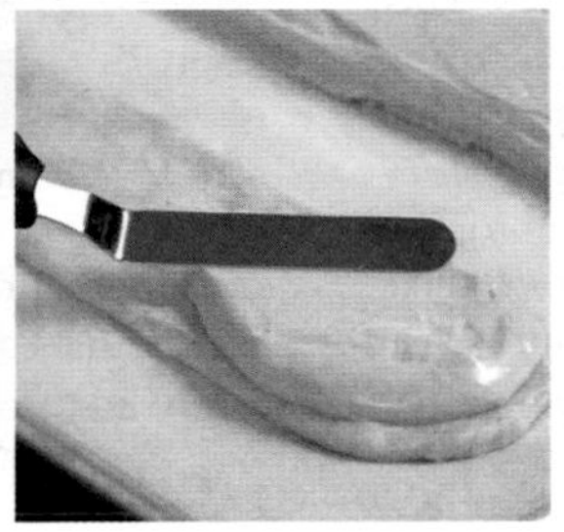

SPREAD AND BAKE
Cover each chilled dough rectangle with half of the warm choux dough. Bake the Danish Puffs for 1½ hours.

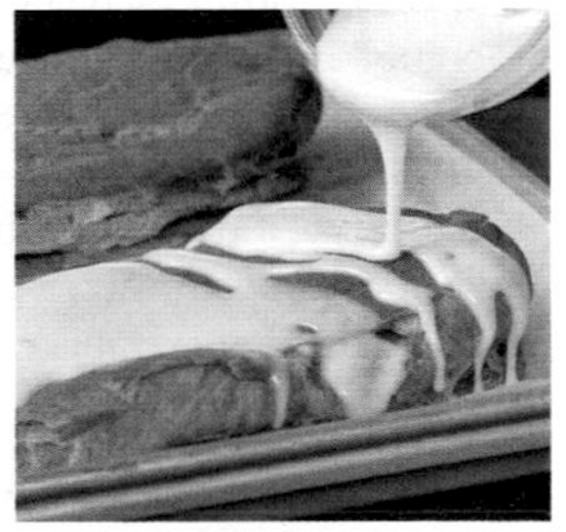

GLAZE PUFFS
After the puffs have baked and cooled, ice them with a simple glaze and sprinkle them with sliced almonds.

proofed, stretching it to the corners was much easier, though it still required a 10-minute rest before the last bit of fitting. In the end, I found that pressing the dough to a 10 by 6-inch rectangle before letting it rise gave me just the head start I needed for easy stretching.

Now I could work on the toppings. Tasters found the plain mozzarella lackluster. A few of the pizzas I'd sampled augmented it with nutty, salty Parmesan cheese. Adding ¼ cup of Parmesan to my 2 cups of mozzarella rounded out the flavor. The diced tomatoes alone tasted bright but unbalanced. Adding ¼ teaspoon of salt, a tablespoon of olive oil, minced garlic, and dried oregano introduced the necessary aromatic depth.

I mixed up one more batch of dough, let it rise on the pan, stretched it out, let it rise a second time, and then topped it with cheese and the seasoned diced tomatoes. I baked it, sprinkled on some basil, slid it onto the wire rack, and called my tasters. Before I could ask what they thought, the pizza was gone.

The American Table
Where Was Grandma Born?

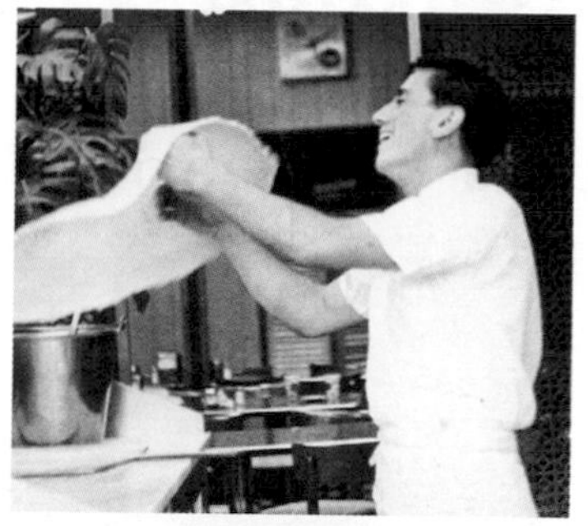

Making the original at Umberto's.

In a 2003 piece in the Long Island newspaper *Newsday*, writer Erica Marcus traced grandma pizza's origins to Umberto's Pizzeria, in New Hyde Park. According to Marcus, in the early 1970s proprietor Umberto Corteo would ask his pizza man to create a simple pizza like the one his mother used to make in Italy. The Corteos opened a second pizzeria, King Umberto's, in nearby Elmont; this was later bought by two former Umberto's pizza makers who built a best-selling item out of their former boss's favorite lunch, naming it grandma pizza sometime in the late-1980s. Within 10 years, other Long Island pizzerias were offering the pie, and a phenomenon was born.

GRANDMA PIZZA Serves 4

If the dough snaps back when you press it to the corners of the baking sheet, cover it, let it rest for 10 minutes, and try again.

DOUGH

- **3 tablespoons olive oil**
- **¾ cup water**
- **1½ cups (8¼ ounces) bread flour**
- **2¼ teaspoons instant or rapid-rise yeast**
- **1 teaspoon sugar**
- **¾ teaspoon salt**

TOPPING

- **1 (28-ounce) can diced tomatoes**
- **1 tablespoon olive oil**
- **2 garlic cloves, minced**
- **1 teaspoon dried oregano**
- **¼ teaspoon salt**
- **8 ounces mozzarella cheese, shredded (2 cups)**
- **¼ cup grated Parmesan cheese**
- **2 tablespoons chopped fresh basil**

1. FOR THE DOUGH: Coat rimmed baking sheet with 2 tablespoons oil. Combine water and remaining 1 tablespoon oil in 1-cup liquid measuring cup. Using stand mixer fitted with dough hook, mix flour, yeast, sugar, and salt on low speed until combined. With mixer running, slowly add water mixture and mix until dough comes together, about 1 minute. Increase speed to medium-low and mix until dough is smooth and comes away from sides of bowl, about 10 minutes.

2. Transfer dough to greased baking sheet and turn to coat. Stretch dough to 10 by 6-inch rectangle. Cover with plastic wrap and let rise in warm place until doubled in size, 1 to 1½ hours. Stretch dough to corners of pan, cover loosely with plastic, and let rise in warm place until slightly puffed, about 45 minutes. Meanwhile, adjust oven rack to lowest position and heat oven to 500 degrees.

3. FOR THE TOPPING: Place tomatoes in colander and drain well. Combine drained tomatoes, oil, garlic, oregano, and salt in bowl. Combine mozzarella and Parmesan in second bowl. Sprinkle cheese mixture over dough, leaving ½-inch border around edges. Top with tomato mixture and bake until well browned and bubbling, about 15 minutes. Slide pizza onto wire rack, sprinkle with basil, and let cool for 5 minutes. Serve.

KEY STEP **Easy Rise**

Our method lets the dough proof right on the sheet. Spread the dough on an oiled baking sheet and then set it aside to rise.

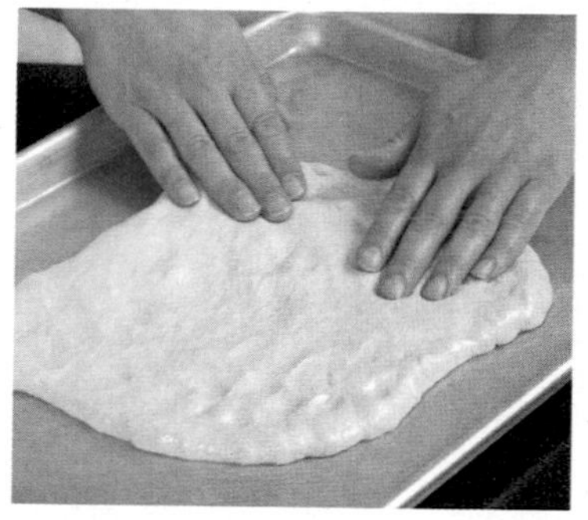

ON THE SIDE

Antipasto Salad

With so many bold ingredients, the challenge is to unify the flavors. BY SARAH GABRIEL

ANTIPASTO SALAD, an Italian American take on chef's salad, is a staple of red-sauce restaurants and pizzerias. The best ones highlight cured meats, marinated vegetables, cheese, and olives on a bed of lettuce with a potent dressing to unite the components. The recipes that I found missed the mark. Some were harsh with onion and vinegar, others greasy. And the flavors never came together.

For a salad that wouldn't be overloaded but still had good fresh-briny balance, we decided on salami, provolone, olives, red onion, artichoke hearts, pepperoncini, cherry tomatoes, and basil to go with the lettuce. Surprisingly, this was showing restraint, as many recipes call for far more.

To soften the onion's bite, I used a test kitchen trick and simmered the slices in red wine vinegar and water. Marinated artichoke hearts were too oily straight out of the jar, even when rinsed. I decided to use frozen artichoke hearts instead. After a few rounds of testing, I realized that I could better integrate the flavors by marinating the onion and artichokes together and then use the marinade as the base of my dressing.

I simmered the onion in vinegar and water as before, but this time I added garlic, oregano, and salt. Once the onion softened a bit, I introduced the thawed artichoke hearts. Then I stirred in the pepperoncini and let the mixture cool. When I was ready to make the salad, I drained the marinade and whisked ¼ cup with olive oil to create a dressing that tied the boldly flavored ingredients together.

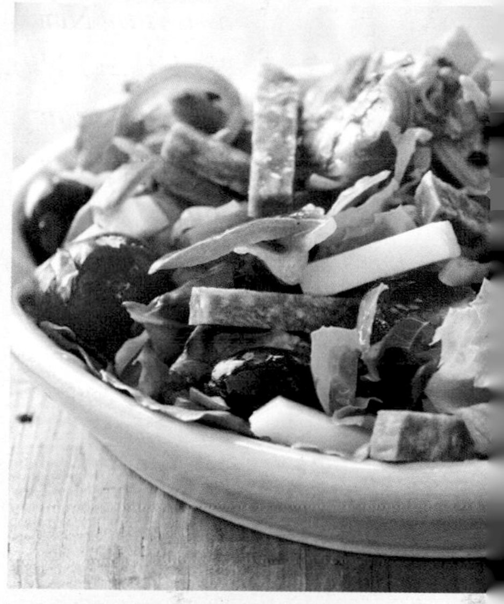

For extra flavor, we marinate the onions, artichokes, and pepperoncini together.

ANTIPASTO SALAD Serves 6 to 8

If you buy whole artichoke hearts, quarter them through the stem after thawing. The drained marinated vegetables and vinaigrette can be refrigerated separately for up to one day. Dress the salad just before serving.

- **⅔ cup red wine vinegar**
- **¼ cup water**
- **2 garlic cloves, minced**
- **2 teaspoons dried oregano Salt and pepper**
- **1 red onion, halved and sliced ¼ inch thick**
- **9 ounces frozen artichoke hearts, thawed and patted dry**
- **⅓ cup jarred sliced pepperoncini**
- **2 tablespoons extra-virgin olive oil**
- **2 romaine lettuce hearts (12 ounces), chopped**
- **12 ounces cherry tomatoes, halved**
- **3 (¼-inch-thick) slices provolone cheese (6 ounces), cut into 1-inch-long matchsticks**
- **3 (¼-inch-thick) slices salami (6 ounces), cut into 1-inch-long matchsticks**
- **⅓ cup pitted kalamata olives**
- **¼ cup fresh basil leaves, chopped**

1. Bring vinegar, water, garlic, oregano, and 1 teaspoon salt to boil in small saucepan over medium-high heat. Add onion, reduce heat to medium-low, and simmer, stirring occasionally, until onion is nearly tender, 5 to 7 minutes. Stir in artichokes and cook until tender, about 3 minutes. Off heat, add pepperoncini, transfer mixture to bowl, and refrigerate until cool, about 20 minutes.

2. Drain marinated vegetables through fine-mesh strainer into bowl; reserve ¼ cup vinegar mixture. Toss marinated vegetables with 1 tablespoon oil in bowl. Whisk remaining 1 tablespoon oil into reserved vinegar mixture until thoroughly incorporated. Toss romaine, tomatoes, provolone, and salami with vinaigrette in large bowl. Season with salt and pepper to taste. Transfer salad mixture to platter and top with marinated vegetables, olives, and basil. Serve.

Danish Puff Pastry

Our first attempts at this two-dough buttery pastry produced Danish slump pastry.
Could we pump up this puff and simplify the process, too? BY SARAH GABRIEL

Danish puff pastry is neither Danish nor puff pastry. It is, however, buttery, almond-y, and incredibly delicious. Inspired by the many-leaved traditional Danish pastry known as kringle, the Betty Crocker kitchens developed Danish puff pastry in 1961, seemingly to capture some of kringle's fancy, layered pastry appeal without the complex, time-consuming process of laminating (that's how pastry chefs say "layer dough with butter"). Even 50 years later, this was a goal I could definitely get behind.

When I collected recipes for Danish puff pastry, I made two surprising discoveries. First, Danish puff pastry is simply ordinary pie crust with flavored *pâte à choux*, or cream puff dough, spread on top of it. And second, all recipes for it are virtually identical. These recipes start with instructions to make basic pie dough. In place of a rolling pin, they call for shaping the dough into two long ropes and then simply patting them flat to form two rectangles. The "topping" is made from typical cream puff dough: Boil a cup of water with half a cup of butter, stir in a cup of flour to make a paste, and then turn off the heat and mix in three eggs. Unlike classic choux paste, Danish puff gets an injection of almond extract. This choux paste is spread over the long, narrow pie dough rectangles, baked in a 350-degree oven for about an hour, cooled, and topped with an almond or vanilla glaze and sliced, toasted almonds.

A pastry made from two completely different doughs seemed really and truly bizarre to me, but my colleague Becky practically drooled as she recalled her mother making Danish puffs for special

Although this unusual pastry looks and tastes like something you purchased at a fancy bakery, it's actually not that difficult to make.

occasions during Becky's childhood. Based on her description, I had visions of a sky-high Danish puff, with a crisp, flaky pie crust supporting a buttery, creamy interior, its labyrinthine network of dough walls and air channels resembling the many layers of a traditional laminated dough. A sweet and easy glaze (basically confectioners' sugar and milk) united the two parts. Unfortunately, my test puffs weren't like that at all. Instead, the choux top was stunted and the pie crust bland and dry.

I quickly remedied the bland flavor by adding salt and sugar to both crust and puff dough. Getting the top to puff up was more complicated. A comparison of the Danish puff topping recipes with cream puff and éclair recipes indicated that more egg would help raise the roof on my puff. One extra egg helped a bit, so I tried two. That knocked the buttery-eggy-almond flavor out of balance, making the puff too eggy. My next idea—bake the puff for a short time in a very hot oven and then decrease the

temperature to finish baking—did give the puff a jump start, as I'd intended, but it still didn't achieve the heights I had in mind.

I was getting a cramp in my forearm from stirring my umpteenth batch of choux paste when I got to wondering if the dough was too stiff: A stiff, dry dough is harder to inflate than a loose, wet dough. To make it looser, I added more water. At the same time, I tried out two standard choux paste techniques that are aimed at drying the interior of

SPANISH CHICKEN CUTLETS WITH YOGURT SAUCE

CAJUN SLOPPY JOES

PAN-FRIED SOLE WITH LEMONY HERB BUTTER

CHIPOTLE CHICKEN TORTILLA SOUP

CAJUN SLOPPY JOES Serves 4

WHY THIS RECIPE WORKS: Blooming the Cajun seasoning with the onions enhances its bold flavor.

- 2 tablespoons vegetable oil
- 1 onion, chopped fine
  Salt and pepper
- 1 tablespoon Cajun seasoning
- ⅛ teaspoon cayenne pepper
- 1 pound 85 percent lean ground beef
- 1 cup tomato puree
- ¼ cup ketchup
- 4 hamburger buns

1. Heat oil in 12-inch skillet over medium heat until shimmering. Add onion and ½ teaspoon salt, cover, and cook, stirring occasionally, until onion is soft, about 5 minutes. Add Cajun seasoning and cayenne and cook until fragrant, about 1 minute. Add meat and cook, breaking up pieces with spoon, until just pink, about 3 minutes.

2. Stir in tomato puree, ketchup, and ¼ teaspoon pepper. Simmer until sauce is slightly thicker than ketchup, 8 to 10 minutes. Season with salt and pepper to taste. Spoon meat onto hamburger buns and serve.

TEST KITCHEN NOTE: Heinz Organic Tomato Ketchup is the test kitchen's taste-test winner.

SPANISH CHICKEN CUTLETS WITH YOGURT SAUCE Serves 4

WHY THIS RECIPE WORKS: The yogurt both helps bind the bread crumbs to the chicken and serves as the base for the sauce.

- 1¼ cups plain yogurt
- 2 teaspoons smoked paprika
  Salt and pepper
- 1½ cups panko bread crumbs
- 4 (6-ounce) chicken cutlets, ½ inch thick, trimmed
- 6 tablespoons olive oil
- 2 garlic cloves, minced
- 2 tablespoons minced fresh parsley

1. Adjust oven rack to middle position and heat oven to 200 degrees. Combine yogurt, paprika, ½ teaspoon salt, and ¼ teaspoon pepper in medium bowl. Reserve ½ cup yogurt mixture. Place bread crumbs in shallow dish. Pat cutlets dry with paper towels and season with salt and pepper. One at a time, coat cutlets in remaining yogurt mixture and dredge in bread crumbs, pressing to adhere.

2. Heat 2 tablespoons oil in 12-inch nonstick skillet over medium-high heat until just smoking. Cook 2 cutlets until golden brown, about 4 minutes per side. Transfer to wire rack set inside rimmed baking sheet and keep warm in oven. Wipe out skillet with paper towels and repeat with 2 tablespoons oil and remaining cutlets.

3. Wipe out skillet with paper towels, and heat remaining 2 tablespoons oil until shimmering. Add garlic and cook until fragrant, about 30 seconds. Remove from heat and let cool slightly. Whisk cooled garlic oil and parsley into reserved yogurt mixture until combined. Season with salt and pepper to taste. Serve chicken with yogurt sauce.

TEST KITCHEN NOTE: Sweet paprika is also tasty in this recipe.

CHIPOTLE CHICKEN TORTILLA SOUP Serves 4

WHY THIS RECIPE WORKS: Picante sauce, a cousin of salsa that contains pureed tomatoes, replaces the more standard tomato puree and onions in this soup.

- 4 (6-inch) corn tortillas, halved and sliced crosswise into ½-inch strips
- 1 tablespoon vegetable oil
- 1 red bell pepper, stemmed, seeded, and chopped
- 4 cups low-sodium chicken broth
- 1 (2½-pound) rotisserie chicken, skin and bones discarded, meat shredded into bite-size pieces (3 cups)
- 1 (8-ounce) jar picante sauce
- 1 tablespoon minced canned chipotle chile in adobo sauce
- 2 tablespoons chopped fresh cilantro
- 1 tablespoon lime juice
  Salt and pepper

1. Adjust oven rack to upper-middle position and heat oven to 450 degrees. Place tortilla strips on rimmed baking sheet and bake until crisp, 6 to 8 minutes.

2. Meanwhile, heat oil in Dutch oven over medium-high heat until shimmering. Cook pepper until well browned, about 8 minutes. Add broth, chicken, picante sauce, and chipotle and bring to simmer. Cook until chicken is heated through, about 2 minutes. Remove from heat and stir in cilantro, lime juice, and tortillas. Season with salt and pepper to taste. Serve.

TEST KITCHEN NOTE: Serve with shredded sharp cheddar cheese and diced avocado.

PAN-FRIED SOLE WITH LEMONY HERB BUTTER Serves 4

WHY THIS RECIPE WORKS: We dress up our fish with a quick compound butter for a dinner you can have on the table in minutes.

- 3 tablespoons unsalted butter, softened
- 3 tablespoons minced fresh chives
- 2 teaspoons grated lemon zest
  Salt and pepper
- ½ cup all-purpose flour
- 4 (6-ounce) skinless sole fillets
- 3 tablespoons vegetable oil

1. Combine butter, chives, lemon zest, ¼ teaspoon salt, and ⅛ teaspoon pepper in bowl; set aside. Place flour in shallow dish. Pat fish dry with paper towels and season with salt and pepper. Dredge fish lightly on both sides in flour, shaking off excess.

2. Heat 1½ tablespoons oil in 12-inch nonstick skillet over medium-high heat until just smoking. Cook 2 fillets until golden, about 2½ minutes per side. Transfer to plate and tent loosely with foil. Wipe out skillet with paper towels and repeat with remaining 1½ tablespoons oil and fish. Top each fillet with 1 tablespoon of herb butter. Serve.

TEST KITCHEN NOTE: You can use flounder in place of the sole.

**CHICKEN BREASTS WITH
PARSLEY-AND-TOMATO COUSCOUS**

WEEKNIGHT SPAGHETTI AND MEATBALLS

SPICY PORK AND BROCCOLI STIR-FRY

ITALIAN SAUSAGE AND POTATO FRITTATA

WEEKNIGHT SPAGHETTI AND MEATBALLS Serves 4

WHY THIS RECIPE WORKS: Cooking everything in the same pan saves on time—and cleanup.

- 1 pound meatloaf mix
- ⅓ cup panko bread crumbs
- 1 large egg, lightly beaten
- 5 garlic cloves, minced
- 1 tablespoon olive oil
- 1 (28-ounce) can crushed tomatoes
- 2 cups water
- 8 ounces spaghetti, broken in half
- ¼ cup chopped fresh basil
- Salt and pepper

1. Combine meat, bread crumbs, egg, and half of garlic in bowl and knead gently until combined. Form mixture into 4 dozen 1-inch meatballs. Heat oil in 12-inch nonstick skillet over medium-high heat until just smoking. Cook meatballs until well browned all over, about 5 minutes. Transfer meatballs to plate.

2. Add remaining garlic to skillet and cook until fragrant, about 30 seconds. Add tomatoes, water, and pasta and bring to boil. Cover, reduce heat to medium-low, and cook, stirring often, until pasta begins to soften, about 7 minutes. Return meatballs to pan and simmer, covered, until meatballs are cooked through and pasta is al dente, about 5 minutes longer. Off heat, stir in basil, and season with salt and pepper to taste. Serve.

TEST KITCHEN NOTE: You can substitute equal parts ground beef and ground pork for the meatloaf mix.

CHICKEN BREASTS WITH PARSLEY-AND-TOMATO COUSCOUS Serves 4

WHY THIS RECIPE WORKS: Cooking the chicken skin side down ensures well-rendered skin. Covering the pan helps it cook faster.

- 4 (12-ounce) bone-in split chicken breasts, halved crosswise
- Salt and pepper
- 1 tablespoon vegetable oil
- 1¼ cups low-sodium chicken broth
- 1 cup couscous
- 1 tomato, cut into ¼-inch dice
- 3 scallions, sliced thin
- 3 tablespoons minced fresh parsley
- 1 tablespoon lemon juice
- ¼ teaspoon red pepper flakes

1. Pat chicken dry with paper towels and season with salt and pepper. Heat oil in 12-inch skillet over medium-high heat until just smoking. Cook chicken, skin side down, until well browned, about 5 minutes. Reduce heat to medium, cover, and cook until meat registers 160 degrees, about 15 minutes. Transfer chicken to platter and tent loosely with foil.

2. Meanwhile, bring broth to boil in medium saucepan. Stir in couscous, cover, and remove from heat. Let stand for 5 minutes. Stir in tomato, scallions, parsley, lemon juice, and red pepper flakes. Season with salt and pepper to taste. Serve chicken with couscous.

TEST KITCHEN NOTE: You can substitute other leafy herbs, like basil or tarragon, for the parsley.

ITALIAN SAUSAGE AND POTATO FRITTATA Serves 4

WHY THIS RECIPE WORKS: Microwaving the potato slices speeds up their cooking time.

- 10 large eggs
- 1½ ounces Parmesan cheese, grated (¾ cup)
- 3 tablespoons half-and-half
- 3 tablespoons minced fresh basil
- ½ teaspoon salt
- ½ teaspoon pepper
- 1 russet potato, peeled and sliced ¼ inch thick
- 6 ounces Italian sausage, casings removed

1. Adjust oven rack to upper-middle position and heat oven to 450 degrees. Whisk eggs, ½ cup Parmesan, half-and-half, basil, salt, and pepper together in bowl; set aside. Place potato in second bowl, cover, and microwave until just tender, about 4 minutes.

2. Cook sausage in 10-inch nonstick skillet over medium-high heat, breaking up pieces with spoon, until brown, 6 to 8 minutes. Stir in potato and reduce heat to medium. Add egg mixture and cook, using spatula to scrape bottom of skillet, until large curds form but eggs are still very wet, about 2 minutes. Shake skillet to distribute eggs evenly and cook, without stirring, until bottom is set, about 30 seconds. Sprinkle with remaining ¼ cup Parmesan and bake until golden brown, 6 to 8 minutes. Serve.

TEST KITCHEN NOTE: Both hot and sweet sausage are delicious here.

SPICY PORK AND BROCCOLI STIR-FRY Serves 4

WHY THIS RECIPE WORKS: Coating the pork strips in cornstarch gives them a velvety texture, keeps them moist, and helps the sauce adhere.

- ¾ cup low-sodium chicken broth
- 2 tablespoons soy sauce
- 2 tablespoons cornstarch
- 1 tablespoon Asian chili-garlic sauce
- 1 teaspoon toasted sesame oil
- 1 (16-ounce) pork tenderloin, cut crosswise into ½-inch-thick slices, each slice cut into ½-inch-thick strips
- 3 tablespoons vegetable oil
- 1 pound broccoli, florets cut into 1-inch pieces, stalks trimmed, peeled, and sliced ¼ inch thick
- 1 tablespoon grated fresh ginger
- 1 garlic clove, minced

1. Whisk ½ cup broth, soy sauce, 1 tablespoon cornstarch, chili-garlic sauce, and sesame oil together in bowl; set aside. Toss pork, 1 tablespoon vegetable oil, and remaining 1 tablespoon cornstarch together in bowl. Heat 2 teaspoons vegetable oil in 12-inch nonstick skillet over medium-high heat until just smoking. Brown half of pork, 3 to 5 minutes. Transfer pork to plate. Repeat with 2 teaspoons vegetable oil and remaining pork.

2. Heat remaining 2 teaspoons oil in now-empty skillet until just smoking. Add broccoli and cook until bright green, about 1 minute. Add remaining ¼ cup chicken broth and cook, covered, until broccoli is tender, about 3 minutes. Add ginger and garlic and cook until fragrant, about 30 seconds. Stir in soy sauce mixture and cook until thickened, about 2 minutes. Return pork and any accumulated juices to skillet and cook until heated through, about 1 minute. Serve.

Easy Mediterranean Chicken and Rice

We wanted lively flavors, moist chicken, and a no-fuss weeknight dinner.
But in most recipes, these goals never align. BY ADAM RIED

IN THE LEXICON of warm, homey, simple suppers, chicken and rice is a classic that often comes up short. Or more precisely, it comes up bland. In many of the recipes we've tried, neither the chicken nor the rice has much personality on its own, and worse, they have little affinity for each other. I wanted to help chicken and rice fulfill its potential as an easy, brightly flavored weeknight dinner, with both components combined into a harmonious whole.

Traditional recipes stew chicken slowly to make a rich broth for cooking the rice, but who has the time on a weeknight? Many modern recipes speed things up by calling for cooking the chicken and rice separately but simultaneously and combining them on the plate. In the end, they taste as though they've never met before. Aiming for the middle ground, I made some initial choices. First, I wanted vivid Mediterranean flavors—from olives, tomatoes, and lemon. Second, to keep things simple, I chose a popular cut of chicken that requires zero preparation: boneless, skinless chicken breast halves.

Since the meat is so mild, I considered flavor-boosting strategies. Brining in salty water lets the muscle fibers release and subsequently reabsorb moisture; the chicken stays juicy when it's cooked, and the salt rides in with that reabsorbed moisture and seasons the meat deeply. Instead of plain brine, I created a salty marinade with garlic, oregano, lemon zest, and olive oil to tie in the Mediterranean flavors. After an hour, I sautéed the chicken and found that it had absorbed the flavors nicely.

I wanted the chicken and rice to spend time cooking together so their flavors could mingle. Rice takes 30 minutes to cook on the stovetop and chicken breast halves about 15, so 45 minutes into the chicken marinating time, I started the rice. Fifteen minutes later, I placed the chicken over it. After another 15 minutes, both were nicely cooked. But while the timing worked, the flavor didn't. Neither chicken nor rice had much depth.

Browning the chicken first provided a double flavor boost, benefiting the chicken itself and providing fond I could deglaze to flavor the rice. I also sautéed an onion in the chicken drippings and added garlic and oregano to mirror the marinade flavors. On the downside, I

had to wait until the chicken had marinated for the full hour before browning it, and only then could I start the rice. Could I recoup the time by starting the rice in the microwave while the chicken browned? Then they could finish cooking together on the stove. After a couple of tests to iron out the timing, this proved a winning technique.

As I stirred in olives, cherry tomatoes, and parsley at the end, I had two last ideas to maximize flavor. First, I replaced some of the salt in the marinade with salty packing brine from the olives. This perked up the chicken noticeably. Second, I revisited the marinade flavors at serving time, adding lemon zest and fresh oregano to the parsley. With just 30 minutes of hands-on cooking, I'd injected an often boring dish with flavor.

LEMONY MEDITERRANEAN CHICKEN AND RICE Serves 4

- ⅓ cup pitted kalamata olives, chopped, plus ¼ cup olive brine
- ¼ cup olive oil
- 2 tablespoons minced fresh oregano
- 4 garlic cloves, minced
- 1 tablespoon grated lemon zest
  Salt and pepper
- 4 (6- to 8-ounce) boneless, skinless chicken breasts, trimmed
- 2 cups low-sodium chicken broth
- 1 cup long-grain white rice
- 1 onion, chopped
- 4½ ounces cherry or grape tomatoes, halved
- ¼ cup minced fresh parsley

1. Combine olive brine, 3 tablespoons oil, 1 tablespoon oregano, half of garlic, 2 teaspoons lemon zest, 1½ teaspoons salt, and ½ teaspoon pepper in zipper-lock bag. Pat chicken dry with paper towels and place in bag. Refrigerate for 1 to 2 hours, turning occasionally.

2. Pat chicken dry with paper towels. Heat 1½ teaspoons oil in 12-inch nonstick skillet over medium-high heat until just smoking. Cook chicken until browned, 3 to 5 minutes per side; transfer to plate. While chicken is cooking, microwave 1¼ cups broth and rice in covered large bowl until liquid is absorbed, 6 to 8 minutes, stirring halfway through cooking.

3. Add remaining 1½ teaspoons oil and onion to now-empty skillet and cook

over medium heat until softened, about 5 minutes. Stir in 2 teaspoons oregano and remaining garlic and cook until fragrant, about 30 seconds. Add remaining ¾ cup broth and parcooked rice and bring to boil, scraping up any browned bits. Return chicken and any accumulated juices to skillet and cook, covered, over medium-low heat until meat registers 160 degrees and rice is tender, 8 to 12 minutes. Transfer chicken to cutting board, tent loosely with aluminum foil, and let rest for 10 minutes.

4. Off heat, stir olives, tomatoes, and 2 tablespoons parsley into rice. Cover and let sit until chicken is ready. Meanwhile, combine remaining 2 tablespoons parsley, remaining 1 teaspoon oregano, and remaining 1 teaspoon lemon zest in bowl. Slice chicken into ½-inch slices, arrange on top of rice, and sprinkle with herb mixture. Season with salt and pepper to taste, and serve.

To give the chicken a boost of flavor, we add olive brine to the marinade.

Introducing Gremolata

A classic Italian garnish for osso *buco* (braised veal shanks), gremolata is made from minced parsley, lemon zest, and garlic. We adapted the idea, sprinkling our Lemony Mediterranean Chicken and Rice with parsley, lemon zest, and oregano for fresh, bright flavor.

SMALL PACKAGE, BIG WALLOP
Herbs + lemon zest = flavor.

Tuna-Noodle Casserole

This homey dish either conjures warm childhood memories or evokes groans. We set out to make a version that even people who thought they hated tuna-noodle casserole would love. BY NICK IVERSON

Our crunchy, salty, flavorful topping is made with potato chips, cheese, bread crumbs, and butter.

KEY STEPS Building a Better Tuna-Noodle Casserole
Small steps lead to big improvements in our Tuna-Noodle Casserole.

1. Rinsing the cooked egg noodles in cold water prevents them from overcooking in the finished casserole.

2. Sautéing the mushrooms develops rich flavor and evaporates their liquid, so it won't water down the sauce.

3. Marinating the tuna briefly in warm, seasoned oil makes the fish moist and flavorful.

THANKS TO CAMPBELL'S and its many corporate cookbooks, by the late 1940s, the efficient, frugal home cook could add a can of cream of mushroom soup to canned tuna, boiled noodles, shredded cheese, and a few vegetables; top the lot with bread crumbs; bake; and presto—dinner. Convincing my fellow test cooks that tuna-noodle casserole tastes good wouldn't be so easy. Judging from the recipes I tested, I could see why. The sauces were bland and set up like paste, the noodles were mushy, and the tuna was dry and unpleasantly fishy. Despite these sorry specimens, I think tuna-noodle casserole gets a bum rap. I was determined to change some minds.

First, I ditched the soup in favor of a homemade white sauce. The improvement was immediate. I whisked in Monterey Jack and cheddar cheese, which melted well and added nice flavor. I sautéed button mushrooms, to develop their flavor and cook off their liquid so they wouldn't water down the sauce.

As for the noodles, I figured overcooking was where recipes went wrong. I drained my noodles the very instant they hit al dente. Even so, they turned to mush in the casserole. It occurred to me that as the noodles drained, they continued to cook. So I rinsed them under cold water to stop the process, which serendipitously washed away the starch; now I could cross "pasty casseroles" off my list of worries, too.

The dry, overly fishy tuna still marred the casserole. As one taster said, "I'd love tuna-noodle casserole—if only it didn't have tuna." When tuna is canned, it's cooked once before canning and a second time to ensure that it's sterile and, thus, safe to eat. In the casserole, it was cooking yet again. It didn't stand a chance. A colleague suggested that I "marinate" the tuna. Following her advice, I bathed the fish in olive oil, lemon juice, and salt and pepper before adding it to the casserole. This trick worked even better when I warmed the marinade: In just 10 minutes, its flavor penetrated, and the fish turned flaky and moist.

Tuna casserole wouldn't be complete without a topping. Bread crumbs alone were bland and boring. I added potato chips for salty crunch, plus a handful of cheese. I made a final casserole that encompassed all my repairs and refinements and called all doubting Thomases to the table. They're believers now.

TUNA-NOODLE CASSEROLE
Serves 8 to 10

- 4 ounces Monterey Jack cheese, shredded (1 cup)
- 4 ounces sharp cheddar cheese, shredded (1 cup)
- 2 cups potato chips, crushed
- 2 slices hearty white sandwich bread, torn into 1-inch pieces
- 6 tablespoons unsalted butter
  Salt and pepper
- 3 (5-ounce) cans solid white albacore tuna packed in water
- 2 tablespoons olive oil
- 2 teaspoons lemon juice
- 12 ounces egg noodles (7¾ cups)
- 10 ounces white mushrooms, trimmed and sliced ¼ inch thick
- 1 onion, chopped fine
- 1 red bell pepper, stemmed, seeded, and chopped fine
- 3 tablespoons all-purpose flour
- 3½ cups half-and-half
- 1½ cups low-sodium chicken broth
- 1½ cups frozen peas

1. Adjust oven rack to middle position and heat oven to 425 degrees. Combine Monterey Jack and cheddar in bowl. Pulse potato chips, bread, ¼ cup cheese mixture, 2 tablespoons butter, ¼ teaspoon salt, and ¼ teaspoon pepper in food processor until coarsely ground, about 8 pulses; set aside.

2. Place tuna in fine-mesh strainer and press dry with paper towels. Transfer to large bowl and flake into coarse pieces with fork. Microwave oil, lemon juice, ½ teaspoon salt, and ½ teaspoon pepper in small bowl until bubbling around edges, about 30 seconds. Stir oil mixture into tuna and let sit for 10 minutes.

3. Bring 4 quarts water to boil in Dutch oven. Add pasta and 1 tablespoon salt and cook until just al dente. Drain pasta and rinse with cold water until cool, about 2 minutes. Drain again and set aside. Melt 1 tablespoon butter in now-empty pot over medium-high heat. Add mushrooms and ¼ teaspoon salt and cook until liquid evaporates and mushrooms are browned, 6 to 8 minutes. Transfer mushrooms to bowl with tuna mixture. Add 1 tablespoon butter, onion, and bell pepper to now-empty pot and cook, stirring occasionally, until softened, about 5 minutes. Transfer to bowl with tuna-mushroom mixture; set aside.

For more than a century American corporations have been pushing their products through recipes. The back-of-the-box recipe was the genius of one Henry Parsons Crowell, who in the 1880s bought an Ohio oat mill that came with a trademark: a man in Quaker garb holding a scroll that bore the word "Pure." But how could Crowell promote a product as ordinary as oats? Each of his three marketing innovations was later copied far and wide: Crowell made his product convenient and reassured consumers who were nervous about germs by packaging it in the recently invented folding paperboard box. He used four-color printing to make Quaker Oats stand out on the shelf. Finally, he made it easy for housewives to use his product by printing a recipe right on the box. The first recipe was for porridge. Over time, he added bread, fried pudding, pancakes, and in 1908 the first oatmeal cookie. A later version, "Famous Oatmeal Cookies," appeared in 1955 and remains on packages to this day.

4. In now-empty pot, melt remaining 2 tablespoons butter over medium heat. Add flour and cook, whisking constantly, until golden, about 1 minute. Slowly whisk in half-and-half and broth and bring to boil. Reduce heat to medium-low and simmer until slightly thickened, 5 to 7 minutes. Off heat, whisk in remaining cheese mixture until smooth. Stir in pasta, tuna-vegetable mixture, peas, ½ teaspoon salt, and ½ teaspoon pepper.

5. Scrape mixture into 13 by 9-inch baking dish (casserole can be refrigerated without topping for up to 24 hours; increase baking time to 25 minutes, adding topping halfway through baking) and top with bread-crumb mixture. Bake until golden brown, 12 to 14 minutes. Let casserole cool on wire rack for 10 minutes. Serve.

Pennies from Heaven

The expression means an unexpected windfall of good fortune. But at first these glazed carrots were anything but a windfall of good flavor. BY NICK IVERSON

IN THE MID-1930s, "candying," or glazing, cheap, naturally sweet vegetables such as sweet potatoes and parsnips was in vogue as a quick way to improve their flavor. One such side dish using carrots was nicknamed "pennies from heaven," after the feel-good Depression-era movie starring Bing Crosby. To make the dish, carrots are cut into coins, cooked, and glazed with orange juice, sugar, cinnamon, butter, and dried apricots until they shine like newly minted pennies.

Recipes typically call for either boiling or steaming the carrots and then stirring in (sticky-sweet) glazes. But when I tried it, this technique produced mushy, washed-out carrots; sugar overload; and leathery chunks of apricots. And where was the orange flavor? Clearly, this recipe needed to be dusted off and revitalized.

Since I wanted the orange flavor to really register, instead of boiling the carrots in water I tried simmering them directly in orange juice. That worked well, so to further punch up the flavor I tossed in the orange zest. Instead of using a pot, it occurred to me to switch to a (nonstick) skillet. That way, once the carrots were tender I could simply crank up the heat to reduce the orange juice for an instant glaze (and save myself the trouble of cleaning a second pan). Unfortunately, this streamlined method exacerbated the original problem of saccharine-sweet glazes: As the orange juice reduced, its sugars concentrated. To compensate for that, I removed the added sugar that's called for in most recipes.

I'd fixed the sugar level—the glaze finally tasted right—but I'd inadvertently messed up its consistency: The glaze was watery and didn't cling to the carrots. (Sugar not only sweetens; it also thickens.) I tried adding apricot

Lemon juice balances the sweetness of the carrots, orange juice, apricots, and sugar.

jam, both to thicken and to reinforce the glaze's fruity flavors. Whoops. Too sweet—again. Not only that, but I'd forgotten that jam thins out when warmed. I reconsidered granulated sugar, this time using a fraction of the amount that I'd started with. Happily, a mere tablespoon restored the glaze's consistency without pushing the dish into dessert territory. To reinforce the carrots' savory qualities, I squirted in lemon juice and sprinkled on black pepper. I added the knob of butter now, which emulsified, helping to turn the juice into a glaze.

The apricots, however, remained tough, chewy afterthoughts—I was adding them at the end, just to heat through. I could have softened them with a little hot liquid, draining it before tossing them with the carrots at the end, but wouldn't it be easier to plump the apricots in the orange juice from the start? A bonus: They lent tang and brightness to the simmering carrots. I added the cinnamon at the same time, to give its harsh edge a chance to mellow.

I wish I could promise you good times to come, but I'm afraid I don't have that kind of power. But here's something I can promise: These pennies from heaven will sweeten your table.

DOUBLE DUTY
Simmering Liquid and Glaze Base
Simmering the carrots in orange juice infuses them with flavor. At the end, we add butter and sugar and reduce the juice to a glossy glaze. We use the zest to add flavor, too.

CITRUS PUNCH

PENNIES FROM HEAVEN Serves 4
We like to use a rasp-style grater to zest citrus fruits.

- 1 **pound carrots, peeled and sliced ¼ inch thick**
- ¼ **teaspoon grated orange zest plus ½ cup juice**
- ¼ **cup dried apricots, chopped**
- 2 **tablespoons lemon juice**
  Salt and pepper
- ⅛ **teaspoon ground cinnamon**
- 1 **tablespoon sugar**
- 1 **tablespoon unsalted butter**

1. Bring carrots, orange zest and juice, apricots, lemon juice, ½ teaspoon salt, ¼ teaspoon pepper, and cinnamon to boil in 12-inch nonstick skillet over medium-high heat. Reduce heat to medium-low, cover, and simmer, stirring occasionally, until carrots are nearly tender, 8 to 10 minutes.

2. Remove lid, increase heat to medium-high, and cook until liquid is reduced to 2 tablespoons, 1 to 2 minutes. Add sugar and butter and cook, stirring frequently, until carrots are tender and glaze is thick and glossy, 1 to 2 minutes. Season with salt and pepper to taste. Serve.

Chinese Chicken Salad

Does "tired, limp, and anemic" sound like something you want to eat? We set out to bring crunch, fresh taste, and boldness to this 1980s favorite. BY REBECCAH MARSTERS

JUICY CHICKEN, STRONG flavors, and crunchy, fresh vegetables—Chinese chicken salad is a good idea with a prestigious pedigree. Wolfgang Puck introduced it to Angelenos at his Chinois on Main restaurant a few decades back. But ever since it trickled down to family-friendly chains and turned up on mall menus across the country, the salad has lost its way. That was abundantly clear when I tested a half-dozen recipes recently and watched my tasters pick at watery lettuce, bland chicken, and a hodgepodge of ingredients, all coated in gloppy, sugary dressing. I wanted to restore the salad to its original dignity, giving it balance, textural contrast, flavorful chicken, and a fresh outlook.

Despite the name, recipes for Chinese chicken salads seem to ignore the chicken. Many call for rotisserie chicken. But to get the Asian flavors to penetrate the poultry, I knew that I'd need to start with marinated raw chicken. I settled on boneless, skinless breasts for convenience, marinating them for an hour in a mixture of soy sauce, rice vinegar, grated ginger, store-bought orange juice, chili-garlic sauce, and a moderate amount of sugar. I sautéed the chicken, let the meat cool, and shredded it. I was pleased with the taste but not the timetable. Could I skip the soak and simply poach the chicken breasts in their marinade? I gave it a try. After I removed and shredded the chicken, I cooked the marinade down to concentrate its flavor. I discovered that if I returned the shredded chicken to the concentrated marinade, it soaked up even more flavor.

As I got to work making my dressing, I realized that it was almost identical in composition to the marinade. To streamline, I created one mixture, using

> To see how to properly section an orange, go to CooksCountry.com/extra.

some of it to poach the chicken and adding sesame and vegetable oils to the remainder for the dressing.

Time to pare down: I vetoed all canned ingredients—baby corn, water chestnuts, and mandarin oranges—and gave the OK to scallions, cilantro, and bell peppers. For crunch, I used flavorful roasted peanuts. I knew that it would

take a substantial green to stand up to the strong flavors in this salad. Napa cabbage worked nicely in tandem with romaine. I tossed all the ingredients with dressing and then tasted . . . a muddle. Where was the fresh, vibrant Chinese chicken salad of my imagination? A colleague suggested that I handle the sturdy chicken and the vegetables separately. So I dressed the vegetables on their own and topped them with the chicken. Made this way, the salad snapped into focus.

A few of my tasters just wouldn't give up on the canned mandarin oranges. I wouldn't budge on the can, but I was willing to add fresh orange segments. While I was at it, I used their juice in the marinade in place of store-bought.

Economists say that China's star is rising. The same goes for this salad.

Fresh oranges brighten the taste and color of our Chinese Chicken Salad.

CHINESE CHICKEN SALAD
Serves 6

You can substitute one clove of minced garlic and ¼ teaspoon of cayenne pepper for the Asian chili-garlic sauce.

- 2 oranges
- ¼ cup rice vinegar
- ¼ cup soy sauce
- 3 tablespoons grated fresh ginger
- 3 tablespoons sugar
- 1 tablespoon Asian chili-garlic sauce
- 3 tablespoons vegetable oil
- 2 tablespoons toasted sesame oil
- 4 (6- to 8-ounce) boneless, skinless chicken breasts, trimmed
- 2 romaine lettuce hearts (12 ounces), sliced thin
- ½ small head napa cabbage, cored and sliced thin (6 cups)
- 2 red bell peppers, stemmed, seeded, and cut into 2-inch-long matchsticks
- 1 cup fresh cilantro leaves
- 1 cup salted, dry-roasted peanuts, chopped
- 6 scallions, sliced thin

1. Cut thin slice from top and bottom of oranges, then slice off rind and pith. Working over bowl, cut orange segments from thin membrane and transfer segments to second bowl; set aside. Squeeze juice from membrane into first bowl (juice should measure ¼ cup).

2. Combine orange juice, vinegar, soy sauce, ginger, sugar, and chili-garlic sauce in bowl; transfer ½ cup orange juice mixture to 12-inch skillet. Slowly whisk vegetable oil and sesame oil into remaining orange juice mixture to make vinaigrette; set aside.

3. Bring orange juice mixture in skillet to boil. Add chicken, reduce heat to medium-low, cover, and simmer until meat registers 160 degrees, 10 to 15 minutes, flipping halfway through cooking. Transfer chicken to plate and let rest for 5 to 10 minutes.

4. Meanwhile, boil pan juices until reduced to ¼ cup, 1 to 3 minutes; set aside. Using 2 forks, shred chicken into bite-size pieces. Off heat, add chicken, any accumulated juices, and 2 tablespoons vinaigrette to skillet. Toss to coat and let sit for 10 minutes.

5. Toss romaine, cabbage, bell peppers, cilantro, peanuts, and scallions with remaining vinaigrette in large bowl. Transfer to serving platter and top with chicken and oranges. Serve.

Shrimp Bisque

Shrimp bisque is a delicious classic, but it can be daunting to make. We wanted a version that didn't involve washing every pot in your kitchen—yet still delivered great shrimp flavor. BY NICK IVERSON

SHRIMP BISQUE IS one of those great "fancy" French soups. When done correctly, it's something to behold—luxuriously rich and creamy, mildly sweet and shrimpy, with a hint of sherry and a handsome pastel hue. But fancy often equals finicky and tedious. The recipes I tested were just that, ranging from antiquated and involved (making a shrimp stock in one pot, whisking a roux in another, sautéing aromatics in a third, and then straining the soup through a French *chinois*) to the downright strange (creating a compound butter from the boiled shells). And then there were those that set the bisque on fire—I'm not kidding. I wanted bisque that didn't chain me to the stove yet still delivered impressive shrimp flavor; I wanted "fancy" without the fuss.

From the initial recipes I tested I could see two things right away: One, like most crustaceans, shrimp carry a lot of their flavor in their shells, and the trick is extracting it. Two, in effort to extract that flavor, recipes wasted as much as 1½ pounds of whole raw shrimp, calling for making stock for the soup from whole, ground, or sautéed shrimp, and in all three cases discarding the spent crustaceans. I wanted the shrimp in my bisque, not in the trash.

> ▶ Learn how to devein and peel shrimp at **CooksCountry.com/extra.**

Seeking to make easy, flavorful stock with no waste, I turned to bottled clam juice, a briny test kitchen staple for seafood soups. But far from highlighting the shrimp flavor, the clam juice screamed "Clam!" and overwhelmed the delicate shrimp. Next, I tried chicken stock, another go-to soup backbone in the test kitchen. Again, tasters vetoed it, gently reminding me that shrimp bisque should taste like, you know, shrimp.

I reconsidered making my own stock. I'd try it, but I'd use just the shells, plus the process would have to be less complicated. I peeled the shrimp and set aside the shells and meat separately. From there, I followed a streamlined basic seafood bisque method: I sautéed onions, carrots, and celery in butter and added flour (to thicken), white wine (for acidity), and tomato paste (a standard shrimp bisque ingredient for color and flavor). I poured in plain water and stirred in the reserved shrimp shells. I let everything simmer for about 30

minutes, and then I strained the pot and pitched the spent shells and vegetables. Finally, I returned my simple, homemade stock to the stove, added lots of cream, and, in the last few minutes, stirred in the chopped shrimp meat.

This approach produced an acceptable bisque but not a great one. Simply boiling the shrimp shells had resulted in meek shrimp flavor. What to do to amplify it? I knew that sautéing and browning any ingredient helps develop its flavor, and I remembered that some of my initial test recipes had done so with the shells. So I changed my order of operations. First, I sautéed the shrimp shells in butter until they were golden brown, about five minutes. Only then did I add the vegetables and continue as before. Now my bisque had pronounced (and delicious) shrimp flavor.

Unfortunately, the shrimp themselves were like rubbery marbles, even though I was adding them to the simmering broth for just three minutes. I tried introducing the shrimp after I turned off the heat, covering the pot, and letting the bisque stand for five minutes. The gentle residual heat cooked the shrimp perfectly. Finished with the classic splash of sherry, my bisque looked and tasted as fancy and as fussy as the recipes I'd started with. Looks are deceiving.

SHRIMP BISQUE Serves 6 to 8
Be sure to buy shell-on shrimp for this recipe.

- 4 tablespoons unsalted butter
- 2 pounds medium-large (31 to 40 per pound) shrimp, peeled and shells reserved, shrimp deveined and chopped
- 2 onions, chopped
- 2 carrots, peeled and chopped
- 2 celery ribs, chopped
- ½ cup all-purpose flour
- 6 tablespoons tomato paste
- 2 garlic cloves, minced
- 2 cups dry white wine
- 6 cups water
- 2 sprigs fresh thyme
- 2 cups heavy cream
- 1 tablespoon dry sherry
  Salt and pepper

1. Melt butter in Dutch oven over medium heat. Cook shrimp shells until spotty brown, about 5 minutes. Add onions, carrots, and celery and cook until browned, 6 to 8 minutes. Stir in

flour and cook, stirring constantly, until golden, about 2 minutes. Add tomato paste and garlic and cook until fragrant and paste begins to darken, about 2 minutes. Stir in wine and simmer, scraping up any browned bits, until thickened, 2 to 3 minutes. Add water and thyme and bring to boil. Reduce heat to medium-low and simmer until slightly thickened, about 30 minutes.

2. Strain contents of pot through fine-mesh strainer into large saucepan, pressing on solids to extract as much liquid as possible; discard solids. Stir in cream and sherry and bring to simmer. Off heat, add chopped shrimp, cover pot, and let sit until shrimp are cooked through, about 5 minutes. Season with salt and pepper to taste, and serve.

To avoid overcooking the shrimp, we add them off heat.

Shell-On Shrimp
For a bisque with real shrimp flavor, you need the shells, not just the meat. After peeling, sauté the shells with vegetables and then add water and wine to make a fast, flavorful shrimp stock.

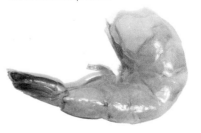

CRUSTACEAN PLUS CARAPACE

Black and White Cookies

These huge, tender cookies may be New York's best-kept secret. We spill it.

CAROLYNN PURPURA MACKAY

*Y*ou would be hard-pressed to find a deli or bakery in New York City that doesn't sell black and white cookies. But if you're not from the Big Apple (or you missed the famous "Sein-feld" episode about them), here's what you need to know: They're tender, gigantic iced cookies with an ardent following. The base is flavored with vanilla or lemon. The icing is half chocolate and half vanilla or lemon. "Cookie" may be a misnomer, as what you get when you mix the ingredients together is closer to cake batter than to cookie dough, and the cookie itself is definitely of the cakey school.

I don't live in New York. But even if I did, bakery black and white cookies rarely live up to their billing. Former *New York Times* food writer Molly O'Neill should know, and here's what she wrote in 2001: "The black-and-white cookie, that frumpy and oversize mainstay of New York City bakeries and delis, has not endured by dint of its taste. Unlike other edible icons, like New York cheesecake or bagels, there is no such thing as a delicious black-and-white cookie. They are either edible or inedible." I took what O'Neill wrote as a personal challenge. I grabbed recipes from every New York City cookbook I could track down and headed into the test kitchen.

These recipes mainly produced cookies about the size of coasters, yet the range of textures was wider than I had expected. Some were like sugar cookies, others resembled sponge cake, and a third group was nearest to tender yellow cake. None was bad (it's a cookie, folks),

Our Black and White Cookies get flipped after they are baked so that the flat bottom, which is easy to glaze, becomes the top.

but none was perfect, either. As a group, they were bland, and even the one we liked best and considered truest to form was too crunchy and coarse, plus it was pocked with air bubbles. Still, it was clear that I didn't have to reinvent the wheel here; my job would be to fine-tune. Before buckling down to work, I made an executive decision: I abandoned the lemon. Lemon and chocolate? Whatever some New Yorkers say, the combination is as wrong as cheering for the Yankees at Fenway Park. I'd stick with vanilla.

The recipe I used as my jumping-off point read like a yellow cake recipe: First cream butter with sugar, next beat in the egg, and then alternate the dry ingredients (all-purpose flour with leavener) with milk. The batter that it produced was thicker than cake batter, though, so the raw cookies would hold their shape. As an experienced baker, I knew that cake flour equals tender crumb and soft interior, so I tried it. It was tender all right—so tender that the cookies fell apart. I went back to all-purpose flour.

Next I substituted sour cream for the milk. Sour cream typically makes for tender baked goods, and it did so here. But the one-for-one swap made the cookies so moist that they stuck to the cookie sheets. I dialed back on the amount of sour cream. Getting rid of the air bubbles in the cookies was as easy as using less baking soda and powder. Finally, I doubled the vanilla extract and sat back as the complaints about blandness disappeared. When I started seeing tasting sheets that said things like

"Killer! So right!" I knew it was time to move on to the icing.

The most heated debate during my early tests had been over which side of the cookies to frost: flat or domed. After a couple of trial runs, I settled on the flat side—simpler to frost and there was less risk of the glaze running down the edges. With that settled, we debated the texture. Should the frosting be creamy or "snap" when a cookie was broken in half? To please everybody, I set myself the goal of making a creamy icing that set up to a hard sheen.

Some recipes for black and white frosting are actually fondant: water and sugar boiled to what candy makers call the "soft-ball stage." I had no intention of making such a fuss and opted for a streamlined approach: I'd combine confectioners' sugar with water, milk, or heavy cream, whisking together a base glaze and adding chocolate to half. The water made the glaze look dull and taste chalky. The cream kept it too soft. Milk proved perfect but for one thing: As the soft cookies sat, the icing soaked in. To prevent that, I peered into my pastry chef's bag of tricks and pulled out corn syrup. I replaced a portion of the milk with syrup for thicker, stickier, and shinier glaze. For the chocolate glaze, I tested chocolate in every form before settling on cocoa power as the simplest. No need to melt: Just open the tin.

As I was wrapping up my testing, a New York friend announced that she was coming to town. I requested a box of black and white cookies. When she (and they) arrived, I pitted them against my homemade version. New York, here I come.

BLACK AND WHITE COOKIES

Makes 12 cookies

Twelve cookies doesn't sound like much, but these cookies are huge. You'll get neater cookies it you spread on the vanilla glaze first. This recipe provides a little extra glaze, just in case.

COOKIES

- 1¾ cups (8¾ ounces) all-purpose flour
- ½ teaspoon baking powder
- ¼ teaspoon baking soda
- ⅛ teaspoon salt
- 10 tablespoons unsalted butter, softened
- 1 cup (7 ounces) granulated sugar
- 1 large egg
- 2 teaspoons vanilla extract
- ⅓ cup sour cream

GLAZE

- 5 cups (20 ounces) confectioners' sugar, sifted
- 7 tablespoons whole milk
- 2 tablespoons corn syrup
- 1 teaspoon vanilla extract
- ½ teaspoon salt
- 3 tablespoons Dutch-processed cocoa powder, sifted

1. FOR THE COOKIES: Adjust oven racks to upper-middle and lower-middle positions and heat oven to 350 degrees. Line 2 baking sheets with parchment paper. Combine flour, baking powder, baking soda, and salt in bowl.

2. Using stand mixer fitted with paddle, beat butter and sugar on medium-high speed until pale and fluffy, about 2 minutes. Add egg and vanilla and beat until combined. Reduce speed to low and add flour mixture in 3 additions, alternating with 2 additions of sour cream, scraping down bowl as needed. Give dough final stir by hand.

3. Using greased ¼-cup measure, drop cookie dough 3 inches apart onto prepared baking sheets. Bake until edges are lightly browned, 15 to 18 minutes, switching and rotating sheets halfway through baking. Let cookies cool on sheets for 5 minutes, then transfer to wire rack to cool completely, about 1 hour.

4. FOR THE GLAZE: Whisk sugar, 6 tablespoons milk, corn syrup, vanilla, and salt together in bowl until smooth. Transfer 1 cup glaze to small bowl; reserve. Whisk cocoa and remaining 1 tablespoon milk into remaining glaze until combined.

5. Working with 1 cookie at a time, spread 1 tablespoon vanilla glaze over half of underside of cookie. Refrigerate until glaze is set, about 15 minutes. Cover other half of cookies with 1 tablespoon chocolate glaze and let cookies sit at room temperature until glaze is firm, at least 1 hour. Serve. (Cookies can be stored at room temperature for up to 2 days.)

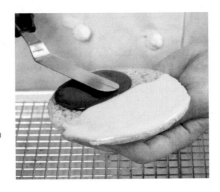

TEST KITCHEN TECHNIQUE
Glazing Black and White Cookies

Using a butter knife or offset mini spatula, glaze half of the underside of each cookie with vanilla. Chill the cookies in the refrigerator for 15 minutes so the glaze can start to harden. Glaze the other half of each cookie with chocolate, and let the cookies sit until the glaze sets, about one hour.

RATING COOKIE JARS

Cookie jars come in shapes and sizes of all sorts: You can buy one that looks like the Cookie Monster, Tinker Bell, or Mr. T. But what about function? We want our jar to keep cookies fresh, intact, and easy to grab. Avoiding novelty jars, we bought four models, one each in glass, plastic, ceramic, and stainless steel, all with at least 4-quart capacity so they could hold plenty of baked goods. We looked for jars with a tight seal to maintain freshness and with openings wide enough to allow us to reach inside for really big cookies (up to 4 inches in diameter). We filled the jars with French tuile cookies (they're brittle, so particularly susceptible to humidity) and inspected them daily for a week: Even the worst performer kept the cookies crisp for a respectable four days. Next we filled each jar with a moisture-sensitive color indicator called Drierite; its crystals change from blue to pink as dampness penetrates. After seven days, we noticed changes in color, which were more drastic in some jars than in others. Only one jar kept the Drierite blue. The OXO Good Grips Pop Storage Container made an airtight seal that can keep our homemade cookies fresh, crisp, and delectable for days—if they last that long. –TAIZETH SIERRA

KEY Good ★★★ Fair ★★ Poor ★

HIGHLY RECOMMENDED	CRITERIA		TESTERS' NOTES
OXO GOOD GRIPS Pop Storage Container, Big Square 4 Quart **Model:** 1071396V1 **Price:** $16.99 **Source:** www.oxo.com 	Performance Ease of Cleaning	★★★ ★★	No other container in our lineup had an airtight seal (activated by a pop-up button on the lid). We also liked that the clear plastic (BPA-free) jar showed off our baking. The container was easy to clean, but the lid's nooks and crannies took more effort, and the lid is not dishwasher-safe. We tested the 4-quart model; the container comes in several sizes and shapes.

RECOMMENDED

OGGI Jumbo 9.5-Inch Ceramic Cookie Jar **Model:** 5326 **Price:** $19.95 **Source:** www.cooking.com	Performance Ease of Cleaning	★★ ★★★	This ceramic jar kept cookies crisp. Our moisture indicator stayed dry, too—until the weather turned damp. Then it discolored slightly, telling us that in spite of a rubber gasket, the jar lacked an airtight seal. This model is easy to clean, with no nooks to trap crumbs.
ANCHOR HOCKING 1-Gallon Heritage Hill Jar with Glass Lid **Model:** 69349T **Price:** $9.99 **Source:** www.bedbathandbeyond.com	Performance Ease of Cleaning	★★ ★★★	This glass model was a looker, bringing to mind a jar you might find on the counter of an old-fashioned general store. The heavy glass lid did a decent job keeping cookies fresh—as long as the humidity was low. Washing was a breeze.

RECOMMENDED WITH RESERVATIONS

BASIC ESSENTIALS English Heritage Cookie Bin **Model:** TTU-17329-EC **Price:** $12.99 **Source:** www.ttustore.com	Performance Ease of Cleaning	★★ ★	This handsome stainless steel tin was the roomiest of the models we tested. Unfortunately, it ranked last for cookie freshness. Also, the deep seams along the bottom and sides filled with crumbs, making cleanup a hassle.

Cooking Class Quicker Chicken Broth

Homemade chicken broth can improve your cooking by leaps and bounds. But traditional chicken broth requires hours of simmering. We found a faster way to a rich, flavorful broth.

QUICKER CHICKEN BROTH

Makes 2½ quarts broth and 3 cups meat

A cleaver is the best tool for hacking through the chicken legs. If you don't have one, use the thick heel end of a heavy-bladed chef's knife or leave the legs whole and double the simmering time. If you're not making soup and don't need meat, you can use any combination of chicken backs and/or wingtips in place of the legs.

- 1 tablespoon vegetable oil
- 4 pounds chicken leg quarters, cut into 2-inch pieces
- 1 onion, chopped
- 2 quarts water
- 2 teaspoons salt
- 2 bay leaves

1. Heat oil in Dutch oven over medium-high heat until just smoking. Add half of chicken and cook until browned all over, about 10 minutes. Transfer to bowl and repeat with remaining chicken. Transfer chicken to bowl with first batch; carefully remove fat from pot and save for another use. (See "Broth Q&A.")

2. Return chicken to pot along with onion, cover, and cook over low heat until chicken releases its juices, about 20 minutes. Add water, salt, and bay leaves, and bring to boil over high heat.

3. Reduce heat to medium-low and simmer, covered, until broth is rich and flavorful, about 20 minutes. Strain broth into large bowl and let stand for 10 minutes before defatting. Remove meat from bones, discarding skin and bones, and reserve meat for another use.

60-MINUTE BROTH
We use only chicken legs, onion, bay leaves, and salt.

Broth in a Jiffy

The traditional method requires a whole chicken, leeks, carrots, celery, parsley sprigs, thyme, bay leaves (the last three tied into a bouquet garni), salt, and peppercorns. And at least 2½ hours of simmering. We prefer to keep it short and simple.

ESSENTIAL EQUIPMENT

Besides the obvious—a stockpot or a Dutch oven—several other kitchen implements will come in handy when making our recipe for Quicker Chicken Broth. The models shown below are our favorites: the winners of our meticulously tested equipment rating stories.

Cleaver If you have a cleaver gathering dust in your kitchen, break it out now. It's designed to chop through bones.

Global 6-Inch Meat Cleaver, $167

Strainer Broth made with hacked bones will contain minute bone particles and must be strained. A fine-mesh strainer is the right tool for the job.

CIA Masters Collection Fine-Mesh Strainer, $28

Fat Separator A fat separator makes defatting hot broth simple—just pour the broth in the top, let it settle, and pour the defatted broth out of the spout, leaving the fat behind.

Trudeau Gravy Separator with Integrated Strainer, $12.99

MAKE AHEAD Freeze with Ease

Once you get used to having homemade chicken broth at the ready in the freezer, you'll wonder how you ever lived without it. Depending on how you'll ultimately use it, you can freeze the broth in portions of different sizes. Here are three ideas for freezing broth; all can be stored for up to three months.

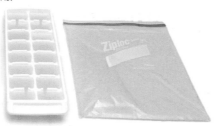

Use ice cube trays for small amounts Pour the broth into ice cube trays. After the cubes have frozen, remove them and store them in a zipper-lock bag. Use cubes for pan sauces, stir-fry sauces, and vegetable braises.

Use muffin tins for medium amounts Nonstick muffin tins create slightly larger portions. After the broth has frozen, store the "cups" in a large zipper-lock bag. "Cups" are good for casseroles and braising/steaming/poaching liquid.

Use zipper-lock bags for large amounts Line a 4-cup measuring cup with a zipper-lock bag (it holds the bag open so you can use both hands to pour) and pour in the cooled broth. Seal the bag (double up if you wish) and lay it flat to freeze. This is a good option for rice, gravy, soup, or stew.

Really Easy Chicken Broth in 12 Really Easy Steps

This
We

BUTTE
crean
rots.
appei
tiona
prope
the b
morr
leftov
pot p
a pro

In
route
vesse
rame
plent
for p
head

Fo
less,
the r
breas
takin
in ch
save
the b
the c
tradi
and f
roux
seasc
brou
poini
cove
thing
the c
the s

Tl
was
som
breas
sauc
that,
sauté
the r
kitch
sauc
norn

N
fresh
fashi
then
befo
just
carrc
and
get v
vidu
sauté

1. HACK CHICKEN
Use a cleaver (or heavy chef's knife) to hack the raw chicken legs into 2-inch pieces.
WHY? To quickly release the bone marrow, which adds richness and body to the stock.

2. HEAT OIL
Heat a tablespoon of oil in a Dutch oven until smoking.
WHY? If the oil isn't hot enough, the chicken won't brown properly (and browning adds flavor).

3. BROWN CHICKEN
Add half of the chicken to the hot oil and brown on both sides. Repeat with the rest of the chicken.
WHY? Browning adds deep flavor quickly.

4. POUR OFF FAT
After removing the last batch of browned chicken, carefully pour off the hot fat.
WHY? To help ensure the finished broth won't be greasy.

5. ADD ONION
Return the browned chicken to the pot and stir in a chopped onion.
WHY? The onion adds aromatic depth to the stock fast. (Carrot and celery need more time to contribute flavor.)

6. COVER AND COOK
Reduce the heat to low, cover the pot, and cook for about 20 minutes. Remove the lid only when the chicken has released its juices.
WHY? The steamy environment encourages the chicken to release its rich, flavorful juices.

7. ADD WATER AND SEASONINGS
Add the water, salt, and bay leaves to the pot.
WHY? Salt and bay leaves are all the seasoning this quick broth needs.

8. SIMMER AND COVER
Bring the broth to a simmer, cover, and cook for just 20 minutes.
WHY? Now is when the magic happens: The broth becomes deeply infused with chicken flavor.

9. STRAIN BROTH
Using a fine-mesh strainer, carefully strain the hot broth into a large, clean bowl or pot.
WHY? To separate the broth from the hunks of chicken and to remove bone particles and other impurities from the liquid.

10. DEFAT BROTH
Let strained broth cool and settle for 10 minutes and then defat in batches using a fat separator.
WHY? To avoid a fatty, greasy broth.

11. TAKE MEAT OFF BONES
When the chicken is cool enough to handle, separate the meat from the bones, discarding the skin and bones.
WHY? Because you don't want to waste moist, delicious chicken leg meat.

12. STORE SEPARATELY
Even if you plan to combine them later, store the meat and broth in separate containers.
WHY? So the chicken doesn't turn wet and soggy.

Broth Q&A

Why not just use canned broth?
Storebought broth is fine for many recipes, but homemade is so much better. To prove it, we held a blind taste test for 15 cooks, pitting our Quicker Chicken Broth against our favorite storebought broth, Swanson Certified Organic Free Range Chicken Broth. The "rich," "meaty" home-made broth won in a landslide.

Is there a difference between broth and stock?
It depends whom you ask. These days, many sources use these terms inter-changeably. But technically, stock is more concentrated and has more body. It's made from meaty bones, which are sometimes roasted before they are simmered to extract even more flavor. Broth is lighter: A whole chicken or chicken parts are simmered until the chicken is done. Recipes for the home cook that call for broth or stock to make, say, rice pilaf rarely distinguish between the two.

Why simmer the broth? Can't I boil it so it's ready even quicker?
No. It's important to simmer, not boil, or the grease will blend into the broth. At that point, it's less likely to separate, making the broth difficult to defat.

What if I don't own a fat separator?
A fat separator makes quick work of defatting hot broth, but you can use these three tools instead: time, your refrig-erator, and a spoon. When you let the broth chill for several hours, the fat solidi-fies on top and can be easily removed.

What can I do with the chicken fat?
Chicken fat is loaded with flavor. If you're making soup, use the fat (called *schmaltz* in Yiddish and used with abandon in Jewish cooking) instead of oil to sauté the aromatics. You can also use it in place of butter when making a roux for gravy or stew. Chicken fat will keep in the refrig-erator for three days; it also freezes well.

▶ Visit **CooksCountry.com/extra**
for our recipe for Chicken Noodle Soup.

Looking for a Recipe

READER TO READER

Did you misplace a favorite recipe? Can you almost taste a chocolate cake from childhood but the recipe is long gone? Ask a reader. While you're at it, answer a reader. Post queries and finds at **CooksCountry.com/magazine**; click on **Looking for a Recipe** (or write to Looking for a Recipe, *Cook's Country*, P.O. Box 470739, Brookline, MA 02447). We'll share all of your submissions online and print several on this page. Include your name and mailing address with each submission.

Plum Cake
Joanne Botzum, Medina, Ohio

My grandmother used to make a simple cake with slices of plums in it. I've seen several recipes for plum cake, but they are not the same. Hers was not frosted, but I believe she sprinkled sugar on it and baked or broiled it to produce a crunchy glaze. The plums poked out through the top of the cake so she was always careful to arrange them attractively. Do you have a recipe for this type of plum cake?

Pork Chops Baked in Cabbage
Margaret Silliker, Chicago, Ill.

I have been trying to find the recipe for pork chops baked in cabbage that came from a 1960s or '70s Time Life series about French cooking. I don't remember the exact name of the recipe, but the pork chops were browned and then baked in a cabbage and white wine cream sauce. The chops came out incredibly tender, while the cabbage dissolved into the delicious creamy sauce.

Scrapple
Gloria Laylin, Dublin, Ohio

My mother used to make scrapple with cornmeal and sausage and put it in a loaf pan. Then she sliced it, fried it in butter, and served it with maple syrup. I've tried several recipes, but none come close. She was from New York, moved to Kansas when she married in 1944, and then moved to Ohio in about 1959, and I don't know where she got the recipe. It was definitely not Philadelphia scrapple. It would be wonderful to duplicate it.

Ginger Cream Cookies
Colleen McMahon, Waconia, Minn.

When I was a child in the 1960s and '70s, my grandma McMahon used to make delicious cookies called ginger creams. They were thick, soft, cakey, dark cookies with creamy white icing. At every family reunion, we reminisce about our wonderful grandmother, and also about the fact that none of us has ever been able to duplicate her ginger cream recipe. It sure would be great to have it back in the family. Thanks.

Steak Fingers
Phyllis Easterling, Fort Collins, Colo.

When I was in high school, the A&W used to serve something they called "steak finger basket." Everyone loved it. I'm curious to know what cut of meat they used and what spices were in the crispy breading so I can try to duplicate the item in my own kitchen.

Chocolate Icebox Cookies
Anna Jo Fischer, Eugene, Ore.

I'm looking for a recipe for chocolate icebox cookies that our housekeeper used to make for us. She would roll the dough into a log, wrap it in waxed paper, and put it in the freezer. The cookies were very thin, cakelike, and very delicious. Please help!

Sugar Cream Pie
Sydne Brewer, Seattle, Wash.

I grew up in a small north-central Indiana town, where we used to eat sugar cream pie. Now my family lives in Seattle, and no one here has even heard of it. In Indiana, we used to buy it at the local grocery store. It's my dad's favorite pie. I have tried several recipes (including David Letterman's mom's recipe), but none is as good as the pie I remember from childhood. Please help me make a great sugar cream pie for my dad.

Burnt Sugar Cake
Barbara Burcham-Ramsay, Central Point, Ore.

Way back when (perhaps as long ago as home-ec class in Westchester, California), I had a great recipe for burnt sugar cake. When cake mixes came on the scene, Duncan Hines had a mix for it. Now, no company that I know of makes a mix for the cake, and I can't locate my old recipe. Can anyone help?

Tomato Dumplings
Debi Varelis, Bradenton, Fla.

My Tennessee grandma used to make this for us when we were children. I know it had stewed tomatoes, with dropped dumplings cooked in the sauce. I would love to have this recipe again.

FIND THE ROOSTER!

A tiny version of this rooster has been hidden in the pages of this issue. Write to us with its location and we'll enter you in a random drawing. The first correct entry drawn will win our top-rated innovative cutting board (see page 30), and each of the next five will receive a free one-year subscription to *Cook's Country*. To enter, visit **CooksCountry.com/rooster** by March 31, 2012, or write to Rooster, *Cook's Country*, P.O. Box 470739, Brookline, MA 02447. Include your name and address. Monica Leichtenberg of Covington, La., found the rooster in the October/November 2011 issue in the Smoky Indoor Ribs photo on page 17 and won our favorite travel mug. Cock-a-doodle-doo.

DATE NUT BARS Makes 12 bars
Sue Shough, Powell, Ohio

The dough may look dry at first, but it will come together as it is mixed. Rolling the bars in confectioners' sugar while they are still slightly warm helps the sugar stick.

- 1 cup packed (7 ounces) brown sugar
- ¾ cup (3¾ ounces) all-purpose flour
- ½ teaspoon baking powder
- ½ teaspoon salt
- 9 ounces pitted dates, chopped (1½ cups)
- 1 cup pecans, toasted and chopped
- 2 large eggs, lightly beaten
- 2 tablespoons unsalted butter, melted and cooled
- ½ cup (2 ounces) confectioners' sugar

1. Adjust oven rack to middle position and heat oven to 350 degrees. Grease and flour 8-inch square baking pan. Combine brown sugar, flour, baking powder, and salt in large bowl. Stir in dates, pecans, eggs, and butter until combined. Scrape batter into prepared pan.

2. Bake until toothpick inserted in center comes out with few crumbs attached, 25 to 30 minutes. Let bars cool in pan on wire rack for 15 minutes. Remove from pan and let cool for 15 minutes. Cut into 12 equal pieces and roll in confectioners' sugar. Transfer to wire rack and let cool completely, about 1 hour. Serve.

FRIED PICKLES Makes 16 pickles
Chad Koerlin, Tampa, Fla.

"I learned to make these pickles from my Uncle Bob. They're perfect dipped in ranch dressing and served with cold beer." Use whole kosher dill pickles that you cut into spears yourself, because they're firmer. With the exception of dark stouts and ales, any beer will work in this recipe—even nonalcoholic.

- ½ cup cornmeal
- 4 whole kosher dill pickles, quartered lengthwise, patted dry with paper towels
- 1 cup all-purpose flour
- 1 cup cornstarch
- 2 teaspoons baking powder
- 1 teaspoon salt
- ½ teaspoon cayenne pepper
- 1 (12-ounce) bottle cold beer
- 3 quarts peanut or vegetable oil

1. Place cornmeal in shallow dish. Dredge pickle spears in cornmeal and transfer to plate. Combine flour, cornstarch, baking powder, salt, and cayenne in large bowl. Slowly whisk in beer until smooth.

2. Heat oil in large Dutch oven over medium-high heat until 350 degrees. Rewhisk batter. Transfer half of pickles to batter. One at a time, remove pickles from batter (allowing excess to drip back into bowl) and fry in hot oil until golden brown, 2 to 3 minutes. Drain pickles on wire rack set in rimmed baking sheet. Bring oil back to 350 degrees and repeat with remaining pickles. Serve.

Raspberry–White Chocolate Bombe

Give your valentine one perfect treat: a giant, cake-size truffle
filled with liqueur-spiked, raspberry–white chocolate mousse. It'll win hearts.

To make this cake you will need:

- ¼ cup raspberry liqueur, such as Chambord
- ¼ cup raspberry-flavored gelatin
- ⅛ teaspoon salt
- 1 pound white chocolate, finely chopped
- 2 cups heavy cream
- 2 cups fresh raspberries
- 1 (9-inch) white cake round*
- White chocolate curls, for decoration*

FOR THE MOUSSE: Line 10-cup-capacity mixing bowl with plastic wrap. Bring liqueur to simmer in small saucepan. Stir in gelatin and salt until dissolved; remove from heat.

Microwave 8 ounces white chocolate and ½ cup heavy cream in medium bowl, stirring every 30 seconds, until chocolate is melted and mixture is smooth, about 1½ minutes. Stir in gelatin mixture and let cool to room temperature, about 30 minutes. Whip remaining 1½ cups cream with electric mixer until soft peaks form, 1 to 3 minutes. Gently fold one-third of whipped cream into cooled white chocolate mixture. Fold in remaining whipped cream until incorporated. Scrape one-third of mousse into prepared bowl and stud with raspberries. Repeat twice with remaining mousse and berries. Place inverted cake round on top of

mousse, trimming cake to fit if necessary. Cover with plastic and chill until mousse is set, about 4 hours (and up to 24 hours).

TO ASSEMBLE: Turn out bombe onto large cake platter. Remove plastic. Microwave remaining 8 ounces chopped chocolate in bowl until melted and gently spread over mousse and cake. Press chocolate curls into white chocolate. Cut cake with warm knife and serve.

*Go to **CooksCountry.com/extra** for our **9-Inch White Cake** recipe and to learn how to make chocolate curls.

Cook's Country

Dear Country Cook,

Years ago, my mother gave me one of her favorite paintings, a modest watercolor of a small West Virginia homestead nestled in a hollow with a winding dirt road. The photo on this page reminds me a great deal of that landscape: a sharp rise of mountain visible from a small front porch. When we built our Vermont cabin in 1955 on the old Ford farm, the view was much the same as the one in that painting. It's odd how landscapes run as constants through our lives, powerful and unrecognized.

Kitchen landscapes have much the same hold on us. For me, it is the warmth of a cast-iron cookstove that radiates like a tiny sun in my own small universe; canning jars shimmering in a bath of steam; lopsided baking powder biscuits set out on a cooling rack; and the constant perfume of wood smoke, wet dog, and maple-cured bacon.

Once the view from the mind's eye is set, it charts our path throughout a lifetime. We think we are headed forward, but we are constantly returning to that small front porch, the one with a familiar view.

Christopher Kimball
Founder and Editor, Cook's Country

Cook's Country

Founder and Editor Christopher Kimball
Editorial Director Jack Bishop
Executive Editor, Magazines John Willoughby
Executive Editor Peggy Grodinsky
Managing Editor Scott Kathan
Senior Editors Lisa McManus, Bryan Roof, Diane Unger
Test Kitchen Director Erin McMurrer
Associate Editors Amy Graves, Sarah Wilson
Test Cooks Sarah Gabriel, Rebeccah Marsters
Assistant Editors Hannah Crowley, Chris Dudley, Shannon Friedmann Hatch, Taizeth Sierra
Assistant Test Cooks Nick Iverson, Carolynn Purpura MacKay
Copy Editors Nell Beram, Megan Chromik
Executive Assistant Christine Gordon
Assistant Test Kitchen Director Gina Nistico
Senior Kitchen Assistants Meryl MacCormack, Leah Rovner
Kitchen Assistants Maria Elena Delgado, Andrew Straaberg Finfrock, Ena Gudiel
Executive Producer Melissa Baldino
Associate Producer Stephanie Stender

Contributing Editors Erika Bruce, Eva Katz, Jeremy Sauer
Consulting Editors Anne Mendelson, Meg Ragland
Science Editor Guy Crosby, Ph.D.
Executive Food Editor, TV, Radio & Media Bridget Lancaster

Online Managing Editor David Tytell
Online Editor Kate Mason
Online Assistant Editors Eric Grzymkowski, Mari Levine
Associate Editor/Camera Operator Nick Dakoulas

Design Director Amy Klee
Art Director Julie Cote
Deputy Art Director Susan Levin
Associate Art Director Lindsey Timko
Staff Photographer Daniel J. van Ackere
Color Food Photography Keller + Keller
Styling Catrine Kelty
Associate Art Director, Marketing/Web Erica Lee
Designers, Marketing/Web Elaina Natario, Mariah Tarvainen
Online Photo Editor Steve Klise

Vice President, Marketing David Mack
Circulation Director Doug Wicinski
Circulation & Fulfillment Manager Carrie Fethe
Partnership Marketing Manager Pamela Putprush
Marketing Assistant Lauren Perkins
Customer Service Manager Jacqueline Valerio
Customer Service Representatives Jessica Amato, Morgan Ryan

Chief Operating Officer David Dinnage
Production Director Guy Rochford
Senior Project Manager Alice Carpenter
Production & Traffic Coordinator Kate Hux
Asset & Workflow Manager Andrew Mannone
Production & Imaging Specialists Judy Blomquist, Heather Dube, Lauren Pettapiece
Technology Director Rocco Lombardo
Systems Administrator Marcus Walser
Software Architect Robert Martinez
Software Project Manager Michelle Rushin
Senior Business Analyst Wendy Tseng
Web Developers Chris Candelora, Cameron MacKenzie
Human Resources Manager Adele Shapiro

VP New Media Product Development Barry Kelly
Social Media Manager Steph Yiu

Chief Financial Officer Sharyn Chabot
Director of Sponsorship Sales Anne Traficante
Retail Sales & Marketing Manager Emily Logan
Client Service Manager, Sponsorship Bailey Snyder
Publicity Deborah Broide

ON THE COVER:
Lemon Snow, Keller + Keller, Catrine Kelty
ILLUSTRATION: Greg Stevenson

Cook's Country magazine (ISSN 1552-1990), number 44, is published bimonthly by Boston Common Press Limited Partnership, 17 Station Street, Brookline, MA 02445. Copyright 2012 Boston Common Press Limited Partnership. Periodicals Postage paid at Boston, Mass., and additional mailing offices. Publications Mail Agreement No. 40020778. Return undeliverable Canadian addresses to P.O. Box 875, Station A, Windsor, Ontario N9A 6P2. POSTMASTER: Send address changes to Cook's Country, P.O. Box 8382, Red Oak, IA 51591-1382. Customer Service: It's easy to subscribe, give a gift subscription, change your address, and manage your subscription online. Visit www.AmericasTestKitchen.com/customerservice for all of your customer service needs or write to us at Cook's Country, P.O. Box 8382, Red Oak, IA 51591-1382. PRINTED IN THE USA

Contents

APRIL/MAY 2012

REDUCED-FAT SCALLOPED POTATOES, 28   PORK CHOPS WITH TOMATO GRAVY, 21   ENGLISH MUFFIN BREAD, 17

Features

In Every Issue

$1,000 GRAND PRIZE

Heirloom Cookie Contest
We're big fans of tradition. So for next Christmas, send us your cherished holiday cookie recipe, the one that's been passed down through the generations. And tell us how the cookie became one of the family. The deadline for entries is April 30, 2012. Submit your heirloom recipe and find contest details at **CooksCountry.com/cookiecontest**. There is one $1,000 grand prize, and six finalists get $100 each.

America's TEST KITCHEN
RECIPES THAT WORK

America's Test Kitchen is a 2,500-square-foot kitchen located just outside of Boston. It is the home of Cook's Country and Cook's Illustrated magazines and is the workday destination of more than 50 test cooks, editors, and cookware specialists. Our mission is to test recipes until we understand how and why they work and arrive at the best version. We also test kitchen equipment and supermarket ingredients in search of brands that offer the best value and performance. You can watch us work by tuning in to Cook's Country from America's Test Kitchen (CooksCountryTV.com) on public television.

Getting to Know Seeds

You may think seeds belong in the garden, but one look around a well-stocked kitchen proves otherwise.

Pumpkin Seeds
HALLOWEEN BONUS

The whole white seeds are sold for snacking; the green hulled versions (pepitas) are popular in Mexico, where they are often ground up for mole sauces. Our tasters described the seeds as having a pleasant "vegetal" taste. To roast pumpkin seeds, spread them out on a lightly oiled rimmed baking sheet, bake at 350 degrees for 10 to 15 minutes, and season with salt and pepper while still hot.

Coriander Seeds
IN A PICKLE

These "seeds" are actually the dried fruits of the coriander plant, which also gives us the herb cilantro. Their "citrusy" flavor enhances spice crusts for meat and fish, and whole seeds are used in pickling. To bring out its flavor, toast coriander in a dry skillet over medium heat for a few minutes, until it's fragrant. Place a splatter screen over the skillet to keep the seeds from popping out of the pan.

Sesame Seeds
BAGEL FRIEND

Look for them on a bagel, in a stir-fry, as a crust for salmon, or ground into tahini. They came to the United States with slaves, who called them benne seeds. The seeds can be grayish ivory, brown, red, or black and are used in both savory and sweet recipes. Their "nutty," subtle "honey" quality suits candies, granola, bread, and sweets, like the classic Southern benne wafers.

Cumin Seeds
WORLD TRAVELERS

Cumin seeds are used in cuisines from India to Asia, Mexico to North Africa, playing a role in both curry blends and chili powders. In America, we often use cumin in its ground form in chili, barbecue sauces, and rubs. Cumin seeds, which resemble caraway, can also add toastiness, crunch, and a distinctive "woodsy aroma" to vegetables like sautéed snap peas or roasted beets.

Flaxseeds
HEALTH FOOD

Health food nuts love these seeds because they're rich in omega-3 fatty acids. The seeds can be toasted, sprouted, or ground; they're most easily digested when eaten ground. Grind them (and other seeds) in a coffee grinder or in a mortar and pestle. Flaxseeds have a "wheaty," "earthy" flavor, making them a nice addition to whole-grain breads. Store them in the refrigerator or freezer.

Poppy Seeds
LEMON'S LOVE

While they come from the same plant that produces opium, we're interested in poppy seeds for their "peppery," "smoky-sweet" flavor, as our tasters described it. Eastern Europeans love them in pastries; in the U.S., we know them from baked treats that have emigrated from that same neck of the woods: bagels, challah, and pretzels. Also, try them in coleslaw, egg noodles, salad dressing, and to add crunch to lemon–poppy seed muffins.

Mustard Seeds
HOT STUFF

These small, acrid seeds put the punch into prepared mustard, be it Dijon, yellow, or whole grain. Whole mustard seeds—the smaller, hotter brown seeds—are common in Indian cuisine, flavoring vindaloo, chutneys, and samosas. In the United States, we use the yellow mustard seeds for pickling and canning. Natural foods stores, as well as some supermarkets, sell spicy mustard seed sprouts near the bean and alfalfa sprouts.

Celery Seeds
LOVAGE CHILD

Celery seeds come from wild celery (or a similar plant called lovage) and have a flavor that our tasters likened to "sweet grass" and "chamomile tea." In the test kitchen, we've used them to lend warm, potent celery flavor to dishes like Chuck Roast in Foil and Catalina Salad Dressing (you can find the recipes for both dishes at CooksCountry.com/recipes).

Caraway Seeds
RYE TOPPER

The Greeks used caraway as a cure for an upset stomach, and it's no coincidence that the seeds are still often paired with notoriously hard-to-digest foods like cabbage, cream sauces, and cheese. They are pungent and herbaceous (tasters picked up "mint" and even "tobacco"), with a slightly bitter finish, making them a natural with fatty meats and in rye bread.

Anise Seeds
BISCOTTI BUDDY

Anise seeds flavor sweets (think biscotti) and such liqueurs as Pernod, pastis, sambuca, and ouzo. They are a close cousin to fennel seeds, which are larger and more savory. Both contain the essential oil anethol, which gives them their licorice flavor. In the test kitchen, we've found that one can usually be substituted for the other, although we prefer to bake with the sweeter anise seeds.

Sunflower Seeds
FOR THE BIRDS

Native Americans cultivated these seeds, collecting them from the huge, bright yellow flowers. Our tasters found them mildly sweet, "dense," and "creamy." Remove the black-and-white streaked shell and then eat the light brown seed out of hand or in salads and slaws. Because of children's peanut allergies, sunflower seed butter has become a common replacement for peanut butter.

Nigella Seeds
BLACK ONION SEEDS

Nigella seeds (also called charnushka) are rarely used in this country but are common in India and the Middle East. The seeds have an "oniony" bite and a slightly astringent, "piney" taste. Get to know them sprinkled on rolls in place of poppy or sesame seeds or stirred into a spicy tomato chutney. Be careful when you're shopping, as they're often mislabeled as black cumin or black caraway.

ARUGULA, RADISH, MINT, AND PEA SALAD

SKILLET KIELBASA MACARONI AND CHEESE

**ROASTED LEMON CHICKEN WITH
ALMOND-PARMESAN BROCCOLI**

**BEEF TENDERLOIN STEAKS WITH
CHIVE BAKED POTATOES**

SKILLET KIELBASA MACARONI AND CHEESE Serves 4

WHY THIS RECIPE WORKS: Homemade macaroni and cheese usually requires using (and washing) multiple dishes. To cut down on the work, we prepare our rich, satisfying macaroni and cheese in just one pan.

1	pound kielbasa sausage, sliced ¼ inch thick
2	cups fresh bread crumbs
	Salt and pepper
3¾	cups water
1	(12-ounce) can evaporated milk
12	ounces (3 cups) elbow macaroni
2	teaspoons hot sauce
1	teaspoon cornstarch
12	ounces sharp cheddar cheese, shredded (3 cups)
8	ounces Monterey Jack cheese, shredded (2 cups)

1. Brown kielbasa in 12-inch nonstick skillet over medium-high heat, 6 to 8 minutes. Transfer to paper towel–lined plate. Add bread crumbs, ¼ teaspoon salt, and ¼ teaspoon pepper to now-empty skillet and cook, stirring frequently, until golden brown, about 5 minutes. Transfer to bowl and wipe out skillet.

2. Bring water, 1¼ cups evaporated milk, and ½ teaspoon salt to simmer in now-empty skillet over medium-high heat. Add pasta and cook, stirring often, until al dente, 8 to 10 minutes.

3. Whisk remaining ¼ cup evaporated milk, hot sauce, and cornstarch together in bowl, then stir into pasta. Bring to simmer and cook until slightly thickened, about 1 minute. Off heat, stir in cheddar, Monterey Jack, and kielbasa. Sprinkle with toasted bread crumbs. Serve.

TEST KITCHEN NOTE: To make fresh bread crumbs, pulse two slices of hearty white sandwich bread in a food processor until coarsely ground.

ARUGULA, RADISH, MINT, AND PEA SALAD Serves 4

WHY THIS RECIPE WORKS: A little mayonnaise and Dijon mustard turn a thin vinaigrette into a light, creamy dressing.

½	cup chopped fresh mint
3	tablespoons white wine vinegar
2	tablespoons extra-virgin olive oil
2	tablespoons mayonnaise
2	tablespoons Dijon mustard
6	ounces (6 cups) baby arugula
10	radishes, trimmed and sliced thin
1	cup frozen peas, thawed
	Salt and pepper
4	large hard-cooked eggs, chopped

1. Whisk mint, vinegar, oil, mayonnaise, and mustard together in bowl until combined.

2. Toss arugula, radishes, and peas together in large bowl. Toss with dressing until combined. Season with salt and pepper to taste. Top with eggs. Serve.

TEST KITCHEN NOTE: Serve with crusty bread and good cheese for a light supper.

BEEF TENDERLOIN STEAKS WITH CHIVE BAKED POTATOES
Serves 4

WHY THIS RECIPE WORKS: By giving the potatoes a head start in the microwave before moving them to a hot oven, we get a fluffy interior and a crisp crust in half the time.

4	small russet potatoes
½	cup sour cream
½	cup chopped fresh chives
2	garlic cloves, minced
	Salt and pepper
4	(6- to 8-ounce) center-cut filets mignons, 1 inch thick
2	tablespoons vegetable oil

1. Adjust oven rack to middle position and heat oven to 450 degrees. Poke several holes in each potato with fork and microwave on high until slightly soft to touch, 6 to 10 minutes. Carefully transfer potatoes directly to oven rack and roast until skewer glides easily through flesh, 15 to 20 minutes.

2. Meanwhile, combine sour cream, 7 tablespoons chives, and garlic in bowl and season with salt and pepper to taste.

3. Pat steaks dry with paper towels and season with salt and pepper. Heat oil in 12-inch skillet over medium-high heat until just smoking. Cook steaks until well browned and meat registers 125 degrees (for medium-rare), 4 to 6 minutes per side. Transfer to platter and tent loosely with aluminum foil.

4. Using tines of fork, make dotted X on top of each potato. Press in at ends of potatoes to push flesh up and out. Top each potato with sour cream mixture and sprinkle with remaining 1 tablespoon chives. Serve with steaks.

ROASTED LEMON CHICKEN
WITH ALMOND-PARMESAN BROCCOLI Serves 4

WHY THIS RECIPE WORKS: As the chicken cooks, the lemons flavor the meat and roast into a tasty garnish.

4	(12-ounce) bone-in split chicken breasts, trimmed and halved crosswise
	Salt and pepper
1	tablespoon olive oil
8	(¼-inch-thick) lemon slices (2 lemons)
1½	pounds broccoli, florets cut into 1-inch pieces, stalks peeled and sliced ½ inch thick, separated
4	garlic cloves, minced
½	cup low-sodium chicken broth
¼	cup grated Parmesan cheese
¼	cup slivered almonds, toasted

1. Adjust oven rack to middle position and heat oven to 500 degrees. Pat chicken dry with paper towels. Season with salt and pepper. Heat oil in 12-inch skillet over medium-high heat until just smoking. Add chicken, skin side down, and cook until browned, about 5 minutes. Transfer chicken skin side up to wire rack set inside aluminum foil–lined rimmed baking sheet, leaving fat in skillet. Arrange lemon slices over chicken and transfer to oven. Roast until chicken registers 160 degrees, 15 to 18 minutes. Transfer chicken and lemons to platter and tent loosely with foil.

2. Meanwhile, return now-empty skillet to medium-high heat. Add broccoli stalks and cook until slightly softened, about 3 minutes. Stir in garlic and cook until fragrant, about 30 seconds. Add broccoli florets and broth and cook, covered, until broccoli is tender, 4 to 6 minutes. Remove lid and cook until liquid evaporates, about 1 minute. Off heat sprinkle with Parmesan and almonds. Season with salt and pepper to taste. Serve with chicken.

BAKED SALMON WITH LIME VINAIGRETTE

SWEET AND SPICY PORK TENDERLOIN

GRILLED TURKEY–MANGO CHUTNEY BURGERS

**POACHED CHICKEN WITH ASPARAGUS
AND HERBED MAYONNAISE**

SWEET AND SPICY PORK TENDERLOIN Serves 4 to 6

WHY THIS RECIPE WORKS: Our dry rub does double duty, serving as a spice rub and flavoring the sauce.

- 2 tablespoons chili powder
- 1 teaspoon smoked paprika
- 1 teaspoon salt
- ½ teaspoon pepper
- 2 (12- to 16-ounce) pork tenderloins, trimmed
- 1 tablespoon vegetable oil
- ¼ cup ketchup
- 2 teaspoons cider vinegar
- 1½ teaspoons sugar

1. Adjust oven rack to middle position and heat oven to 450 degrees. Combine chili powder, paprika, salt, and pepper in bowl. Reserve 1 tablespoon spice mixture. Pat pork dry with paper towels and season with remaining spice mixture.

2. Heat oil in 12-inch nonstick skillet over medium-high heat until just smoking. Cook tenderloins until browned on all sides, 5 to 7 minutes. Transfer pork to wire rack set inside aluminum foil–lined rimmed baking sheet. Bake until meat registers 140 degrees, 15 to 18 minutes. Transfer meat to a platter, tent with foil, and let rest 5 minutes.

3. Combine reserved spice mixture, ketchup, vinegar, and sugar in bowl and brush over pork. Slice pork and serve.

TEST KITCHEN NOTE: Serve with your favorite barbecue sides.

BAKED SALMON WITH LIME VINAIGRETTE Serves 4

WHY THIS RECIPE WORKS: Starting the salmon on a super-heated baking sheet renders some of its fat; roasting it at 275 degrees keeps the fish moist.

- 1 (1½-pound) skin-on center-cut salmon fillet, sliced crosswise into 4 equal pieces
- ¼ cup extra-virgin olive oil
  Salt and pepper
- ¼ cup minced fresh cilantro leaves
- 3 tablespoons lime juice (2 limes)
- 1 shallot, minced
- 1 jalapeño chile, stemmed, seeded, and minced
- 1 small garlic clove, minced
- ½ teaspoon sugar

1. Adjust oven rack to lowest position, place rimmed baking sheet on rack, and heat oven to 500 degrees. Make 4 or 5 shallow cuts about 1 inch apart along skin side of each piece of salmon, being careful not to cut into flesh.

2. Pat salmon dry with paper towels, rub with 1 tablespoon olive oil, and season with salt and pepper. Reduce oven to 275 degrees and remove baking sheet. Place salmon skin side down on baking sheet. Roast until thickest part of fillets registers 125 degrees, 9 to 13 minutes.

3. Meanwhile, whisk cilantro, remaining 3 tablespoons oil, lime juice, shallot, jalapeño, garlic, and sugar together in bowl. Season with salt and pepper to taste. Transfer salmon to platter. Top with vinaigrette. Serve.

TEST KITCHEN NOTE: Buy a whole center-cut fillet and cut it into four uniform pieces that cook at the same rate.

POACHED CHICKEN WITH ASPARAGUS AND HERBED MAYONNAISE Serves 4

WHY THIS RECIPE WORKS: Gently poaching the chicken makes it tender and juicy. Cooking the asparagus in the chicken poaching liquid infuses it with flavor.

- Salt and pepper
- 4 (6-ounce) boneless, skinless chicken breasts, trimmed
- 1½ pounds asparagus, trimmed
- ½ cup mayonnaise
- 2 tablespoons chopped fresh dill
- 2 tablespoons chopped fresh tarragon
- 2 tablespoons chopped fresh parsley
- 1 tablespoon Dijon mustard
- 1 tablespoon lemon juice

1. Bring 2 cups water and 1 tablespoon salt to boil in 12-inch skillet. Add chicken, reduce heat to medium, and simmer, covered, until chicken registers 160 degrees, 12 to 15 minutes, flipping once halfway through cooking. Transfer to platter and tent loosely with aluminum foil.

2. Add asparagus to skillet, cover, and simmer until tender and bright green, about 4 minutes, redistributing once during cooking. Transfer to serving platter with chicken.

3. Meanwhile, whisk mayonnaise, dill, tarragon, parsley, mustard, and lemon juice together and season with salt and pepper to taste. Spoon herbed mayonnaise over chicken and serve with asparagus.

TEST KITCHEN NOTE: Asparagus spears of medium thickness work best in this recipe.

GRILLED TURKEY–MANGO CHUTNEY BURGERS Serves 4

WHY THIS RECIPE WORKS: Turkey burgers can be dry. To moisten them, we added mango chutney to the meat. Not only does the chutney take these burgers from dry to juicy, but it boosts the flavor of the turkey, too.

- ½ cup mayonnaise
- 3 garlic cloves, minced
- ¼ teaspoon cayenne pepper
  Salt and pepper
- 1½ pounds ground turkey
- 1 cup panko bread crumbs
- ½ cup mango chutney
- 4 hamburger rolls
- 4 leaves Bibb lettuce

1. Whisk mayonnaise, 1 garlic clove, and cayenne together in bowl. Season with salt and pepper to taste; set aside.

2. Combine turkey, panko, chutney, and remaining 2 garlic cloves in large bowl. Pat turkey mixture into four ¾-inch-thick patties. Season with salt and pepper. Grill over medium-hot fire until burgers register 160 degrees, 7 to 10 minutes, flipping halfway. Transfer burgers to rolls and top with mayonnaise mixture and lettuce. Serve.

TEST KITCHEN NOTE: The test kitchen prefers Silver Palate Mango Chutney.

English Muffin Bread

We love English muffins for their crunchy crust, chewy interior, and many nooks and crannies. We looked for the same great qualities in a quick, easy loaf bread. BY SARAH WILSON WITH CHRIS DUDLEY

WITH THEIR CHEWY interior, crunchy crust, and craggy, dimpled texture that sops up butter and jam, English muffins are the perfect companion to that first cup of coffee. I wanted a no-fuss recipe that would give me everything good about English muffins without any of the hassles—specifically, the kneading, rolling, cutting, and griddling.

Fortunately, someone had thought of this before me—ergo, English muffin bread. The bread, a type known as "yeasted batter breads," is easy by definition: You scrape the wet, sticky batter directly into a loaf pan (or pans) and let it rise. No kneading or shaping required. To my surprise, I discovered recipes for these loaves that dated all the way back to the turn of the 19th century. Old or new, most were made from flour, milk, salt, sugar, and yeast. One of the older recipes heated the flour before adding it. Weird. Another added baking soda. Odd enough, but even stranger was how the soda was incorporated (more on that later). Beyond that, some recipes used milk and others dry milk powder; some called for all-purpose flour and others bread flour. I'd test every detail in our quest for the easiest, chewiest, most satisfying English muffin bread ever.

I started by baking eight test loaves, following an assortment of recipes. The bread that used baking soda was swirled with weird, nasty-tasting streaks of brown. The others were tasty enough but noticeably short on nooks and crannies; they seemed more like ordinary white bread than like an English muffin. The newer recipes resembled one another closely, so I picked one as my starting point, combining all-purpose flour with yeast, salt, and sugar

Sure, you could eat this bread plain, but it really shines when toasted—and buttered.

(to help the bread brown and give the yeast a kick start); pouring in "hot" milk (110 degrees, the test kitchen standard to activate the yeast); stirring for less than a minute; and leaving the batter to rise. Once it had doubled in size, I scraped it into the loaf pans for a second rise and then baked the

loaves. The results were mixed: While the crumb was nice and moist, when I slathered the bread with butter, it lacked the proper porous quality and the proper chew.

Fixing the latter was easy. High-gluten bread flour turned the texture satisfyingly chewy. While I was making simple swaps, I wondered which made for a more perfect loaf: milk or dry milk powder. I couldn't tell the difference, so I opted for milk, which is always in my kitchen. Since I wanted larger holes, and more of them, I took a second look at baking soda. Before, following instructions, I'd mixed it with liquid and added it to the thick batter just before the second rise. It had been impossible to stir in effectively. After more research, I found recipes that mixed the soda in with the other dry ingredients. That technique yielded loaves that were appropriately coarse and honeycombed.

Earlier, I'd dismissed as bizarre the directions in an old recipe for warming

flour. On reflection, might warm flour speed the rise? To see, I heated the flour in the oven. It did shorten the proofing, and I was considering adding the step to my recipe when I realized it'd be simpler to adjust the temperature of the hot milk. Since I mixed the yeast with the other dry ingredients before adding the milk, those combined ingredients would dilute the heat, preventing dangerously hot milk from killing the yeast. I slowly increased the temperature and watched the proofing time melt away. Ultimately, using milk 10 to 20 degrees hotter than usual let me cut the first rise in half.

I baked two final loaves, counted the minutes until they cooled, and then toasted a slice. It turned an attractive speckled brown, walked the line between crunch and chew, and soaked up butter like nobody's business. It tasted like the store-bought English muffins we know and love. Only better. Much better.

ENGLISH MUFFIN BREAD
Makes 2 loaves

    Cornmeal
  5 cups (27½ ounces) bread flour
4½ teaspoons instant or rapid-rise yeast
  1 tablespoon sugar
  2 teaspoons salt
  1 teaspoon baking soda
2½ cups whole milk, heated to 120 degrees

1. Grease two 8½ by 4½-inch loaf pans and dust with cornmeal. Combine flour, yeast, sugar, salt, and baking soda in large bowl. Stir in hot milk until combined and dough pulls away from sides of bowl, about 1 minute. Cover dough with greased plastic wrap and let rise in warm place for 30 minutes, or until dough is bubbly and has doubled.

2. Stir dough and divide between prepared loaf pans, pushing into corners with greased rubber spatula. (Pans should be about two-thirds full.) Cover pans with greased plastic and let dough rise in warm place until it reaches edge of pans, about 30 minutes. Adjust oven rack to middle position and heat oven to 375 degrees.

3. Discard plastic and transfer pans to oven. Bake until bread is well browned and registers 200 degrees, about 30 minutes, rotating and switching pans halfway through baking. Turn bread out onto wire rack and let cool completely, about 1 hour. Slice, toast, and serve.

The American Table
A Well-Dressed Table

By the end of the 19th century, the English were losing their taste for English-style muffins, but in the U.S. they had become such a popular breakfast bread that the properly set breakfast table required special dishes for serving them. Victorians, of course, were ardent believers that the correct home environment shaped correct behavior; proper dining and tableware, especially, equated with proper civilization. So wealthy families had specific dishware for everything, from glass or silver vases for celery to custom dishes to hold bananas to specialized vessels and utensils for serving sardines. And don't forget asparagus forks.

Antique English muffin serving dish.

Cook's Country

Dear Country Cook,

I have fond and lasting memories of Holsteins, since I spent many summers in Vermont helping out with the afternoon milking. This was a small mountain farm operation with 25 head (fewer milkers at any one time), a barn filled with flies, and an overhead manure bucket on rails.

I soon learned each of the Holsteins' names and personalities. Some hauled off and swatted their tails more than others; some liked a nice scratch behind the ears, like a dog. I can still feel their warmth; the swollen bellies; the heavy, bony heads; the supple, silky skin of the udders; and the rhythmic pumping of the machine.

I also learned where food comes from. The last pail of milk was brought into the farmhouse, so I drank raw milk in summers, knowing every step of its production, from calling in the herd to shutting the barn door once the cows had returned to pasture.

We have lost the intimacy between farm and table. Farm kids are lucky. They press cider, they dig up carrots and hill potatoes, they milk cows, and they may even help with the taking of a life, gratefully putting food on the table.

Cooking does not exist apart from fields and barns. If you have never milked a cow, it is hard to appreciate the taste of milk. A cold glass still reminds me of a small red barn on a mountain farm a very long time ago.

Cordially,

Christopher Kimball
Founder and Editor, Cook's Country

Cook's Country

Founder and Editor Christopher Kimball
Editorial Director Jack Bishop
Executive Editor, Magazines John Willoughby
Executive Editor Peggy Grodinsky
Managing Editor Scott Kathan
Senior Editors Lisa McManus, Bryan Roof, Diane Unger
Test Kitchen Director Erin McMurrer
Associate Editors Chris Dudley, Amy Graves, Sarah Wilson
Test Cooks Sarah Gabriel, Carolynn Purpura MacKay, Rebeccah Marsters
Assistant Editors Hannah Crowley, Shannon Friedmann Hatch, Taizeth Sierra
Assistant Test Cook Nick Iverson
Copy Editors Nell Beram, Megan Chromik
Executive Assistant Christine Gordon
Assistant Test Kitchen Director Gina Nistico
Test Kitchen Manager Leah Rovner
Senior Kitchen Assistant Meryl MacCormac
Kitchen Assistants Maria Elena Delgado, Andrew Straaberg Finfrock, Ena Gudiel
Executive Producer Melissa Baldino
Associate Producer Stephanie Stender

Contributing Editors Erika Bruce, Eva Katz, Jeremy Sauer
Consulting Editors Anne Mendelson, Meg Ragland
Science Editor Guy Crosby, Ph.D.
Executive Food Editor, TV, Radio & Media Bridget Lancaster

Online Managing Editor Christine Liu
Online Associate Editors Eric Grzymkowski, Mari Levine
Senior Video Editor Nick Dakoulas

Design Director Amy Klee
Art Director Julie Cole
Deputy Art Director Susan Levin
Associate Art Director Lindsey Timko
Staff Photographer Daniel J. van Ackere
Color Food Photography Keller + Keller
Styling Catrine Kelty
Deputy Art Director, Marketing/Web Erica Lee
Designers, Marketing/Web Elaina Natario, Mariah Tarvainen
Photo Editor Steve Klise

Vice President, Marketing David Mack
Circulation Director Doug Wicinski
Circulation & Fulfillment Manager Carrie Fethe
Partnership Marketing Manager Pamela Putprush
Marketing Assistant Lauren Perkins
Customer Service Manager Jacqueline Valerio
Customer Service Representatives Jessica Amato, Morgan Ryan

Chief Operating Officer David Dinnage
Production Director Guy Rochford
Senior Project Manager Alice Carpenter
Project Manager Kate Hux
Asset & Workflow Manager Andrew Mannone
Production & Imaging Specialists Judy Blomquist, Heather Dube, Lauren Pettapiece
Systems Administrator Marcus Walser
Software Architect Robert Martinez
Software Project Manager Michelle Rushin
Senior Business Analyst Wendy Iseng
Web Developers Chris Candelora, Cameron MacKenzie
Human Resources Manager Adele Shapiro

VP New Media Product Development Barry Kelly
Social Media Manager Steph Yiu

Chief Financial Officer Sharyn Chabot
Director of Sponsorship Sales Anne Traficante
Retail Sales & Marketing Manager Emily Logan
Client Service Manager, Sponsorship Bailey Snyder
Publicity Deborah Broide

ON THE COVER:
Potato Chip Cookies, Keller + Keller, Catrine Kelty
ILLUSTRATION: Greg Stevenson

Cook's Country magazine (ISSN 1552-1990), number 45, is published bimonthly by Boston Common Press Limited Partnership, 17 Station Street, Brookline, MA 02445. Copyright 2012 Boston Common Press Limited Partnership. Periodicals Postage paid at Boston, Mass., and additional mailing offices. Publications Mail Agreement No. 40020778. Return undeliverable Canadian addresses to P.O. Box 875, Station A, Windsor, Ontario N9A 6P2. POSTMASTER: Send address changes to Cook's Country, P.O. Box 6018, Harlan, IA 51593-1518. Customer Service: It's easy to subscribe, give a gift subscription, change your address, and manage your subscription online. Visit www.AmericasTestKitchen.com/customerservice for all of your customer service needs or write to us at Cook's Country, P.O. Box 6018, Harlan, IA 51593-1518. PRINTED IN THE USA

Contents

FLUFFY CORNMEAL PANCAKES, 22   BLT POTATO SALAD, 19   BARBECUED PULLED CHICKEN, 6

America's TEST KITCHEN
RECIPES THAT WORK®

America's Test Kitchen is a 2,500-square-foot kitchen located just outside of Boston. It is the home of Cook's Country and Cook's Illustrated magazines and is the workday destination of more than 50 test cooks, editors, and cookware specialists. Our mission is to test recipes until we understand how and why they work and arrive at the best version. We also test kitchen equipment and supermarket ingredients in search of brands that offer the best value and performance. You can watch us work by tuning in to Cook's Country from America's Test Kitchen (CooksCountryTV.com) on public television.

Getting to Know Asian Condiments

The condiment shelves of Asian grocery stores can be mystifying. Don't let that keep you away. These sauces and pastes inject tremendous flavor into food with virtually no effort on the part of the cook.

Soy Sauce
BEAN JUICE

The Chinese invented it nearly 3,000 years ago, fermenting soybeans with wheat or barley and special molds and yeasts. But soy transcends Asian cuisine; we rely on its *umami* character to add savory, complex depth to dishes like beef stroganoff and French onion soup. Our preferred brand for cooking is Lee Kum Kee Tabletop Soy Sauce.

Teriyaki Sauce
AMERICAN FAVORITE

Popularized some 40 years ago in the United States by the Benihana chain, teriyaki sauce—which is from Japan—is made from soy sauce, sake or mirin (sweet Japanese wine), sugar, ginger, and garlic. The glaze gives food a glossy look and a sweet finish. Our favorite brand is Annie Chun's All Natural Teriyaki Sauce.

Sweet-and-Sour Sauce
EGG ROLL DIPPER

In China, this term encompasses a range of dipping sauces that are typically freshly prepared from vinegar and sugar. In the States, sweet-and-sour sauce has evolved (some would say devolved) into something thicker and sweeter. Western versions may include pineapple, ketchup, cornstarch, and corn syrup. Sweet-and-sour sauce is the classic dip for egg rolls.

Hoisin Sauce
MU SHU MATE

This thick, reddish-brown sauce—made from soybeans, sugar, garlic, and spices—is the classic sauce for Chinese mu shu dishes. Variation among brands is dramatic. The test kitchen picked "smoky," "malty" Kikkoman Hoisin Sauce as our favorite, noting its balanced flavors. Hoisin can be used in dipping sauces, glazes, and marinades.

Black Bean Sauce
FERMENTED AND FUNKY

This thick, robust sauce is made from fermented, salted black soybeans (either pureed or left whole) that are mixed with soy sauce, sugar, and sometimes MSG. Tasted by itself, black bean sauce is powerfully sharp, "nutty," and "yeasty." It adds instant depth to stir-fries, spareribs, noodles, and fish. You can buy versions with spice and garlic, too.

Wasabi
JAPANESE HORSERADISH

The gnarled, brown wasabi root is a relative of horseradish, and at nice restaurants in Japan the fresh root is grated to order. In America, your sushi probably comes with the premade stuff from a tube or a powder (which often contains no real wasabi). Our tasters found that fresh wasabi or paste made from the real item is best (no surprise).

Plum Sauce
CHINESE CHUTNEY

The Chinese have cultivated plums since ancient times. To extend its life after the harvest, the fruit was preserved with salt, sugar, spices, garlic, ginger, and sweet potato, giving the sauce a sweet-and-sour quality. Nowadays, peaches and apricots are used, too. You may know plum sauce as duck sauce, as it's often served with Peking duck.

Fish Sauce
PISCATORY PERFUME

Don't let the strong smell dissuade you: The pungent, "meaty," almost "cheesy" flavor adds wonderful complexity to dishes like pad thai and Vietnam's catfish in a clay pot. The sauce is made from fermented fish or, more often, anchovy extract, and the lighter the sauce the lighter the flavor. "Dark and pungent" Tiparos Fish Sauce is our favorite brand.

Chili Sauce
ASIAN HEAT

Almost every Asian cuisine has its own version of chili sauce; the three you're likely to encounter in the States are Sriracha, chili-garlic sauce, and Indonesia's sambal oelek. They all contain chiles and salt; many feature vinegar, sugar, and garlic, too. Want to make Sriracha yourself? Go to CooksCountry.com/sriracha for our recipe.

Oyster Sauce
THE PEARL OF SAUCES

This southern Chinese specialty is made from boiled oysters and adds salty tang to such dishes as kung pao chicken and sesame noodles. Buy oyster-flavored sauce that contains just oyster extractives and seasonings—sauces with extra ingredients have muddled flavor. Our favorite brand is Lee Kum Kee's Premium Oyster Flavored Sauce.

Miso
JAPANESE MAIN SQUEEZE

Chances are you've sipped the soup (dashi broth mixed with miso paste) as a preamble to a Japanese meal. The paste itself is made from fermented soybeans and grain—usually rice or barley—and Japanese cooks use it nearly every day. White, or *shiro*, miso (pictured above) is sweeter, with "floral," "fruity" flavors, while red, or *aka*, miso is saltier and "earthier."

Kecap Manis
INDONESIAN SOY SAUCE

Kecap is the catchall term for sauces in Indonesia, and kecap manis is the sweetest. It's made from soybeans, palm sugar, and seasonings. Salty-sweet kecap manis looks like tar but tastes like "caramel," "burnt sugar," and "coffee," our tasters found. Marinate steaks in it or brush chicken wings with the thinned sauce toward the end of grilling.

EASY SUMMER VEGETABLE PASTA

GRILLED ASIAN SHORT RIBS WITH CUCUMBER SALAD

**PORK TENDERLOIN WITH
GRILLED PEACHES AND RED ONIONS**

**SHRIMP AND LEMON SKEWERS WITH
JALAPEÑO DRESSING**

GRILLED ASIAN SHORT RIBS WITH CUCUMBER SALAD Serves 4

WHY THIS RECIPE WORKS: Butterflying the ribs speeds up the cooking time and allows you to remove more fat from the meat before cooking.

- 1 cup rice vinegar
- 1 cup sugar
- ¾ cup soy sauce
- 6 garlic cloves, minced
- 2 tablespoons grated fresh ginger
- 4 (6- to 8-ounce) boneless beef short ribs, trimmed and butterflied
  Salt and pepper
- 2 seedless English cucumbers, peeled, halved lengthwise, and sliced thin
- ½ onion, sliced thin
- 2 tablespoons vegetable oil

1. Whisk ½ cup vinegar and ⅓ cup sugar together until sugar is dissolved; set aside. Combine soy sauce, remaining ⅔ cup sugar, remaining ½ cup vinegar, garlic, and ginger in small saucepan and bring to simmer. Cook until sugar is dissolved and mixture has thickened, about 10 minutes. Reserve ½ cup soy sauce mixture for serving.

2. Pat ribs dry with paper towels and season with salt and pepper. Grill ribs over hot fire, brushing with soy sauce mixture, until temperature reaches 125 degrees, about 3 minutes per side. Transfer ribs to cutting board, tent loosely with aluminum foil, and let rest for 5 minutes.

3. Meanwhile, toss cucumbers, vinegar mixture, onion, and oil together in bowl. Slice short ribs thinly against grain and transfer to serving platter. Serve cucumber salad with short ribs, passing reserved soy sauce mixture separately.

EASY SUMMER VEGETABLE PASTA Serves 4

WHY THIS RECIPE WORKS: Boursin cheese thinned with starchy pasta cooking water makes a quick, flavorful sauce for pasta and vegetables.

- 1 pound penne
  Salt and pepper
- 1 tablespoon olive oil
- 1 red onion, halved and sliced thin
- 3 garlic cloves, minced
- 2 zucchini, halved lengthwise and sliced ¼ inch thick
- 1 summer squash, halved lengthwise and sliced ¼ inch thick
- 12 ounces cherry tomatoes, halved
- 1 (5.2-ounce) package Garlic & Herb Boursin cheese
- ½ cup chopped fresh basil

1. Bring 4 quarts water to boil in Dutch oven. Add penne and 1 tablespoon salt to boiling water and cook until al dente. Reserve ¾ cup pasta cooking water and drain pasta.

2. Heat oil in now-empty Dutch oven over medium-high heat until shimmering. Add onion and cook until softened, about 3 minutes. Add garlic and cook until fragrant, about 30 seconds. Add zucchini, summer squash, and ¼ cup reserved pasta water and cook, covered, until vegetables are tender, about 6 minutes. Stir in cooked pasta, tomatoes, Boursin, remaining ½ cup pasta water, and basil until pasta is heated through. Season with salt and pepper to taste. Serve.

TEST KITCHEN NOTE: Serve with grated Parmesan cheese.

SHRIMP AND LEMON SKEWERS WITH JALAPEÑO DRESSING Serves 4

WHY THIS RECIPE WORKS: Brushing shrimp with butter and sprinkling them with sugar ensures browning despite the short grilling time.

- 1½ pounds extra-large shrimp (21 to 25 per pound), peeled and deveined
- 3 lemons, quartered and sliced ½ inch thick, plus 1 teaspoon grated lemon zest plus 1 tablespoon juice
- 2 tablespoons unsalted butter, melted
- 1 tablespoon sugar
  Salt and pepper
- 6 tablespoons olive oil
- 1 jalapeño chile, stemmed, seeded, and minced
- 2 tablespoons chopped fresh cilantro

1. Pat shrimp dry with paper towels. Thread shrimp onto skewers (you will need about 12 skewers), alternating with lemon slices. Brush with butter and sprinkle with sugar. Season with salt and pepper. Combine olive oil, jalapeño, cilantro, and lemon zest and juice in bowl.

2. Grill skewers over hot fire, covered, until lightly charred, about 3 minutes. Flip skewers and continue to cook until shrimp are just opaque, about 2 minutes. Transfer to platter and spoon jalapeño dressing on top. Serve.

TEST KITCHEN NOTE: You can replace the lemons with limes.

PORK TENDERLOIN WITH GRILLED PEACHES AND RED ONIONS Serves 4

WHY THIS RECIPE WORKS: The sweetness of the peaches is balanced by the heat of the cayenne and red onion.

- 1 tablespoon ground cumin
- 1 tablespoon packed brown sugar
- 1½ teaspoons ground coriander
- ½ teaspoon cayenne pepper
  Salt and pepper
- 2 (12- to 16-ounce) pork tenderloins, trimmed
- 2 peaches, halved and pitted
- 2 small red onions, quartered
- 2 tablespoons olive oil
- 1 tablespoon granulated sugar

1. Combine cumin, brown sugar, coriander, cayenne, and ½ teaspoon salt in bowl. Rub tenderloins with spice mixture. Grill over hot fire until browned on all sides and meat registers 145 degrees, about 12 minutes. Transfer to carving board, tent loosely with aluminum foil, and let rest for 10 minutes.

2. While pork rests, brush peaches and onions with oil and sprinkle with granulated sugar. Season with salt and pepper to taste. Grill over hot fire until caramelized and tender, about 3 minutes per side. Transfer to platter. Slice pork ½ inch thick and serve with peaches and onions.

TEST KITCHEN NOTE: Leave the root end of the onions intact so the petals don't separate when grilled.

CHICKEN CAESAR SALAD WRAPS

**GRILLED T-BONE STEAKS WITH
LEMON-GARLIC SPINACH**

**GRILLED CHICKEN WITH RED CURRANT GLAZE
AND QUICK WILD RICE**

SUMMER DINNER SALAD WITH SCALLOPS

GRILLED T-BONE STEAKS WITH LEMON-GARLIC SPINACH

Serves 4

WHY THIS RECIPE WORKS: Microwaving the spinach speeds up the cooking time.

- 18 ounces (18 cups) baby spinach
- 2 (20-ounce) T-bone or porterhouse steaks, 1½ inches thick, trimmed
  Salt and pepper
- 3 tablespoons extra-virgin olive oil
- 3 garlic cloves, minced
- 1 teaspoon grated lemon zest plus 2 tablespoons juice, plus lemon wedges for serving

1. Place spinach and ¼ cup water in large bowl. Cover and microwave until spinach is wilted and decreased in volume by half, about 4 minutes. Transfer spinach to colander; use rubber spatula to gently press spinach to release liquid. Move spinach to cutting board and roughly chop. Return to colander and press again to release any remaining liquid.

2. Pat steaks dry with paper towels. Season with salt and pepper. Grill over hot fire until cooked to desired doneness, 6 to 8 minutes per side for medium-rare. Transfer steaks to carving board, tent loosely with aluminum foil, and let rest for 5 to 10 minutes.

3. Meanwhile, heat 2 tablespoons oil in 12-inch nonstick skillet over medium heat until shimmering. Add garlic and lemon zest and cook until fragrant, about 30 seconds. Add spinach to skillet and cook until heated through, about 2 minutes. Stir in 1 tablespoon lemon juice and season with salt and pepper to taste; cover and keep warm.

4. Slice meat off bones, then slice thinly against grain. Arrange slices on platter and drizzle with remaining 1 tablespoon oil and remaining 1 tablespoon lemon juice. Serve with spinach and lemon wedges.

CHICKEN CAESAR SALAD WRAPS Serves 4

WHY THIS RECIPE WORKS: This Caesar-inspired dressing does double duty, flavoring the salad greens as well as the chicken.

- ¼ cup mayonnaise
- ¼ cup grated Parmesan cheese
- 2 tablespoons lemon juice
- 1 tablespoon Worcestershire sauce
- 1 tablespoon Dijon mustard
- 1 garlic clove, minced
- ¼ cup olive oil
- 1 (2½-pound) rotisserie chicken, skin and bones discarded, meat shredded into bite-size pieces (3 cups)
- 1 romaine lettuce heart (6 ounces), torn into bite-size pieces
- 4 (10-inch) flour tortillas

1. Whisk mayonnaise, Parmesan, lemon juice, Worcestershire, mustard, and garlic together until combined. Whisk in oil slowly until thoroughly incorporated.

2. Toss chicken with half of dressing and toss romaine with remaining dressing. Lay tortillas on counter. Divide chicken equally among tortillas. Top chicken on each tortilla with 1 cup dressed lettuce mixture and roll into wraps. Serve.

TEST KITCHEN NOTE: Take care to tear your romaine into bite-size pieces.

SUMMER DINNER SALAD WITH SCALLOPS Serves 4

WHY THIS RECIPE WORKS: Sea scallops cook in minutes and add substance to a simple salad, turning it into dinner.

- 1½ tablespoons red wine vinegar
- 2½ teaspoons minced shallot
- 1 teaspoon Dijon mustard
- ½ teaspoon mayonnaise
  Salt and pepper
- 7 tablespoons extra-virgin olive oil
- 10 ounces (10 cups) mesclun greens
- 4 carrots, peeled and sliced ⅛ inch thick
- 12 ounces snap peas, strings removed, halved crosswise
- 1½ pounds large sea scallops, tendons removed

1. Combine vinegar, shallot, mustard, mayonnaise, ¼ teaspoon salt, and ¼ teaspoon pepper in bowl. Slowly whisk in 5 tablespoons oil until incorporated. Toss greens, carrots, and snap peas with dressing. Divide salad among 4 individual bowls.

2. Pat scallops dry with paper towels and season with salt and pepper. Heat 1 tablespoon oil in 12-inch nonstick skillet over high heat until just smoking. Add half of scallops in single layer and cook, without moving, until well browned, 1½ to 2 minutes. Flip and continue to cook until sides of scallops are firm and centers are opaque, 30 to 90 seconds longer (remove smaller scallops as they finish cooking). Transfer scallops to plate and tent loosely with aluminum foil. Wipe out skillet with wad of paper towels and repeat with remaining 1 tablespoon oil and remaining scallops. Divide scallops among salads. Serve.

TEST KITCHEN NOTE: Buy "dry" scallops, which have no chemical additives. Distinguish them by color: Dry scallops are ivory or pinkish, while wet scallops are bright white.

GRILLED CHICKEN WITH RED CURRANT GLAZE AND QUICK WILD RICE Serves 4

WHY THIS RECIPE WORKS: With minimal cooking, currant jam transforms into a thick, clingy glaze for the chicken.

- 2 packages Uncle Ben's Long Grain and Wild Ready Rice
- 1 teaspoon grated orange zest plus ⅔ cup juice (2 oranges)
- ½ cup red currant jam
- 1 shallot, minced
- 1 tablespoon minced fresh thyme
  Salt and pepper
- 1½ teaspoons cornstarch dissolved in 1 tablespoon cold water
- 8 (5- to 7-ounce) bone-in chicken thighs, skin removed, trimmed
- ½ cup golden raisins
- ¼ cup sliced almonds, toasted

1. Cook rice according to package directions. Meanwhile, combine orange zest and juice, jam, shallot, thyme, ½ teaspoon salt, and ½ teaspoon pepper in small saucepan and bring to boil. Whisk cornstarch mixture into boiling glaze. Reduce heat to low and simmer until thickened, about 5 minutes.

2. Season chicken with salt and pepper. Grill chicken skinned side up over medium-hot fire, covered, until underside is browned and sides are beginning to firm up, 8 to 10 minutes. Flip chicken and cook until well-browned and chicken registers 175 degrees, 6 to 8 minutes. Brush chicken all over with ¼ cup of glaze and transfer to platter; tent loosely with aluminum foil and let rest for 5 minutes.

3. Transfer rice to bowl and stir in raisins and almonds. Season with salt and pepper to taste. Serve rice with chicken, passing remaining glaze separately.

Macaroni and Cheese Casserole

With satisfying heft and bright flavor, this custard-based mac and cheese has lots going for it—as long as you can keep the eggs from scrambling. BY SARAH GABRIEL

I
test
chic
pest
side
grill
coal
the
ther
F
disti
Plea
hon
witl
fresl
the
neel
incr
and
to s
loos
tenc
this
up t

GR
Not
thre
stuff

3/
1¹/

1
lem
pro
scra
¼ c
for
to p
inc
¼ c

TES
To f
stuf

Sta
bre
eac

SAYING THAT YOU adore smooth, creamy, gooey macaroni and cheese is like saying you're in favor of world peace. Who doesn't? Who isn't? But recently, I heard about a different version—a firm yet moist mac and cheese casserole bound with an eggy custard. A colleague who was familiar with it described the taste as pleasantly sharp, with more heat, heft, and depth (it's flavored with dry mustard, onion, and Worcestershire) than your typical plain-Jane mac and cheese. Sign me up.

Most recipes for this style call for whisking together eggs, milk, flour, grated cheese or Velveeta, minced onion, and flavorings. This cold custard is mixed with boiled macaroni in a casserole, topped with bread crumbs, and baked. After attempting an array of recipes, I raised an eyebrow at my colleague. He'd never mentioned waxy Velveeta, sour onion, overcooked macaroni, and lumps of scrambled egg in weepy, broken custard. And either my edges were nicely set and the middle soupy or the middle perfect and my edges dry.

It wasn't a total loss, though. I learned that I needed to undercook the pasta so it wouldn't turn to mush once baked into the casserole, to use sharp cheddar (combined with the Worcestershire and dry mustard, it added excellent piquant flavor), and to sauté the onion in butter to soften and sweeten it. Now I baked a casserole to assess my progress. Perfectly cooked noodles? Check. Mellow onion? Check. Good flavor? Check. But the custard continued to break and the eggs to scramble.

The cheese exchange had exacerbated the breaking, as the emulsifiers in Velveeta cover a multitude of sins. To keep the cheese from breaking, I tossed it with cornstarch before melting it, and traded the milk for heavy cream. (The extra fat helps prevent separation. The cream was too rich, so I thinned it with water. It still had more fat than the milk did, so the custard stayed creamy.) Finally, I exchanged the sharp cheddar for moister, less-prone-to-break mild cheddar. My custard held.

But this mac and cheese still tasted bland. I devised a workaround by cutting back on the mild cheddar in the custard and then sprinkling the top of the casserole with sharp cheddar.

Up until now, I'd been using four whole eggs for ½ pound of pasta.

What makes this mac different? Besides the eggs, it's boldly seasoned with onion, dry mustard, and Worcestershire sauce.

Because whites curdle at a lower temperature than yolks, I was able to prevent the eggs from scrambling by losing one whole egg plus one white. The remaining more dilute eggs didn't link and clump (i.e., scramble), yet they still firmed the casserole.

But the uneven cooking persisted. If the custard were hot before the casserole went into the oven, I could cut down the baking time, which would minimize the difference between center and edge. But when I heated the cream mixture, I got lumps of cornstarch and flour. Fine, I'd make white sauce so that the thickeners would be incorporated from the start. I whisked in the cheese, then the eggs, combined the sauce with the parcooked macaroni, sprinkled on buttery crumbs, and baked it. Later, I sat down to a plate of firm yet creamy, gently spicy, altogether delicious mac 'n' cheese casserole.

Mac and Cheese Meets Eggs

Most mac and cheese casseroles have four eggs. We use two eggs and one yolk for our casserole, making it less prone to scramble; egg whites curdle at a lower temperature than yolks. Also, the more dilute the egg proteins are in proportion to the liquid in the casserole, the less likely they are to scramble.

OUR RATIO
Two whole eggs plus one yolk prevent scrambling.

MACARONI AND CHEESE CASSEROLE Serves 4 to 6

The macaroni will still be firm after cooking according to the directions in step 1 (it will finish cooking in the oven). Barilla Elbows won the test kitchen's taste test of elbow macaroni.

- 8 ounces (2 cups) elbow macaroni
  Salt and pepper
- 8 ounces mild cheddar cheese, shredded (2 cups)
- 2 teaspoons cornstarch
- 4 tablespoons unsalted butter
- ½ cup panko bread crumbs
- ½ cup finely chopped onion
- 3 tablespoons all-purpose flour
- 2 teaspoons dry mustard
- ⅛ teaspoon cayenne pepper
- 2 cups water
- 1 cup heavy cream
- 2 large eggs plus 1 large yolk, lightly beaten
- 2 teaspoons Worcestershire sauce
- 4 ounces sharp cheddar cheese, shredded (1 cup)

1. Adjust oven rack to upper-middle position and heat oven to 375 degrees. Bring 4 quarts water to boil in large saucepan. Add macaroni and 1 tablespoon salt and cook for 5 minutes. Drain macaroni; set aside. Toss mild cheddar with cornstarch; set aside.

2. In now-empty saucepan, melt 1 tablespoon butter over medium-low heat. Add panko and cook, stirring constantly, until golden, about 4 minutes. Transfer to bowl and reserve.

3. Return saucepan to medium heat and melt remaining 3 tablespoons butter. Add onion and cook until beginning to soften, about 3 minutes. Stir in flour, mustard, ½ teaspoon salt, ¾ teaspoon pepper, and cayenne and cook, stirring constantly, until fragrant, about 1 minute. Whisk in water and cream and bring to boil. Reduce heat to medium-low. Simmer until thickened, about 5 minutes.

4. Remove cream sauce from heat and whisk in mild cheddar–cornstarch mixture until melted. Whisk in eggs, yolk, and Worcestershire. Stir in parcooked macaroni. Transfer macaroni and cheese to 8-inch square baking dish. Sprinkle with sharp cheddar cheese, then panko. Bake until well browned and set, 20 to 25 minutes. Let rest for 20 minutes. Serve.

Looking for a Recipe

Cowboy Bread
Nicholas Wayne, Allston, Mass.

I'm looking for a recipe for a bread/coffee cake that I used to eat growing up in Rapid City, South Dakota. It's made in a sheet pan and has a cinnamon-streusel topping. It was served in my elementary school cafeteria and was one of my favorite treats.

Armenian Lamb Casserole
Richie Sheehan, Trenton, N.J.

When I was growing up—this would be in the early 1960s—my sister learned to make a delicious lamb, eggplant, tomato, and rice casserole from an Armenian friend. I know it also used red wine and Parmesan cheese. I think her friend got the recipe from a small, learn-to-cook series of books that were popular at the time. The casserole could be made ahead, and it was a great, comforting meal when the weather was cold. I'd love to be able to enjoy this recipe again.

Cinnamon Toast
Mary Zoll, Carlisle, Mass.

At the summer camp I attended in the 1950s (Birch Hill Camp in New Hampshire), the cook used to serve a wonderful cinnamon toast that I've never been able to reproduce. He coated slices of white bread with a thick layer of sticky, cinnamon-flavored liquid that was the consistency of warm honey. A thin cinnamon crust topped the warm cinnamon layer. I suspect the cinnamon toast had been broiled, because you had to wait for it to cool before you could eat it. It was unusual and really delicious. Does anyone have any suggestions for making it?

Noodles Romanoff
Tracey Campbell, Lafayette, Ind.

Years ago, the Betty Crocker company came out with a fantastic noodle dish called Noodles Romanoff. I fell in love with it the first time I tried it. The company hasn't made this product in more than 30 years, and I'd like to be able to re-create it. Please help find this delicious recipe, for me and for all those other folks who have been searching for it as long as I have.

Cream of Celery Soup
LouAnne Dunster, Fargo, N.D.

When I was a kid, Saturdays weren't complete without a grilled cheese sandwich and a hot bowl of cream of celery soup. I know it most likely came from a can, but I'd love to be able to make a homemade version. Does anyone have a recipe?

Blueberry–Lemon Custard Pie
Gretchen Turner, Alexandria, Va.

As a child, I attended a potluck picnic where I was served a blueberry-lemon pie so unusual that I remember it to this day. It was a double-crust pie, with blueberries and a lemon custard filling. The blueberries floated to the top of the filling, giving each slice of pie a layered look. I've been unable to find a recipe for such a pie. Can you help?

No-Bake Chocolate Oatmeal Drops
Marjorie Raymond, Duluth, Minn.

When I was a Girl Scout in the early 1960s, a super-easy recipe for chocolate oatmeal drop cookies made the rounds. I think it started in a saucepan and then the no-bake batter was dropped by the spoonful onto sheets of waxed paper. Once the cookies had cooled, they were fudgy and delicious. I've lost the recipe and can't remember where it originated. Can anyone please help me enjoy these delicious cookies again?

Lancaster County Chicken-Corn Soup
Amy Williard, Conifer, Colo.

Several years ago, we used to frequent mud sales in Lancaster County, Pennsylvania. These are garage sale–type auctions held in early spring at area fire companies where many Mennonite and Amish people come to sell or buy goods. There is almost always a group selling an incredible chicken-corn soup, which is jam-packed with delicious sweet corn. Otherwise, the soup contains only chicken, broth, and salt and pepper—no noodles. I would love to have the recipe to help bring back some wonderful memories.

FIND THE ROOSTER!

TAMARI ALMONDS
Makes 4 cups
Elizabeth Muldoon, San Jose, Calif.

Although this recipe requires more effort than others for tamari almonds (the almonds get bathed in a seasoned tamari mixture four times), the flavor penetrates, yielding especially tasty nuts. Be sure to use low-sodium tamari or the nuts will be too salty. Tamari is a darker, thicker version of soy sauce that is traditionally made without wheat.

    4   cups (1¼ pounds) raw whole almonds
    ½   cup reduced-sodium tamari
    2   teaspoons vegetable oil
    1   teaspoon sugar
    ¼   teaspoon cayenne pepper

1. Adjust oven rack to middle position and heat oven to 325 degrees. Line rimmed baking sheet with aluminum foil and spray with vegetable oil spray.

2. Toss all ingredients together in bowl until thoroughly combined. Drain almonds in colander set over second bowl, shaking to remove excess liquid; reserve liquid. Transfer almonds to prepared baking sheet, spread into even layer, and bake for 15 minutes.

3. Remove almonds from oven and repeat process of tossing with reserved liquid, draining, and baking three more times (baking 15 minutes for each of next 2 rounds and 8 to 10 minutes, until deep mahogany, for final round).

4. Cool almonds to room temperature, about 1 hour. Serve immediately or store in airtight container at room temperature for up to 1 week.

CHOCOLATE GRAVY FOR BISCUITS
Makes about 4 cups
Helen Young, Lovell, Wyo.

"My family was from Oklahoma, and when we were kids (there were five of us), this was our favorite thing to eat. We had it often, and we still do when we get together. Enjoy." This chocolate sauce is called "gravy" because it uses flour as a thickener. For our recipe for Cream Cheese Biscuits (which taste fabulous with the Chocolate Gravy), visit **CooksCountry.com/jul12**; the recipe will be free online for 4 months.

    1   cup (7 ounces) sugar
    ½   cup (2½ ounces) all-purpose flour
    6   tablespoons (1⅛ ounces) Dutch-processed cocoa
    ¼   teaspoon salt
    4   cups whole milk
    1   teaspoon vanilla extract

Whisk sugar, flour, cocoa, and salt together in large saucepan. Slowly whisk in milk until smooth. Bring to simmer over medium heat, stirring constantly, and simmer until thickened, 2 to 3 minutes. Remove from heat and whisk in vanilla. Serve over biscuits.

S'mores Ice Cream Cake

No campfire handy? Not to worry. We've translated the summertime thrill of hot, gooey s'mores into a satisfying chocolate ice cream cake—complete with toasted marshmallows.

To make this cake you will need:

- **4** ounces bittersweet chocolate, chopped fine
- **½** cup heavy cream
- **¼** cup light corn syrup
- **8** whole graham crackers, crushed into crumbs (1 cup), plus 8 quartered along dotted seams
- **4** tablespoons unsalted butter, melted
- **1** tablespoon sugar
- **1** cup marshmallow crème
- **1½** quarts chocolate ice cream, softened
- **22–26** large marshmallows, halved crosswise

FOR THE FUDGE LAYER: Combine chocolate, cream, and corn syrup in medium bowl and microwave until melted and smooth, about 1 minute, stirring halfway through. Cool to room temperature, about 30 minutes.

FOR THE CRUST: Adjust oven rack to middle position and heat oven to 325 degrees. Spray 9-inch springform pan with vegetable oil spray and line sides with 2½-inch-wide strip of parchment paper. Combine graham cracker crumbs, butter, and sugar in bowl until mixture resembles wet sand. Using bottom of measuring cup, press crumbs into even layer on prepared pan bottom. Bake until fragrant and beginning to brown, about 12 minutes. Cool completely.

TO ASSEMBLE: Pour cooled chocolate mixture over crust and smooth into even layer; freeze until firm, about 30 minutes. Spread marshmallow crème over fudge in even layer; freeze until firm, about 15 minutes. Spread ice cream evenly over marshmallow layer. Cover with plastic wrap; freeze until very firm, at least 4 hours. Adjust oven rack 6 inches from broiler element and heat broiler. Place cake on baking sheet; discard plastic; and arrange marshmallow halves, cut side down, in snug layer over top. Broil until marshmallows are lightly browned, 30 to 60 seconds, rotating cake halfway through. (Refreeze cake if necessary.) Working quickly, remove pan ring and parchment and place graham cracker quarters vertically along sides of cake. Serve.

Recipe Index

Cook's Country

AUGUST/SEPTEMBER 2012

Best Peach Melba Crisp

London Broil on the Grill

Wine-and-Herb Grilled Chicken

Make-Ahead Coffee Cake
Quick Enough for Weekdays

Oklahoma Onion Burger
Unique Burger Technique

Slow-Cooker Beer Brats
Game-Day Classic Made Easy

Honey Fried Chicken
Crisp Skin, Sweet Glaze

Tasting Steak Sauces
We Crown a New Champ

Salt-and-Vinegar Potatoes
Better than the Chips

Banana Cream Pie
Silky, Smooth, and Sliceable

Low-Fat Gumbo
No Sacrifice Required

Skillet-Fried Corn
Southern Classic Perfected

www.CooksCountry.com
$4.95 U.S./$6.95 CANADA

When peach Melba was created in London in the 1890s, it became an instant classic. We decided its peach-raspberry pairing was too good to leave to a single dessert, so we spent a couple of weeks perfecting a very American dish: **Peach Melba Crisp.** PAGE 15

Cook's Country

Dear Country Cook,

My mother always told me that pigs are smart and naturally clean animals, although they usually stand in the feeding trough while eating, and a cool mud bath on a hot day is often just the thing. They scare horses. They like a scratch behind the ears. They are enthusiastic. And they can make short work of a small pasture, turning it into a riot of stones, roots, and bare earth in just days. They are particularly cute as piglets; a 300-pound sow does lose much of her charm.

Cows and beefers just don't have the same appeal, although I do admit to a silly infatuation with chickens. The birds may not be intelligent or cuddly, but they remind me of short-sighted punk rockers with spiky hair and odd, jerky manners. Of course, hens provide the most value for the money on a farm, their prodigious egg-laying ability a matter of record.

So, here's to all things pig. If you have a chance, rub him behind the ears. He'll raise his snout and smile that silly smile. It just might be enough to make your day.

Christopher Kimball
Founder and Editor, Cook's Country

Cook's Country

Founder and Editor Christopher Kimball
Editorial Director Jack Bishop
Editorial Director, Magazines John Willoughby
Executive Editor Peggy Grodinsky
Managing Editor Scott Kathan
Senior Editors Lisa McManus, Bryan Roof, Diane Unger
Test Kitchen Director Erin McMurrer
Associate Editors Chris Dudley, Amy Graves, Sarah Wilson
Test Cooks Sarah Gabriel, Carolynn Purpura MacKay, Rebeccah Marsters, Cristin Walsh
Assistant Editors Hannah Crowley, Shannon Friedmann Hatch, Taizeth Sierra
Assistant Test Cook Nick Iverson
Copy Editors Nell Beram, Megan Chromik
Executive Assistant Christine Gordon
Assistant Test Kitchen Director Gina Nistico
Test Kitchen Manager Leah Rovner
Senior Kitchen Assistant Meryl MacCormack
Kitchen Assistants Maria Elena Delgado, Andrew Straaberg Finfrock, Ena Gudiel
Executive Producer Melissa Baldino
Associate Producer Stephanie Stender

Contributing Editors Erika Bruce, Eva Katz, Jeremy Sauer
Consulting Editors Anne Mendelson, Meg Ragland
Science Editor Guy Crosby, Ph.D.
Executive Food Editor, TV, Radio & Media Bridget Lancaster

Online Managing Editor Christine Liu
Online Associate Editors Eric Grzymkowski, Mari Levine
Senior Video Editor Nick Dakoulas

Design Director Amy Klee
Art Director Julie Cote
Deputy Art Director Susan Levin
Associate Art Director Lindsey Timko
Staff Photographer Daniel J. van Ackere
Color Food Photography Keller + Keller
Styling Catrine Kelty
Deputy Art Director, Marketing/Web Erica Lee
Designers, Marketing/Web Elaina Natario, Mariah Tarvainen
Photo Editor Steve Klise

Vice President, Marketing David Mack
Circulation Director Doug Wicinski
Circulation & Fulfillment Manager Carrie Fethe
Partnership Marketing Manager Pamela Putprush
Customer Service Manager Jacqueline Valerio
Customer Service Representatives Jessica Amato, Morgan Ryan

Chief Operating Officer David Dinnage
Production Director Guy Rochford
Senior Project Manager Alice Carpenter
Workflow & Digital Asset Manager Andrew Mannone
Production & Imaging Specialists Judy Blomquist, Heather Dube, Lauren Pettapiece
Systems Administrator Marcus Walser
Senior Business Analyst Wendy Tseng
Web Developer Chris Candelora
Human Resources Manager Adele Shapiro

VP New Media Product Development Barry Kelly
Social Media Manager Steph Yiu

Chief Financial Officer Sharyn Chabot
Director of Sponsorship Sales Anne Traficante
Retail Sales & Marketing Manager Emily Logan
Client Service Associate Kate May
Publicity Deborah Broide

ON THE COVER:
Peach Melba Crisp, Keller + Keller, Catrine Kelty
ILLUSTRATION: Greg Stevenson

Cook's Country magazine (ISSN 1552-1990), number 46, is published bimonthly by Boston Common Press Limited Partnership, 17 Station Street, Brookline, MA 02445. Copyright 2012 Boston Common Press Limited Partnership. Periodicals postage paid at Boston, Mass., and additional mailing offices. Publications Mail Agreement No. 40020778. Return undeliverable Canadian addresses to P.O. Box 875, Station A, Windsor, Ontario N9A 6P2. POSTMASTER: Send address changes to Cook's Country, P.O. Box 6018, Harlan, IA 51593-1518. Customer Service: It's easy to subscribe, give a gift subscription, change your address, and manage your account online. Visit www.AmericasTestKitchen.com/customerservice for all of your customer service needs or write to us at Cook's Country, P.O. Box 6018, Harlan, IA 51593-1518. PRINTED IN THE USA

AUGUST/SEPTEMBER 2012

Contents

FRIED ONION BURGERS, 14

SUMMER TOMATO GRATIN, 21

BANANA CREAM PIE, 22

Features

In Every Issue

America's TEST KITCHEN

RECIPES THAT WORK®

America's Test Kitchen is a 2,500-square-foot kitchen located just outside of Boston. It is the home of Cook's Country and Cook's Illustrated magazines and is the workday destination of more than 50 test cooks, editors, and cookware specialists. Our mission is to test recipes until we understand how and why they work and arrive at the best version. We also test kitchen equipment and supermarket ingredients in search of brands that offer the best value and performance. You can watch us work by tuning in to Cook's Country from America's Test Kitchen (CooksCountryTV.com) on public television.

Getting to Know Noodles

Fifty years ago, a plate of spaghetti constituted ethnic cuisine. Nowadays, Americans are getting to know noodles from all over the planet. How lucky are we?

Dried Italian Pasta
MISS POPULARITY

Cook dried pasta in plenty of salted water: Use 4 quarts of water and 1 tablespoon of salt per pound of pasta. Don't add oil, and don't rinse the pasta after you've drained it, but do save some of the starchy cooking water to thin your sauce. And do try our Skillet Penne with Chicken and Broccoli (page 20), in which we cook the pasta directly in the sauce.

Fresh Italian Pasta
SOFT TOUCH

Fresh pasta (made from a softer wheat than dried) is sold refrigerated in most supermarkets. It cooks faster than dried—in three to five minutes, depending on its shape. If you're willing to invest a little time, homemade pasta is unbeatable. All you need is flour, salt, and eggs—and a little time. A pasta machine expedites the process, but a rolling pin works, too.

Whole-Wheat Pasta
GOOD CARB

A lot of what's sold as "wheat" pasta is actually a blend containing little whole grain. (Our favorite, Bionaturae Spaghetti, is 100 percent whole durum wheat.) Nutty and hearty, whole-wheat pasta is firmer than ordinary pasta, and it takes a few extra minutes to cook. It's best with thick sauces and robust flavors like pancetta, mushrooms, and strong cheese.

Egg Noodles
SOUP SLURPER

Egg noodles contain up to 20 percent eggs, so it's not surprising that our tasters found them "eggy." They can be wide or narrow and are usually cut into short ribbons. Our favorite product is Light 'n Fluffy Wide Egg Noodles. Serve them in soup or bake them into a tuna-noodle casserole. Find the recipe (free for four months) at CooksCountry.com/ tunanoodlecasserole.

Gnocchi (NYOH-kee)
PLUMP DUMPLINGS

In Italy, gnocchi are any dumplings, but Americans are most familiar with those made from flour, mashed potato, and sometimes egg. Our top supermarket pick is Gia Russa Gnocchi with Potato, which is a shelf-stable product; we like it better than frozen or refrigerated. Boil gnocchi in salted water until they float to the surface (about four minutes), drain, and serve with sauce or bake with cheese.

Couscous
MOROCCAN MAINSTAY

Though it is often mistaken for a grain, couscous is, in fact, pasta made of durum semolina, just like the Italian stuff. Most cooks use instant couscous rehydrated with boiling water. After five minutes and a quick fluff, it's ready to eat. We improve on the basic method by first toasting the grains in butter and then steeping them in a mix of broth and water; use a 1:1 ratio of couscous to liquid.

Ramen
CHEAP EATS

In Japan, "ramen" refers to a whole category of brothy noodle dishes. But many Americans know only cheap, convenient instant ramen: cellophane-wrapped blocks of curly noodles with seasoning. Ramen is deep-fried before being dried, so it cooks in minutes. To upgrade instant ramen, ditch the MSG-spiked seasoning packet; cook the noodles in broth; and top with meat, tofu, or a fried egg.

Soba
ALL-WEATHER NOODLE

Buckwheat flour accounts for the dark color of these Japanese noodles, which contain at least 30 percent buckwheat. Soba made with 100 percent buckwheat looks even darker and tastes "smoky," and "mushroomy," our tasters said. In Japan, soba is served hot in broth or, come summer, chilled with a dipping sauce. If you're eating cold noodles, toss them with a little oil to prevent sticking.

Udon
JAPANESE STAPLE

Udon are fat, chewy noodles made of wheat flour that are sold dried or semi-dried. They can contain a lot of sodium, so don't salt their cooking water. In Japan, udon are often served in miso broth, a dish replicated at many an American noodle bar. Udon are starchy and "sweet" and stand up well to rich, savory sauces. Boil for 10 to 12 minutes, drain, and rinse under cold water.

Bean Threads
SEE-THROUGH NOODLES

These translucent, delicate-looking threads, made from mung bean starch, are also called cellophane or glass noodles. Their neutral taste (a taster likened them to "slippery air") is a virtue: They pick up flavor from whatever they're added to, be it hot pots, stir-fries, soups, or even sweet drinks and desserts. Soak dry bean threads in hot water for 20 minutes and drain before using.

Wonton Skins
CHINESE WRAPPERS

These sheets of fresh egg pasta are the wrappers for wontons. Look for them in the refrigerated section of the supermarket, near the tofu. After filling the wrapper, moisten its edges for a tight seal and then boil, steam, or fry to make potstickers, shu mai and, of course, wontons for soup. To keep the sheets from drying out, cover the stack with a damp towel while working with them.

Rice Noodles
PHO FILLER

These translucent noodles are made from water and rice powder. To maintain their chew, we soak them in hot water rather than boiling them. (The soaking time depends on the noodles' thickness.) For stir-fries, add soaked, drained noodles to a hot pan with the other ingredients and cook, tossing often. Rice noodles feature in pad thai, pho, and hundreds of other Asian dishes.

**SHRIMP AND ARUGULA SALAD
WITH LEMON VINAIGRETTE**

SPICY GRILLED FLANK STEAK WITH ZUCCHINI

BLT WRAPS

KUNG PAO CHICKEN

SPICY GRILLED FLANK STEAK WITH ZUCCHINI Serves 4

WHY THIS RECIPE WORKS: The compound butter flavors both the meat and the zucchini.

- 4 tablespoons unsalted butter, softened
- 1 shallot, minced
- 1 teaspoon honey
- ½ teaspoon cayenne pepper
- 1 (1½-pound) flank steak, 1 inch thick, trimmed
  Salt and pepper
- 4 small zucchini (6 ounces each), halved lengthwise
- 2 teaspoons vegetable oil

1. Combine butter, shallot, honey, and cayenne in bowl; set aside. Season steak with salt and pepper. Grill steak over hot fire until medium-rare (125 degrees), 4 to 6 minutes per side. Transfer to carving board, tent loosely with aluminum foil, and let rest while zucchini cooks.

2. Brush zucchini with oil, season with salt and pepper to taste, and grill until tender, about 2½ minutes per side; transfer to platter. Slice steak thin against grain and move to platter with zucchini. Top steak and zucchini with butter mixture. Serve.

TEST KITCHEN NOTE: You can substitute summer squash for the zucchini.

SHRIMP AND ARUGULA SALAD WITH LEMON VINAIGRETTE
Serves 4

WHY THIS RECIPE WORKS: Fast-cooking shrimp adds protein to this simple and satisfying salad.

- 3 slices hearty white sandwich bread, cut into ½-inch pieces
- 2 ounces Parmesan cheese, 1 ounce grated (½ cup), 1 ounce shaved with vegetable peeler
- ½ cup extra-virgin olive oil
- 3 garlic cloves, minced
- 1 pound jumbo shrimp (16 to 20 per pound), peeled and deveined
  Salt and pepper
- 2 teaspoons balsamic vinegar
- 1 teaspoon Dijon mustard
- ½ teaspoon lemon zest plus 1 teaspoon juice
- 8 ounces (8 cups) baby arugula

1. Toss bread, grated Parmesan, 3 tablespoons oil, and 2 garlic cloves together in bowl. Transfer to 12-inch nonstick skillet and cook over medium-low heat, stirring constantly, until croutons are toasted, about 8 minutes; transfer to plate and let cool.

2. Season shrimp with salt and pepper. Heat 2 tablespoons oil in now-empty skillet over medium-high heat until just smoking. Add shrimp and cook, stirring occasionally, until pink and cooked through, 3 to 5 minutes; transfer to plate and let cool.

3. Combine vinegar, mustard, remaining garlic clove, lemon zest and juice, 1 teaspoon salt, and ½ teaspoon pepper in large bowl and slowly whisk in remaining 3 tablespoons oil until incorporated. Toss arugula and dressing together in large bowl. Top salad with shrimp, croutons, and shaved Parmesan. Serve.

KUNG PAO CHICKEN Serves 4

WHY THIS RECIPE WORKS: Just four ingredients—broth, oyster sauce, hot sauce, and cornstarch—make an easy and tasty sauce for the chicken.

- 1 cup low-sodium chicken broth
- 3 tablespoons oyster sauce
- 2 teaspoons hot sauce
- 2 teaspoons cornstarch
- 3 tablespoons vegetable oil
- 1½ pounds boneless, skinless chicken thighs, trimmed and cut into 1-inch pieces
- ½ cup dry-roasted peanuts
- 1 red bell pepper, stemmed, seeded, and cut into ½-inch pieces
- 3 garlic cloves, minced
- 1 tablespoon grated fresh ginger

1. Whisk broth, oyster sauce, hot sauce, and cornstarch together in medium bowl; set aside. Heat 2 tablespoons oil in 12-inch nonstick skillet over medium-high heat until just smoking. Add chicken and peanuts and cook until chicken is lightly browned, about 4 minutes. Transfer chicken and peanuts to plate.

2. Heat remaining 1 tablespoon oil in now-empty skillet over medium-high heat until just smoking. Add bell pepper and cook until lightly browned, about 3 minutes. Stir in garlic and ginger and cook until fragrant, about 30 seconds. Stir in broth mixture and bring to boil. Add chicken, peanuts, and any accumulated juice from plate and simmer until sauce has thickened and chicken is cooked through, about 4 minutes. Serve.

TEST KITCHEN NOTE: Serve with rice and steamed broccoli.

BLT WRAPS Serves 4

WHY THIS RECIPE WORKS: Microwaving the bacon is an easy hands-off cooking method.

- 12 ounces thick-cut bacon
- ¼ cup mayonnaise
- 1 tablespoon Dijon mustard
- 2 romaine lettuce hearts (12 ounces), leaves trimmed to 8 inches long
- 1 pint cherry tomatoes, halved
- 4 (10-inch) flour tortillas

1. Place half of bacon on paper towel–lined plate. Top with paper towels and repeat with remaining bacon. Microwave until crispy, 7 to 9 minutes.

2. Whisk mayonnaise and mustard together in large bowl until combined. Add lettuce and tomatoes and toss to coat evenly with dressing. Lay tortillas on counter and divide lettuce, tomatoes, and bacon among tortillas. Roll tightly and serve.

TEST KITCHEN NOTE: The test kitchen's winning brand of bacon is Farmland Hickory Smoked.

SPICY GRILLED CHICKEN TENDERS WITH CUCUMBER-CORIANDER SALAD

SPINACH, BELL PEPPER, AND SAUSAGE PASTA

GRILLED BEEF AND RED PEPPER SKEWERS

GRILLED CHEESY CHICKEN BREASTS WITH PROSCIUTTO AND WATERCRESS-APRICOT SALAD

SPINACH, BELL PEPPER, AND SAUSAGE PASTA Serves 4

WHY THIS RECIPE WORKS: Hot Italian sausage adds lots of flavor and deep seasoning to this simple pasta dish.

- 1 pound rotini
  Salt and pepper
- 1 pound hot Italian sausage, casings removed
- 1 red bell pepper, stemmed, seeded, and cut into ½-inch pieces
- 4 tablespoons unsalted butter
- 5 ounces (5 cups) baby spinach
- 1 ounce Parmesan cheese, grated (½ cup), plus extra for serving

1. Bring 4 quarts water to boil in Dutch oven. Add pasta and 1 tablespoon salt to water and cook until al dente. Reserve 1 cup pasta cooking water, then drain pasta. Return pasta to pot.

2. Meanwhile, cook sausage in 12-inch nonstick skillet over medium heat, breaking up pieces with spoon, until cooked through, about 10 minutes. Add bell pepper and cook, stirring occasionally, until beginning to brown, about 5 minutes. Remove from heat and stir in butter.

3. Add sausage mixture, spinach, Parmesan, and ½ cup reserved pasta cooking water to pasta and toss to combine, adding additional reserved water as needed. Season with salt and pepper to taste. Serve, passing extra Parmesan separately.

TEST KITCHEN NOTE: Any short pasta can be substituted for the rotini.

SPICY GRILLED CHICKEN TENDERS WITH CUCUMBER-CORIANDER SALAD Serves 4

WHY THIS RECIPE WORKS: Seasoning the chicken in a bag evenly coats the chicken and saves time on cleanup.

- 2 tablespoons sugar
- 1 tablespoon coriander seeds, cracked
- 2 teaspoons ground ginger
- 2 teaspoons turmeric
  Salt and pepper
- ½ teaspoon cayenne pepper
- 1½ pounds chicken tenderloins, trimmed
- ¼ cup rice vinegar
- 1 seedless English cucumber, sliced very thin
- 6 scallions, white and green parts sliced thin on bias
- ½ cup fresh cilantro leaves

1. Combine 1 tablespoon sugar, 2 teaspoons cracked coriander seeds, ginger, turmeric, 1 teaspoon salt, ½ teaspoon pepper, and cayenne in large zipper-lock bag. Add chicken to bag and shake to evenly coat with spice mixture.

2. Whisk vinegar and remaining 1 tablespoon sugar together in large bowl. Add cucumber, scallions, cilantro, and remaining 1 teaspoon coriander seeds and toss to combine. Season with salt and pepper to taste.

3. Grill chicken over medium-hot fire until browned all over and chicken registers 160 degrees, 6 to 8 minutes. Transfer to platter, tent with aluminum foil, and let rest for 5 minutes. Serve chicken with cucumber salad.

TEST KITCHEN NOTE: Crack the coriander seeds inside a zipper-lock bag with a small skillet or a flat meat mallet.

GRILLED CHEESY CHICKEN BREASTS WITH PROSCIUTTO AND WATERCRESS-APRICOT SALAD Serves 4

WHY THIS RECIPE WORKS: The tangy cheese and salty prosciutto boost the mild flavor of the chicken breasts.

- 4 (6-ounce) boneless, skinless chicken breasts, trimmed
- 2 ounces Taleggio cheese, cut into 4 sticks
  Salt and pepper
- 8 thin slices prosciutto (3 ounces)
- 3 tablespoons extra-virgin olive oil
- 2 tablespoons lemon juice
- 1 tablespoon honey
- 10 ounces (10 cups) watercress
- 1½ pounds apricots, halved, pitted, and cut into 1-inch wedges

1. Working with 1 piece at a time, cut pocket in thickest part of chicken breast. Insert 1 piece of Taleggio into pocket. Season chicken with salt and pepper. Lay 2 slices prosciutto on work surface, slightly overlapping each other. Place chicken breast in center of prosciutto slices and fold prosciutto up around it. Repeat with remaining chicken, Taleggio, and prosciutto. Brush wrapped chicken all over with 1 tablespoon oil.

2. Grill chicken over medium fire until chicken registers 160 degrees, about 8 minutes per side. Transfer chicken to platter, tent with aluminum foil, and let rest for 5 minutes.

3. Meanwhile, whisk remaining 2 tablespoons oil, lemon juice, and honey in large bowl. Add watercress and apricots and toss until combined. Season with salt and pepper to taste. Serve salad with chicken.

TEST KITCHEN NOTE: Aged fontina is a good substitute if you can't find Taleggio. You can use fresh peaches or nectarines instead of apricots in the salad.

GRILLED BEEF AND RED PEPPER SKEWERS Serves 4

WHY THIS RECIPE WORKS: A quick marinade is used to flavor both the meat and the peppers.

- 3 tablespoons lime juice (2 limes)
- 2 tablespoons soy sauce
- 1 tablespoon fish sauce
- 1 tablespoon packed dark brown sugar
- 3 garlic cloves, minced
- ½ teaspoon curry powder
- ¼ teaspoon red pepper flakes
- 1½ pounds sirloin steak tips, trimmed and cut into 1-inch chunks
- 2 red bell peppers, stemmed, seeded, and cut into 1-inch pieces

1. Whisk lime juice, soy sauce, fish sauce, sugar, garlic, curry powder, and pepper flakes together in large bowl. Add meat and bell peppers, toss to coat, and let sit for 10 minutes. Thread meat and bell peppers onto four 12-inch skewers.

2. Grill skewers over hot fire until bell peppers are lightly charred and meat is cooked to medium-rare, 5 to 7 minutes, turning every minute to brown all sides. Transfer to platter. Serve.

TEST KITCHEN NOTE: Serve with rice.

Chilled Leek and Potato Soup

What's the key to vichyssoise with great leek and potato flavor and velvety texture?
Surprisingly, it's cutting the fat. BY NICK IVERSON

DESPITE ITS DECIDEDLY French name, vichyssoise, or chilled leek and potato soup, was born in the USA. Louis Diat, chef at New York's famed Ritz-Carlton Hotel, is credited with creating this soup in 1917, when he upgraded and then chilled a batch of the humble leek and potato soup that he'd grown up eating near Vichy, France. It is believed he served his chilled soup at a party celebrating the hotel's new rooftop garden.

I first tasted vichyssoise in culinary school and can tell you from experience that—when well prepared—it's delicious, silken, and refreshing. I collected seven recipes (including the classic Ritz-Carlton version), hauled out soup pots and blenders, and got to work.

Most of these recipes work in a similar way: Leeks are softened in butter, and then cubed potatoes and chicken broth are added. When the potatoes have simmered to tenderness, the soup is pureed, strained, finished with cream, and chilled. Alas, the recipes I tested left something to be desired. Some of the soups were gritty and pasty, some wan and watery, and others the opposite extreme: much too rich. Also, as the soup chilled, the flavor faded. This classic needed sprucing up.

It wasn't surprising that both the type and amount of potatoes had a big impact on the texture of the soup. I tested russet, Red Bliss, Yukon Gold, and fingerling potatoes. The higher-starch potatoes made the soup gummy. Our science editor explained that as the potatoes cook, the starch granules swell, escape, and burst, releasing starch molecules. That accounted for the soup's gummy quality. In the end, a surprisingly small number of low-starch Red Bliss potatoes—blended and strained—produced a light, smooth soup.

Come to think of it, was straining necessary? *Absolutely* necessary? No. Could I streamline and stop after blending? Yes. But vichyssoise is an elegant, refined soup, and pushing it through a fine-mesh sieve gave it a beautiful silkiness. It was worth the extra step.

Leeks contribute texture as well as flavor, adding silkiness to soups. To capitalize on that and let their mild oniony flavor shine, I worked my way up from two leeks to four. "Still meek," my tasters said. To satisfy them, I introduced a chopped onion and then proceeded as before: Add potatoes and broth, simmer, blend, stir in cream, and strain. I let the soup chill and dipped in a spoon. Still meek—huh? Was the fatty cream muting the flavor?

I made the soup once more, and this time I tried something heretical: I omitted the cream. Just like that, the leek and potato flavor snapped into focus. Unfortunately, my tasters and I missed the sweetness that the cream had provided. I checked my research folder and noticed that one of the recipes I'd clipped called for boiling the raw leeks and potatoes in milk. I made my recipe again, borrowing that idea and using milk in place of some of the broth I had been including. The milk provided a well-rounded sweetness without masking the leek and potato flavor. The soup was delightfully silky, and it tasted rich, too—even without any cream. I reinforced the onion flavor with a sprinkle of chives. Now I had an easy soup with an unusual mission: beating the heat.

VICHYSSOISE Serves 4 to 6
Using white pepper means your soup won't be flecked with black.

- 2 tablespoons unsalted butter
- 2 pounds leeks, white and light green parts only, halved lengthwise, sliced thin, and washed thoroughly
- 1 onion, chopped fine
  Salt and white pepper
- 2½ cups whole milk
- 2 cups low-sodium chicken broth
- 8 ounces red potatoes, peeled and cut into ½-inch pieces
- 2 tablespoons minced fresh chives

1. Melt butter in Dutch oven over medium-low heat. Add leeks, onion, and 1½ teaspoons salt; cover and cook, stirring occasionally, until soft, about 10 minutes. Add milk, broth, potatoes, and ⅛ teaspoon white pepper; increase heat to medium-high; and bring to boil. Reduce heat to medium-low and simmer, covered, until potatoes are completely tender, about 20 minutes.

2. Let soup cool for 10 minutes. Working in batches, process soup in blender until smooth, 1 to 2 minutes. Strain soup through fine-mesh strainer into large bowl. Refrigerate until completely chilled, at least 4 hours or up to 2 days. Season with salt and white pepper to taste. Serve, garnished with chives.

For brighter flavor, we augment the leeks with a chopped onion and use milk instead of cream.

TEST KITCHEN TECHNIQUE
Ensuring Velvety Vichyssoise

For the smoothest soup, we puree it in a blender and then pass it through a fine-mesh strainer.

Season When Cold
Have you ever noticed that food tastes better when it's hot than when it's cold? That's why we often reseason our vichyssoise (and other cold soups) after it's chilled. Cold food seems less flavorful for two reasons: First, certain of our taste receptors are less sensitive at temperatures below about 60 degrees. Second, more aroma molecules float into the air and then our noses when food is hot. And as anybody who has ever suffered from a cold knows from personal experience, smelling food is a large part of what enables us to taste it.

Looking for a Recipe

Apple-Cranberry Cookies
Anna Creelman, Drexel Hill, Pa.

Years ago I found a recipe for apple-cranberry cookies in a cookbook I borrowed from a friend. I made two batches, and my husband and I ate almost all of them as they came out of the oven—they were that good. I no longer have the recipe and can't find one that comes even close. If it's any help, they had the texture of the brown-edged wafers that I believe Nabisco used to make. Any ideas?

Seven-Minute Fudge
Gretchen Cowan, Leavenworth, Kan.

A friend of mine lost her recipe for seven-minute fudge—her favorite fudge recipe. Hers had no milk in it (which was unusual). I've scoured my cookbooks and have not found a similar recipe. I'd love to be able to surprise her with it one day.

Carrot Salad
Doris McCowan, Fort Fairfield, Maine

When I was growing up, my grandmother's holiday table wasn't complete without a relish tray. Among the dishes on it was a carrot-raisin salad with tiny bits of pineapple. I've tried to re-create the sweet dressing that she made for that carrot salad, with no luck. Any ideas?

Old-Fashioned Frozen Custard
Linda Snyder, Medina, Ohio

I'm looking for a recipe for ice cream custard like the one my mom used to make back in the 1950s. It had the flavor of the stuff that's sold at local mom-and-pop custard stands in Milwaukee. I think it was made with evaporated milk. I'd love to make it for my grandkids.

Rappie Pie
Helen Brewster, Bath, Maine

I'm trying to find a recipe for a dish I enjoyed while on vacation in Nova Scotia. It's called rappie pie. It was similar to chicken pot pie, but instead of having a pastry crust, it was layered with shredded potato. It definitely had bacon and lots of onion in a rich, thickened chicken broth. If anyone has an easy recipe for rappie pie, I'd love to have it.

Carrot-Walnut Bread
Elaine Desmet, Woonsocket, R.I.

My granddaughter used to like to play with my recipe box, and now my recipe for a delicious carrot-walnut bread has disappeared. It had a lemon glaze that you drizzled over the top after it cooled. I'm pretty sure I clipped the recipe from a magazine in the early 1990s. If you could find this recipe, I would consider it a miracle.

Magic Peach Cobbler
Jennifer Bridges, North Hollywood, Calif.

I'm looking for a recipe for a peach cobbler that is made without eggs and uses canned peaches. You make the batter and place sliced canned peaches on top; then, while the cobbler bakes, the batter and peaches trade places. Magic!

Old-Fashioned Maple Doughnuts
Whitney Thomas, Boston, Mass.

Ever since moving to the Boston area about a year and a half ago, I have been trying to find old-fashioned maple doughnuts, but so far my search has been fruitless. I used to get them all the time in California (far from the land of sugar maples). They are an odd shape, and they have a delicious maple glaze. If I can't buy them, I'd love to be able to make them at home. Can you help?

Goody Goody Hamburger Sauce
Sharyn Fireman, Hull, Mass.

In Dayton, Ohio, Goody's used to be the place to go for hamburgers. The burgers were small and served on toasted buns with lots of thinly sliced dill pickles and the restaurant's special sauce. That sauce was exquisite. It was richly red, sweet, and thick, with undertones of spice and celery. For 70 years, this wonderful place made this sauce fresh every day. Then a fire tragically destroyed the restaurant. I hope someone can re-create the sauce. All the Midwest would be at your feet, and Chris Kimball would get a big hug!

HOMEMADE CORN DOGS Makes 8 corn dogs
Annabelle Stella, Raleigh, N.C.

1½	cups yellow cornmeal
1½	cups all-purpose flour
1	tablespoon baking powder
1	teaspoon baking soda
2	teaspoons sugar
1½	teaspoons salt
½	teaspoon cayenne pepper
1¾	cups buttermilk
4	large eggs, lightly beaten
8	hot dogs
3	quarts peanut or vegetable oil

1. Set wire rack inside rimmed baking sheet. Whisk cornmeal, 1 cup flour, baking powder, baking soda, sugar, salt, and cayenne together in bowl. Whisk in buttermilk and eggs until incorporated. Place remaining ½ cup flour in shallow dish. Dredge hot dogs in flour and shake to remove excess. Thread hot dogs lengthwise onto eight 8-inch skewers.

2. Add oil to large Dutch oven until it measures about 2 inches deep and heat over medium-high heat to 350 degrees. Stir batter to recombine, then transfer half of batter to tall drinking glass. Working with one at a time, submerge hot dog in glass and twirl to coat with batter. Allow excess batter to drip back into glass and place corn dog in hot oil. Repeat immediately with 3 more hot dogs. Fry corn dogs, turning occasionally, until golden brown, 4 to 6 minutes. Transfer to wire rack. Return oil to 350 degrees and repeat with remaining batter and hot dogs. Serve.

TOMATO DUMPLINGS Makes 16 dumplings
Lily Julow, Gainesville, Fla.

"This is one of the wonderful Amish recipes I learned to make during my childhood when we lived in Lancaster, Pennsylvania." These dumplings are delicious served with grated Parmesan.

3	tablespoons unsalted butter, plus 2 tablespoons melted
½	cup finely chopped onion
¼	cup minced celery
1	(28-ounce) can diced tomatoes
2	teaspoons packed brown sugar
½	teaspoon salt
½	teaspoon pepper
¼	cup minced fresh parsley
1	cup all-purpose flour
1½	teaspoons baking powder
½	cup whole milk
1	large egg, lightly beaten

1. Melt 3 tablespoons butter in Dutch oven over medium heat. Add onion and celery and cook until translucent, about 3 minutes. Stir in tomatoes and their juice, sugar, salt, and pepper. Bring to simmer and cook until vegetables are softened, about 5 minutes. Remove from heat and stir in 2 tablespoons parsley.

2. Combine remaining 2 tablespoons parsley, flour, and baking powder in large bowl. Stir in milk, egg, and melted butter until combined and batter is smooth. Return tomato mixture to simmer over medium heat.

3. Using greased tablespoon measure, drop heaping tablespoon-size dumplings on top of tomato mixture, leaving about ½ inch between dumplings. Cover and cook over low heat until dumplings are firm and cooked through, about 20 minutes. (Do not uncover during cooking.) Serve.

Peanut Butter and Jam Cake

We sandwiched fluffy white cake layers with sweet peanut butter frosting and raspberry jam to turn this brown-bag classic into a very special after-school treat.

To make this cake you will need:

Batter for White Layer Cake*
16   **tablespoons unsalted butter, softened**
1   **cup creamy peanut butter**
3   **tablespoons heavy cream**
1   **teaspoon vanilla extract**
2   **cups (8 ounces) confectioners' sugar**
1¼   **cups seedless raspberry jam**
1   **cup dry-roasted peanuts, chopped**

FOR THE CAKE: Adjust oven rack to middle position and heat oven to 350 degrees. Generously grease two 8-inch square baking pans and cover pan bottoms with squares of parchment paper. Grease and flour parchment. Divide batter equally between prepared pans. Bake until cake tops are light golden and toothpick inserted in center comes out clean, about 25 minutes. Cool on wire rack for 10 minutes. Run knife around pans to loosen cakes. Invert cakes onto large plates, peel off parchment, and reinvert onto lightly greased rack. Cool completely.

FOR THE FROSTING: Using stand mixer fitted with whisk, whip butter, peanut butter, cream, and vanilla on medium-high speed until combined, about 30 seconds. Reduce speed to medium-low and slowly add sugar until smooth, 1 to 2 minutes. Increase speed to medium-high and whip frosting until light and fluffy, about 5 minutes.

TO ASSEMBLE: Slice each cake in half horizontally; spread ½ cup jam over each bottom half and replace top half. Place 1 reassembled cake on cake plate, then spread 1 cup frosting in even layer over top. Place second reassembled cake on top of frosting. Spread remaining frosting over top and sides of cake. Press peanuts onto sides of cake. Heat remaining ¼ cup jam in bowl in microwave until melted and smooth, about 20 seconds. Transfer to piping bag or small plastic sandwich bag with 1 corner cut off. Pipe jam in straight lines over top of cake and lightly drag paring knife through lines to create marbled appearance. Serve.

*Go to **CooksCountry.com/sept12** for our **White Layer Cake** recipe.

Cook's Country

Dear Country Cook,

Once one reaches a certain age, one becomes a bridge between history and the present. Yes, I actually did bob for apples at a birthday party when I was seven or eight. Our first phone in Vermont was attached to the wall and had a party line—we had to ring up the operator to contact a neighbor. Floyd Bentley used a team of horses to cut hay and mules to cut and bind the corn, and there was one cow behind the Yellow Farmhouse that gave milk to support the extended family of farmers who lived inside. That farmhouse also had an outhouse and no running water—just a green hand pump in the pantry sink.

You probably expect me to extol the virtues of the simple life, how we enjoyed the passage of time without computers, iPhones, and the Internet. The problem is that the past is gone and the future never arrives—we only live in the moment. And nothing lasts forever; you can't fake it.

Technology can't buy happiness, but cooking can. You can cook for your kids, make a homemade birthday cake, bring a casserole to a sick neighbor, or throw together an impromptu covered-dish supper. The kitchen is a form of time travel since cooking for others is eternal. A good Sunday supper always has and always will bring people together.

Just grab a spoon, a bowl, and a recipe, and turn on the oven. It might be 1920, 1960, or 2012—it doesn't really matter. You are now part of history, connected to all the cooks who have come before and all those who are yet to be born. You don't even need a time machine.

Christopher Kimball
Founder and Editor, Cook's Country

Cook'sCountry

Founder and Editor Christopher Kimball
Editorial Director Jack Bishop
Editorial Director, Magazines John Willoughby
Executive Editor Peggy Grodinsky
Managing Editor Scott Kathan
Senior Editors Lisa McManus, Bryan Roof, Diane Unger
Test Kitchen Director Erin McMurrer
Associate Editors Chris Dudley, Amy Graves, Rebeccah Marsters, Sarah Wilson
Test Cooks Sarah Gabriel, Nick Iverson Carolynn Purpura MacKay, Cristin Walsh
Assistant Editors Hannah Crowley, Shannon Friedmann Hatch, Taizeth Sierra
Copy Editors Nell Beram, Megan Chromik
Executive Assistant Christine Gordon
Assistant Test Kitchen Director Gina Nistico
Test Kitchen Manager Leah Rovner
Senior Kitchen Assistant Meryl MacCormack
Kitchen Assistants Marla Elena Delgado, Ena Gudiel, Andrew Straaberg Finfrock
Executive Producer Melissa Baldino
Associate Producer Stephanie Stender
Production Assistant Kaitlin Hammond

Contributing Editors Erika Bruce, Eva Katz, Jeremy Sauer
Consulting Editors Anne Mendelson, Meg Ragland
Science Editor Guy Crosby, Ph.D.
Executive Food Editor, TV, Radio & Media Bridget Lancaster

Managing Editor, Web Christine Liu
Associate Editors, Web Eric Grzymkowski, Mari Levine, Roger Metcalf
Senior Video Editor Nick Dakoulas

Design Director Amy Klee
Art Director Julie Cote
Deputy Art Director Susan Levin
Associate Art Director Lindsey Timko
Staff Photographer Daniel J. van Ackere
Color Food Photography Keller + Keller
Styling Catrine Kelty
Designer, Marketing/Web Mariah Tarvainen
Photo Editor Steve Klise

Vice President, Marketing David Mack
Circulation Director Doug Wicinski
Circulation & Fulfillment Manager Carrie Fethe
Partnership Marketing Manager Pamela Putprush
Marketing Assistant Joyce Liao
Customer Service Manager Jacqueline Valerio
Customer Service Representatives Jessica Haskin

Chief Operating Officer David Dinnage
Production Director Guy Rochford
Senior Project Manager Alice Carpenter
Workflow & Digital Asset Manager Andrew Mannone
Production & Traffic Coordinator Brittany Allen
Production & Imaging Specialists Judy Blomquist, Heather Dube, Lauren Pettapiece
Systems Administrator Marcus Walser
Helpdesk Support Technician Brianna Brothers
Senior Business Analyst Wendy Tseng
Web Developer Chris Candelora
Human Resources Manager Adele Shapiro

VP New Media Product Development Barry Kelly
Social Media Manager Steph Yiu
Assistant Editor, New Media Amy Scheuerman
Chief Financial Officer Sharyn Chabot
Director of Sponsorship Sales Anne Traficante
Retail Sales & Marketing Manager Emily Logan
Client Service Associate Kate May
Publicity Deborah Broide

ON THE COVER:
Porketta, Keller + Keller, Catrine Kelty
ILLUSTRATION: Greg Stevenson

 Follow us on **Twitter**
twitter.com/TestKitchen

 Find us on **Facebook**
facebook.com/CooksCountry

Cook's Country magazine (ISSN 1552-1990), number 47, is published bimonthly by Boston Common Press Limited Partnership, 17 Station Street, Brookline, MA 02445. Copyright 2012 Boston Common Press Limited Partnership. Periodicals Postage paid at Boston, Mass., and additional mailing offices. Publications Mail Agreement No. 40020778. Return undeliverable Canadian addresses to P.O. Box 875, Station A, Windsor, Ontario N9A 6P2. POSTMASTER: Send address changes to Cook's Country, P.O. Box 6018, Harlan, IA 51593-1518. Customer Service: It's easy to subscribe, give a gift subscription, change your address, and manage your subscription online. Visit AmericasTestKitchen.com/customerservice for all of your customer service needs or write to us at Cook's Country, P.O. Box 6018, Harlan, IA 51593-1518. PRINTED IN THE USA

Contents

SUPER-MOIST ROAST TURKEY, 4

FRUIT CHUTNEYS, 29

SWEET POTATO CASSEROLE, 8

Features

In Every Issue

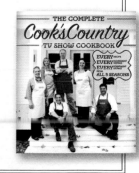

America's TEST KITCHEN

RECIPES THAT WORK®

America's Test Kitchen is a 2,500-square-foot kitchen located just outside Boston. It is the home of *Cook's Country* and *Cook's Illustrated* magazines and is the workday destination of more than 50 test cooks, editors, and cookware specialists. Our mission is to test recipes until we understand how and why they work and arrive at the best version. We also test kitchen equipment and supermarket ingredients in search of brands that offer the best value and performance. You can watch us work by tuning in to *Cook's Country from America's Test Kitchen* (CooksCountryTV.com) on public television.

Getting to Know Cooking Cheeses

Whether crystalline or creamy, sharp or mild, blue or orange, cheese shows up in too many recipes to count here in the test kitchen. We're profiling a dozen that we reach for often. BY REBECCAH MARSTERS

Mild Cheddar
CROWD PLEASER

Whether British or American, all cheddars are made by a process called cheddaring, in which curds are cut into slabs, stacked, and pressed. American cheddar may be white or yellow, depending on the region it's from. We blindfolded our cooks and tasted both; no one could reliably tell the difference. The yellow (it's actually orange) is dyed with annatto seeds. Mild, young cheddar is moister and a better melter than its older siblings.

Sharp Cheddar
ALL GROWN UP

As cheddar ages, its texture firms and dries, and its flavor concentrates. While the U.S. Department of Agriculture (USDA) has no guidelines for aging and labeling, extra-sharp cheddar (at the far end of the cheddar spectrum) is usually nine to 18 months old. Older cheddar can curdle when melted. To prevent that, we shred it and toss it with cornstarch or combine it with better melters, such as Monterey Jack or American cheese.

Monterey Jack
MASTER MELTER

When it comes to creamy melting and mild flavor, Monterey Jack sets the gold standard. A California native, it's also called Cali Jack, or just Jack cheese, and is rarely aged. Pepper Jack is its spicy cousin. Cabot makes our favorite Monterey Jack, which we use in everything from enchiladas to stuffed meatloaf to scalloped potatoes. For easier shredding, spray your grater with vegetable oil spray.

American Cheese
SANDWICH SQUARE

The USDA labels it "process cheese product" for a reason: Most American cheese is only part cheese. Stabilizers and emulsifiers account for the remainder. Eating it showed patriotism during World War II, and we remain fond of it in a grilled cheese sandwich or melted over a cheesesteak. For the best flavor, look for brands with "cultured pasteurized milk" as the first ingredient or try making your own (we're not kidding): **CooksCountry.com/ makeamericancheese**.

Block-Style Mozzarella
PIZZA PAL

Heat brings out the best in this low-moisture mozzarella, which, though rubbery when raw, melts beautifully. You can use part skim and full fat interchangeably in recipes for calzones, lasagnas, and pizza, but avoid preshredded. Our favorite product is Sorrento Whole Milk Mozzarella, which we've found "clean" and "mellow," "practically like drinking milk." Don't confuse block-style with fresh mozzarella, which is usually packed in water.

Parmesan
CHEESE WITH A PAST

True Parmigiano-Reggiano is a cow's-milk cheese made in Northern Italy by strictly governed methods that have been around for 800 years. We love its "buttery," "nutty" flavor and crystalline texture, a product of up to two years of aging. (American Parmesans are younger and use different rennet and pasteurized milk so may be sour, salty, and rubbery.) Save the rinds, storing them in a zipper-lock bag in the refrigerator or freezer, to flavor soup, such as minestrone.

Ricotta
LASAGNA LOVE

Fluffy, buttery, and slightly sweet, ricotta is versatile enough to use both in savory classics, like lasagna and manicotti, and in desserts, such as cheesecake and cannoli. Our taste-test winner is "creamy," "clean" Calabro Part Skim Ricotta. If you can't find it, look for a brand of fresh ricotta that has no gums or stabilizers. Or make it yourself: **CooksCountry.com/ makericotta**. In the test kitchen, we sometimes smooth out ricotta destined for pasta dishes with hot pasta water.

Feta
GREEK GIFT

No need to beware of this salty, sharp, and deliciously crumbly Greek gift. In Greece, real feta must be made from at least 70 percent sheep's milk (goat's milk is also traditional). In the United States, though, feta often uses cow's milk and may come from France or Romania, among other places. The test kitchen favorite is from Greece—Mt. Vikos Traditional Feta. To keep feta moist and fresh, store it in its brine.

Supermarket Blue Cheese
STRONG STUFF

Blue cheese is made by treating cow's-, goat's-, or sheep's-milk cheeses with a (harmless) mold. Bacteria grows in the ripening cheese, giving it a pungent, distinctive flavor and smell. Use the tines of a fork to crumble wedges of cheese and toss it in salads, stir it into dips, or mix it with softened butter and chives to melt over grilled steak or burgers. Blue cheese pairs well with grapes, apples, and pears.

Fresh Goat Cheese (Chèvre)
NEW ARRIVAL

Just 30 years ago, America was a land largely bereft of goat cheese. Today, thanks in part to pioneering Californians Laura Chenel (cheesemaker) and Alice Waters (restaurateur), goat cheese is produced (and eaten) all over the country. Precrumbled is often dry and chalky, so buy it in logs and use unflavored dental floss to slice it into neat medallions.

Swiss Cheese
THE EYES HAVE IT

The name aside, many Swiss cheeses you'll find in the supermarket are actually made in America. The real deal is Emmentaler Swiss cheese, which is nutty and complex when eaten out of hand and a classic for fondue. The holes, or "eyes," in Swiss cheese are formed when (good) bacteria release carbon dioxide as the cheeses age. Older cheeses have a stronger flavor—and larger eyes.

Gruyère
FONDUE FRIEND

Dense, creamy Gruyère, produced in France and Switzerland, is made from raw cow's milk and aged for about a year. Tasters described it as "assertively salty" and "nutty." Our favorite is the Reserve Wheel from Peney-le-Jorat, Switzerland (but we liked every import we tasted). Domestic Gruyères pale in comparison. Find our recipe for Slow-Cooker French Onion Soup (with Gruyère) at **CooksCountry.com/ slowcookeronionsoup**.

BAKED HADDOCK WITH GARLIC GREEN BEANS

WHOLE-WHEAT PENNE WITH BABY SPINACH

CHICKEN PARMESAN SUBS

GINGER BEEF AND RAMEN NOODLE SOUP

WHOLE-WHEAT PENNE WITH BABY SPINACH Serves 4

WHY THIS RECIPE WORKS: To save time and dishes, we cook the pasta and the sauce in the same pan.

- 1 slice hearty white sandwich bread, torn into pieces
- 3 tablespoons unsalted butter
- 3 garlic cloves, minced
- ¼ teaspoon red pepper flakes
- 3¾ cups low-sodium chicken broth
- 1 cup heavy cream
  Salt and pepper
- 12 ounces (3¾ cups) whole-wheat penne
- 6 ounces (6 cups) baby spinach, chopped
- 2 ounces Parmesan cheese, grated (1 cup)

1. Process bread in food processor until coarsely ground, about 5 seconds. Melt 1 tablespoon butter in 12-inch nonstick skillet over medium heat. Add one-third of garlic and cook until fragrant, about 30 seconds. Add bread crumbs and cook, stirring frequently, until golden brown, about 5 minutes. Transfer to bowl.

2. Melt remaining 2 tablespoons butter in now-empty skillet over medium-high heat. Add remaining garlic and pepper flakes and cook until fragrant, about 30 seconds. Stir in broth, cream, ½ teaspoon salt, and ¼ teaspoon pepper and bring to simmer. Add penne and cook, stirring occasionally, until al dente, about 10 minutes.

3. Off heat, stir in spinach and Parmesan. Season with salt and pepper to taste. Sprinkle with toasted bread crumbs. Serve.

TEST KITCHEN NOTE: You can substitute baby arugula for the baby spinach.

BAKED HADDOCK WITH GARLIC GREEN BEANS Serves 4

WHY THIS RECIPE WORKS: Crushed crackers add crunch to the topping.

- 4 (6- to 8-ounce) skinless haddock fillets, 1 inch thick
  Salt and pepper
- 20 Ritz crackers, crushed to coarse crumbs (1 cup)
- 2 tablespoons minced fresh parsley
- ¼ cup olive oil
- 1 tablespoon Dijon mustard
- 1 tablespoon lemon juice
- ⅛ teaspoon cayenne pepper
- 1 pound green beans, trimmed
- 2 garlic cloves, minced

1. Adjust oven rack to middle position and heat oven to 450 degrees. Spray 13 by 9-inch baking dish with vegetable oil spray. Pat haddock dry with paper towels and season with salt and pepper. Place haddock in prepared baking dish.

2. Combine cracker crumbs with 1 tablespoon parsley. In separate bowl, combine 3 tablespoons oil, remaining 1 tablespoon parsley, mustard, lemon juice, and cayenne. Coat top and sides of haddock with oil mixture, then press cracker crumbs onto haddock. Bake until cracker crumbs are golden brown and haddock is opaque, about 15 minutes.

3. Meanwhile, heat remaining 1 tablespoon oil in saucepan over medium-high heat until shimmering. Add green beans and cook, stirring occasionally, until spotty brown, about 8 to 10 minutes. Stir in ¼ cup water and ½ teaspoon salt, cover, and reduce heat to medium-low. Cook until green beans are nearly tender, 3 to 5 minutes. Remove lid and cook until liquid evaporates, about 1 minute. Add garlic and cook until fragrant, about 30 seconds. Season with salt and pepper to taste. Serve green beans with haddock.

GINGER BEEF AND RAMEN NOODLE SOUP Serves 4

WHY THIS RECIPE WORKS: Simmering chicken broth with lime zest and ginger is a shortcut to Asian flavor.

- 1 (1-pound) flank steak, trimmed
  Salt and pepper
- 1 teaspoon vegetable oil
- 8 cups low-sodium chicken broth
- 1 (2-inch) piece ginger, halved lengthwise and smashed
- 3 (2½-inch) strips lime zest plus 1 tablespoon juice
- 4 packages instant ramen noodles (seasoning packets discarded)
- 5 scallions, sliced thin
- ¼ cup soy sauce
- ¼ cup fresh cilantro leaves

1. Pat steak dry with paper towels and season with salt and pepper. Heat oil in 12-inch skillet over medium-high heat until just smoking. Add steak and cook until well browned and temperature registers 125 degrees for medium-rare, 6 to 8 minutes, flipping once. Transfer to cutting board, tent loosely with aluminum foil, and let rest for 5 minutes. Slice steak in half lengthwise, then slice thin against grain.

2. Meanwhile, bring broth, ginger, and lime zest to boil in Dutch oven over medium-high heat. Reduce heat to medium-low, cover, and simmer for 10 minutes.

3. Remove ginger and lime zest from broth with slotted spoon. Add noodles and cook until tender, about 3 minutes. Stir in scallions, soy sauce, and lime juice. Ladle noodles and broth into 4 serving bowls and divide steak and cilantro evenly among bowls. Serve.

TEST KITCHEN NOTE: Smash the ginger with the flat side of a chef's knife.

CHICKEN PARMESAN SUBS Serves 4

WHY THIS RECIPE WORKS: The pan-fried panko coating stays crisp, even when smothered in sauce and cheese.

- ½ cup all-purpose flour
- 3 large eggs
- 1 cup panko bread crumbs
  Salt and pepper
- 4 (4-ounce) chicken cutlets
- ¼ cup vegetable oil
- 2 garlic cloves, minced
- 1 (14.5-ounce) can diced tomatoes
- 4 (6-inch) sub rolls, split lengthwise
- 4 ounces shredded Italian cheese blend (1 cup)

1. Adjust oven rack to middle position and heat oven to 400 degrees. Place flour in shallow dish. Beat eggs in second shallow dish. Combine panko, ¼ teaspoon salt, and ¼ teaspoon pepper in third shallow dish.

2. Pat cutlets dry with paper towels and season with salt and pepper. Dip each cutlet in flour, dunk in eggs, and dredge in panko mixture, pressing to adhere. Heat 3 tablespoons oil in large nonstick skillet over medium-high heat until shimmering. Add cutlets, lower heat to medium, and cook until golden brown and crisp, about 2 minutes per side. Transfer cutlets to paper towel–lined plate and let rest for 5 minutes. Slice each cutlet in half lengthwise.

3. Meanwhile, heat remaining 1 tablespoon oil in medium saucepan over medium-high heat until shimmering. Add garlic and cook until fragrant, about 30 seconds. Stir in tomatoes and their juice and simmer until slightly thickened, about 7 minutes. Mash mixture until only small chunks of tomato remain. Season with salt and pepper. Place rolls on rimmed baking sheet. Lay 2 pieces of cutlet inside each roll. Cover cutlets with tomato sauce, then sprinkle with cheese. Bake until cheese is melted, 3 to 5 minutes. Serve.

EASY CHICKEN EMPANADAS

TWO-BEAN CHILI

SPICED PORK TENDERLOIN WITH PINEAPPLE SALSA

**CHEDDAR-CRUSTED CHICKEN
WITH GARLICKY SPINACH**

TWO-BEAN CHILI Serves 4

WHY THIS RECIPE WORKS: Pureeing some of the bean and tomato mixture gives the chili body.

- 1 tablespoon vegetable oil
- 1 onion, chopped fine
- 3 tablespoons chili powder
- 1 tablespoon minced canned chipotle chile in adobo sauce
- 2 teaspoons ground cumin
- 4 (10-ounce) cans Ro-tel Diced Tomatoes & Green Chilies
- 2 (15-ounce) cans red kidney beans, rinsed
- 2 (15-ounce) cans black beans, rinsed
- ¼ cup minced fresh cilantro
  Salt and pepper

1. Heat oil in Dutch oven over medium-high heat until shimmering. Add onion and cook until starting to soften, about 2 minutes. Add chili powder, chipotle, and cumin and cook until fragrant, about 30 seconds. Stir in tomatoes and their juice and beans and bring to boil. Reduce heat to medium-low and simmer, covered and stirring occasionally, for 15 minutes.

2. Process 2 cups chili in blender until smooth, about 1 minute. Return puree to pot along with cilantro and stir to combine. Season with salt and pepper to taste. Serve.

TEST KITCHEN NOTE: Serve with tortilla chips, cheddar cheese, and lime wedges.

EASY CHICKEN EMPANADAS Serves 4

WHY THIS RECIPE WORKS: Store-bought pie dough makes short work of empanadas.

- 1 tablespoon vegetable oil
- 1 onion, chopped fine
- 2 jalapeño chiles, stemmed, seeded, and minced
- 1 teaspoon ground cumin
- 1 pound ground chicken
  Salt and pepper
- ¼ cup minced fresh cilantro
- ¼ cup pitted green olives, chopped
- ¼ cup raisins
- 2 (9-inch) store-bought pie dough rounds

1. Adjust oven rack to middle position and heat oven to 450 degrees. Line rimmed baking sheet with parchment paper.

2. Heat oil in 12-inch nonstick skillet over medium-high heat until shimmering. Add onion and jalapeños and cook until starting to soften, about 2 minutes. Add cumin and cook until fragrant, about 30 seconds. Add chicken, ¾ teaspoon salt, and ¼ teaspoon pepper and cook until no longer pink, about 4 minutes. Transfer chicken mixture to bowl and stir to cool slightly, about 2 minutes. Stir in cilantro, olives, and raisins. Season with salt and pepper to taste.

3. Cut each dough round in half. Arrange one quarter of filling on 1 side of each dough half, leaving ½-inch border. Brush edges of dough with water, fold dough over filling, and crimp edges with fork to seal. Transfer to prepared baking sheet. Using fork, pierce each empanada twice to allow steam to escape. Bake until golden brown, 15 to 20 minutes. Serve.

TEST KITCHEN NOTE: Serve with salad.

CHEDDAR-CRUSTED CHICKEN WITH GARLICKY SPINACH
Serves 4

WHY THIS RECIPE WORKS: Crushed rice cereal and shredded cheese make a crunchy, flavorful coating.

- 1½ cups crispy rice cereal, crushed
- 6 ounces sharp cheddar cheese, shredded (1½ cups)
- 4 (6-ounce) boneless, skinless chicken breasts, trimmed
  Salt and pepper
- 18 ounces (18 cups) baby spinach
- 2 tablespoons olive oil
- 4 garlic cloves, minced

1. Adjust oven rack to middle position and heat oven to 400 degrees. Spray rimmed baking sheet with vegetable oil spray. Combine cereal and cheddar in shallow dish. Season chicken with salt and pepper. Dredge both sides of breasts in cereal-cheddar mixture, pressing to adhere, and arrange on prepared baking sheet. Bake until chicken registers 160 degrees and coating is golden brown, about 20 minutes. Transfer to serving platter and tent loosely with aluminum foil.

2. Meanwhile, place spinach and ¼ cup water in large bowl, cover, and microwave until spinach is wilted and decreased in volume by half, about 4 minutes. Transfer spinach to colander and, using rubber spatula, press to release liquid. Transfer spinach to cutting board and roughly chop.

3. Heat oil in 12-inch nonstick skillet over medium heat until shimmering. Add garlic and cook until fragrant, about 30 seconds. Add spinach to skillet and cook until uniformly wilted and glossy green, about 2 minutes. Season with salt and pepper to taste. Transfer spinach to platter and serve with chicken.

TEST KITCHEN NOTE: Grate the cheese yourself. Store-bought shredded cheese contains cornstarch and may not adhere.

SPICED PORK TENDERLOIN WITH PINEAPPLE SALSA Serves 4

WHY THIS RECIPE WORKS: The sweet pineapple balances the spiciness of the jalapeño and the spice rub.

- 2 teaspoons ground coriander
- 2 teaspoons ground cumin
- 1 teaspoon ground allspice
  Salt and pepper
- ¼ teaspoon cayenne pepper
- 2 (12-ounce) pork tenderloins, trimmed
- 2 cups pineapple, cut into ½-inch pieces
- 2 tablespoons chopped fresh cilantro
- 1 jalapeño chile, stemmed, seeded, and minced
- ½ teaspoon grated lime zest plus 2 tablespoons juice

1. Adjust oven rack to upper-middle position and heat oven to 475 degrees. Set wire rack inside rimmed baking sheet and place on oven rack. Combine coriander, cumin, allspice, ½ teaspoon salt, ¼ teaspoon pepper, and cayenne in bowl.

2. Pat pork dry with paper towels and coat evenly with spice mixture. Transfer pork to preheated wire rack and roast until meat registers 145 degrees, about 20 minutes, flipping halfway through cooking. Transfer to carving board, tent loosely with aluminum foil, and let rest for 5 minutes. Meanwhile, combine pineapple, cilantro, jalapeño, and lime zest and juice in bowl. Season with salt and pepper to taste. Slice pork into ¼-inch-thick slices and serve with salsa.

TEST KITCHEN NOTE: For more heat, include the jalapeño seeds in the salsa.

Butterscotch Cookies

Few flavors are as familiar as butterscotch. Replicating that flavor in a cookie, however, is like having a clear destination but no map. BY SARAH GABRIEL

WHILE IT DOESN'T have the star power of chocolate or the ubiquity of vanilla, butterscotch is a classic. In pudding, candies, or ice cream topping, I'd take butterscotch's sweet-salty complexity over chocolate any day, so when my editors handed me an assignment for butterscotch icebox cookies, I couldn't wait to get started.

I mixed, chilled, sliced, and baked more than nine dozen cookies from six different recipes (all formed into logs, for convenient slice-and-bake cookies); poured some milk; and called tasters to rank the cookies in order of butterscotch flavor. When I compared the rankings with the recipes, I found that the more brown sugar and butter the better the ranking. If more of those meant more butterscotch flavor, I could just up the two ingredients and I'd be done, right? Wrong.

Our favorite recipe from round one called for ½ cup of brown sugar and 10 tablespoons of butter. I increased both in 2-tablespoon increments and didn't get far before I ran into problems: The extra sugar and butter caused excessive spreading and greasiness. Adding a little extra flour sopped up the grease and decreased spreading, but still, I had maxed out at ¾ cup of brown sugar and 12 tablespoons of butter. It wasn't so much more brown sugar I wanted as more brown sugar flavor. Could I get more flavor by exchanging light brown sugar for dark? More? Yes. Enough? Definitely not.

Before continuing in my quest to amp up butterscotch flavor, I headed to the library to research what, precisely, butterscotch is. I knew that butterscotch, like caramel, is a cooked sugar confection, but some sources said that butterscotch is simply brown sugar cooked with butter, while others indicated that it must contain salt, cane syrup, or an acid like lemon juice—or be cooked to a specific temperature. I had exhausted the butter and brown sugar possibilities, but cooking the two together seemed worth a try. I boiled and then cooled the dark brown sugar with the butter and beat the mixture. Unfortunately, this didn't amp up butterscotch flavor; it made the cookies hard rather than crispy and was a big pain in the neck.

Maybe I needed one of the myriad butterscotch-flavored confections—hard candies, toffee, or chips. Hard candies

were too . . . well, hard. Toffee bits tasted good—just not like butterscotch. Butterscotch chips tasted powerfully butterscotchy, but it was difficult to cut even slices from a dough log studded with chips. I had found the flavor I needed; if I could just figure out how to incorporate it . . .

I started by melting ½ cup of chips and adding them to my softened butter. The melted chips melted the butter—not good, as I couldn't cream melted butter, a step that's necessary to incorporate air to give the cookies structure and tenderness. I tried adding the melted chips to cold butter, but they seized into hard pellets. I went ahead and shaped and baked the cookies anyhow. They came out pockmarked, but that didn't deter tasters a bit. The whole batch was reduced to crumbs within seconds. I was on the right track. Melting the chips along with a few tablespoons of the butter proved the answer: It prevented the mixture from seizing when I mixed in the cold butter. Finally, the cookies were freckle-free and, very soon after I called the tasters, gone.

BUTTERSCOTCH COOKIES
Makes about 32 cookies

Use chilled butter so it won't melt when you add the melted chips in step 2. If the chilled dough begins to split as you slice it, soften it on the counter for 10 minutes.

- ½ cup (3 ounces) butterscotch chips
- 3 tablespoons unsalted butter, plus 9 tablespoons cut into 9 pieces, chilled
- 2 teaspoons vanilla extract
- ¾ cup packed (5¼ ounces) dark brown sugar
- ½ teaspoon salt
- 1 large egg yolk
- 1¾ cups (8¾ ounces) all-purpose flour
- 1 teaspoon baking powder

1. Microwave butterscotch chips and 3 tablespoons butter in bowl until melted, about 1 minute, stirring halfway through. Whisk in vanilla until mixture is smooth; let cool for 10 minutes.

2. Using stand mixer fitted with paddle, beat remaining 9 tablespoons butter, sugar, and salt on medium-high speed until pale and fluffy, about 3 minutes. Add cooled butterscotch mixture and beat until thoroughly combined, about 1 minute, scraping down bowl as needed. Add egg yolk and beat until

incorporated, about 30 seconds. Reduce speed to low, add flour and baking powder, and mix until dough forms, about 1 minute.

3. Turn out dough onto counter and roll into 9-inch log. Wrap tightly with parchment paper and roll to form even cylinder. Refrigerate until firm, at least 2 hours or up to 3 days. (Dough can be wrapped in aluminum foil and frozen for up to 1 month.)

4. Adjust oven racks to upper-middle and lower-middle positions and heat oven to 325 degrees. Line 2 baking sheets with parchment paper. Slice chilled dough with sharp knife into ¼-inch-thick rounds and place 1 inch apart on prepared baking sheets (16 cookies per sheet). Bake until edges have darkened slightly, about 15 minutes, switching and rotating sheets halfway through baking. Let cool for 10 minutes on baking sheets, then transfer cookies to wire rack to cool completely. (Cookies can be stored in airtight container at room temperature for up to 3 days.)

Form this easy dough into logs, chill, and then slice and bake the cookies.

Are Chips Cheating?

At its most basic, butterscotch is butter cooked with brown sugar. After testing, tasting, and rejecting several recipes that rely on this traditional approach, we realized that (artificial) commercial butterscotch flavor—think hard candies and chips—has come to define butterscotch flavor for most of us. To get that flavor to permeate easy-to-slice refrigerator cookies, we melted chips with a little butter, cooled the mixture, and then creamed it right into our dough.

Atlanta Brisket

Brisket braised in cola is a Southern tradition. The sweetness and mellow spice of the cola are nice contrasts to the rich beef. So how come the recipes we tried missed the mark? BY NICK IVERSON

Coca-Cola is such a global presence these days that few people realize it was once just a local specialty, created by an Atlanta pharmacist and sold for a nickel a drink. The company is still head-quartered in Atlanta. Today, Southerners drink more soda than people in other parts of the country (so says the U.S. Department of Agriculture). Or maybe they're cooking with the stuff. It could be that the kola nuts and essence of coca leaf rumored to be in Coke's secret formula give recipes a pleasing extra dimension. Recently, one recipe in partic-ular caught my eye: braised Coca-Cola brisket, also called Atlanta brisket. Truthfully, I was wondering if it could be any good.

A colleague persuaded me to drop my skepticism and give it a try. Don't think warm soda pop, she insisted. Imagine brisket in a sweet-yet-savory sauce with the caramelized complexity of cola. Most of the recipes I found were dead simple: Sear the brisket on both sides in oil in a hot pan; put it in a baking dish; pour a combination of onion soup mix, cola, and ketchup over the meat; cover; and bake. Following these recipes, I braised several briskets. I appreciated the simplicity of the recipes but not the results. The briskets were difficult to sear well, the meat was tough and dry, and the gravies were unpleasantly sweet. On the plus side, these were problems I knew I could fix.

Problem No. 1: A 3½-pound brisket is a big, flat piece of meat that curls up in a hot skillet, which means it doesn't

To ensure a juicy brisket, we salt the raw meat and let it sit for at least six hours before braising. Poking the meat with a fork helps the salt penetrate.

get a uniform sear—and a good sear not only adds flavor to the meat but also cre-ates fond in the pan to enrich the sauce. To produce a sear, I tried a technique we've used before to make panini sand-wiches with really crispy edges. I placed a Dutch oven on top of the brisket to weigh it down and increase its contact with the hot pan (you can wrap the bottom of the Dutch oven in foil for easier cleanup). It worked very well here, too, yielding a nicely browned brisket

and plenty of flavorful fond. Now my problems were down to two: the texture of the meat and the flavor of the sauce.

A few of the recipes I'd found called for marinating (and then cooking) in cola, the idea being that the sweet, acidic soda tenderizes and flavors the brisket. This premise seemed worth testing. I got two briskets and mari-nated both in cola, one overnight and the other for two hours. I braised both in the basic cola, ketchup, and onion

soup mixture; sliced them; and tasted them. The acidic, sugary cola definitely had an impact on the texture of the meat—in a bad way. The briskets were spongy and dry. I tried adding salt to the cola marinade, hoping the salt would help keep the brisket juicy (as with a brine), but to no avail. At the end of the day, all the briskets that I marinated in sugary, acidic cola turned out dry. I'd save the cola for braising.

Although adding salt to the cola

those can be hard to find ⟨…⟩
against them. But what ab⟨…⟩
bulbs? Fresh fennel wasn't ⟨…⟩
able in supermarkets in the ⟨…⟩
is now, so I tried finely ch⟨…⟩
(after cutting out the tou⟨…⟩
adding it to the pork. Tast⟨…⟩
fresh, mild licorice flavor, ⟨…⟩
supplementing it with fen⟨…⟩
added depth and complexi⟨…⟩

Next, I tried several typ⟨…⟩
chopped fresh cloves, gran⟨…⟩
garlic powder. Granulated ⟨…⟩
in part because its coarse g⟨…⟩
were easy to apply in a con⟨…⟩
across the butterflied roast⟨…⟩
ing to more even seasonin⟨…⟩
few additional tests, I foun⟨…⟩
introduce the fennel seeds ⟨…⟩
and granulated garlic to th⟨…⟩
the finished porketta was r⟨…⟩
when this mixture sat on t⟨…⟩
least six hours (and up to ⟨…⟩
cooking. Then I chopped ⟨…⟩
the fresh fennel right befor⟨…⟩

I butterflied, stuffed, ro⟨…⟩
and roasted another pork l⟨…⟩
as I was cutting the twine ⟨…⟩
secure it, I wondered why ⟨…⟩
were rolled in the first plac⟨…⟩
thing to roll and tie an ele⟨…⟩
roast that you're going to ⟨…⟩
table, but porketta is serve⟨…⟩
Skipping the rolling and ty⟨…⟩
only easier, but it shaved ⟨…⟩
hour off the cooking time, ⟨…⟩
exposed more of the meat'⟨…⟩
to crisp up in the oven.

I made one last importa⟨…⟩
when I noticed all the mea⟨…⟩
left behind in the roasting ⟨…⟩
any seasoned cook knows, ⟨…⟩
pings equal flavor. I ran th⟨…⟩
through a fat separator an⟨…⟩
½ cup of the savory juices ⟨…⟩
warm shredded pork. This ⟨…⟩
both amplified the flavor o⟨…⟩
and made the meat more n⟨…⟩

I'll still go back and visi⟨…⟩
Range. But now I can have ⟨…⟩
whenever I want—and so ⟨…⟩

KEY STEPS **Prepping the**
We butterfly and crosshatch ⟨…⟩

1. BUTTERFLY Slice throug⟨…⟩
parallel to the counter, stopp⟨…⟩
from the edge. Then open th⟨…⟩
like a book.

---

marinade hadn't worked, I had one
more salt test up my sleeve. Salting
large cuts of meat is an established test
kitchen technique to improve seasoning and, key here, the texture of meat.
Would rubbing salt into the brisket
and resting it overnight before braising
yield moist meat? Thankfully, it did—
and after a few more tests I found that I
could salt just six hours (although overnight is preferable) and that poking the
meat with a fork before salting helped
the salt penetrate more effectively.

I was ready to move on to the
braising liquid. Several of the recipes
I'd made at the beginning called for
2 cups of cola, 1½ cups of ketchup, and
one packet of onion soup mix for one
3½-pound brisket. I'd start with those
ratios, but the packet of hyper-salty,
artificial-tasting onion soup mix would
definitely have to go. I've overhauled
recipes designed to use packaged onion
soup mix before, so I knew that onion
and garlic powders, brown sugar, and a
little dried thyme would provide a similar flavor with none of the bad stuff. I
whisked this new spice mixture into the
ketchup and cola and set it aside. I salted
a brisket and let it sit and then seared it,
poured the cola mixture over it, covered
the pan with foil, and put it in the oven.

Though still lacking depth and
complexity, this brisket was much better.
To add savor and reinforce the flavor of
the onion powder, I sautéed chopped
onions in the drippings left from searing
the brisket. The sautéed-then-braised
onions practically melted into the result-
ing gravy, supplying the missing balance
and depth. We gave this brisket a taste.
It was tender, and the sweet, caramelized flavor of the cola offset the oniony,
savory meatiness. The formula for Coca-
Cola may be famously top secret, but
the formula for good Atlanta brisket is
now yours.

ATLANTA BRISKET Serves 6

Parchment paper provides a nonreactive
barrier between the cola-based braising
liquid and the aluminum foil.

- 1 (3½-pound) beef brisket, flat cut, fat
  trimmed to ¼ inch
  Salt and pepper
- 4 teaspoons vegetable oil
- 1 pound onions, halved and sliced
  ½ inch thick
- 2 cups cola
- 1½ cups ketchup
- 4 teaspoons onion powder
- 2 teaspoons packed dark brown sugar
- 1 teaspoon garlic powder
- 1 teaspoon dried thyme

1. Using fork, poke holes all over
brisket. Rub entire surface of brisket
with 1 tablespoon salt. Wrap brisket in
plastic wrap and refrigerate for at least
6 or up to 24 hours.

2. Adjust oven rack to lower-middle
position and heat oven to 325 degrees.
Pat brisket dry with paper towels and
season with pepper. Heat 2 teaspoons
oil in 12-inch nonstick skillet over
medium-high heat until just smoking.
Place brisket fat side down in skillet;
weigh down brisket with heavy Dutch
oven or cast-iron skillet and cook
until well browned, about 4 minutes.
Remove Dutch oven, flip brisket, and
replace Dutch oven on top of brisket;
cook on second side until well browned,
about 4 minutes longer. Transfer brisket
to plate.

3. Heat remaining 2 teaspoons oil
in now-empty skillet over medium heat
until shimmering. Add onions and
cook, stirring occasionally, until soft
and golden brown, 10 to 12 minutes.
Transfer onions to 13 by 9-inch baking
dish and spread into even layer.

4. Combine cola, ketchup, onion
powder, sugar, garlic powder, thyme,
1 teaspoon salt, and 1 teaspoon
pepper in bowl. Place brisket fat side
up on top of onions and pour cola
mixture over brisket. Place parchment
paper over brisket and cover dish tightly
with aluminum foil. Bake until tender
and fork easily slips in and out of meat,
3½ to 4 hours. Let brisket rest in liquid,
uncovered, for 30 minutes.

5. Transfer brisket to carving board.
Skim any fat from top of sauce with
large spoon. Slice brisket against grain
into ¼-inch-thick slices and return to
baking dish. Serve brisket with sauce.

TO MAKE AHEAD

Follow recipe through step 4. Allow
brisket to cool in sauce, cover, and
refrigerate overnight or up to 24 hours.
To serve, slice brisket, return to sauce,
and cover with parchment paper. Cover
baking dish with aluminum foil and
cook in 350-degree oven until heated
through, about 1 hour.

Swiss Chard

The impediment to great
sautéed chard wasn't
in the vegetable
but in the technique.

BY SARAH GABRIEL

I COOK A LOT of Swiss chard but have
always been plagued by two problems
with the sauté method. First, this
hearty green cooks down so much
that I have to pile it high in the pan
to make sure I end up with enough,
which in turn makes it hard to stir
without chard ending up all over the
stove and floor. Next, Swiss chard
releases a deluge of liquid as it cooks,
causing it to steam in the pan and then
flood my plate. It was time to work on
my technique.

I collected a variety of recipes calling for a range of tools and methods.
Recipes requiring Dutch ovens yielded
more than those requiring sauté pans
because of the roomier pot, but when
uncovered, the chard was still hard
to stir, and when covered, the chard
came out dripping liquid and tasting steamed. Once the chard wilted,
however, it was compact enough that
I could easily stir it around. What
about a hybrid steam-sauté method?
After cooking in a covered pot over
high heat for about three minutes,
the chard had wilted and released a
lot of liquid, but it was still bright
green. I could definitely keep cooking
without overdoing it, so I continued
cooking with the lid off. Six more
minutes over high heat, while stirring,
allowed the liquid to evaporate.

Because the stems are tougher
than the leaves, some recipes call for
simply discarding them; others call for
boiling them before sautéing, and still
others for giving them a head start in
the sauté pan. Boiling before sautéing
seemed a bother for a side dish, so I
tried the head start sauté method and
it worked fine, but I had a better idea.
Instead of cutting the stems and leaves
into same-size pieces, I simply cut the
tougher stems slightly smaller than the
leaves. This way, I could just throw
them all in together.

I had the cooking method down.
Now my chard needed dressing up.
I began by cooking six minced cloves
of garlic over low heat and adding
red pepper flakes along with the salt
before introducing the chard and
turning up the heat. A drizzle of olive
oil and vinegar just before serving
finished it off.

Sliced small, the tougher stems can cook
with the more tender leaves.

GARLICKY SWISS CHARD

Serves 4 to 6

You can use any variety of chard for this
recipe. The recipe is easily doubled and
cooked in two batches.

- 2 tablespoons plus 1 teaspoon
  olive oil
- 6 garlic cloves, minced
- 2 pounds Swiss chard, stems sliced
  crosswise ¼ inch thick, leaves
  sliced into ½-inch-wide strips
  Salt and pepper
- ⅛ teaspoon red pepper flakes
- 1 teaspoon white wine vinegar

1. Heat 2 tablespoons oil and garlic
in Dutch oven over medium-low heat,
stirring occasionally, until garlic is
lightly golden, about 3 minutes. Stir
in chard, ¼ teaspoon salt, and pepper
flakes. Increase heat to high and cook,
covered, stirring occasionally, until
chard is wilted but still bright green,
2 to 4 minutes.

2. Uncover and continue to cook,
stirring frequently, until liquid evaporates, 4 to 6 minutes. Add vinegar and
remaining 1 teaspoon oil and toss to
combine. Season with salt and pepper
to taste. Serve.

ASIAN-STYLE SWISS CHARD

Add 1 tablespoon grated fresh ginger
to pot along with chard in step 1.
In step 2, substitute 1 tablespoon
sesame oil for olive oil and substitute
4 teaspoons soy sauce for vinegar.
After transferring chard to platter,
sprinkle with 3 tablespoons sliced
scallion and ¼ cup chopped, salted,
dry-roasted peanuts.

▶ Want more options for this recipe?
Go to CooksCountry.com/nov12 for
variations with **Feta and Walnuts** and
with **Goat Cheese and Golden Raisins.**

Looking for a Recipe

READER TO READER

Did you misplace a favorite recipe? Would you like to taste a chocolate cake from childhood but can't because the recipe is long gone? Ask a reader. While you're at it, answer a reader. Post queries and finds at **CooksCountry.com/magazine**; click on **Looking for a Recipe** (or write to Looking for a Recipe, *Cook's Country*, P.O. Box 470739, Brookline, MA 02447). We'll share all of your submissions online and print several on this page. Include your name and mailing address with each submission.

Coronado Salad Ring
Victoria Rodgers, San Antonio, Texas

My great-aunt Elsie used to bring her signature dish to every family reunion. She called it Coronado Salad Ring. It was made with lemon-lime Jell-O, pineapple chunks, cottage cheese, chopped walnuts, and horseradish. She often filled the center of the mold with fresh strawberries. It was perfect on hot summer days. I've lost her recipe, and I'm wondering if anyone has heard of this delicious, long-forgotten salad.

Sweet-and-Sour Braised Red Cabbage
Brit Hagland, Somerville, Mass.

Years ago, my husband and I frequented Lenora Restaurant, a now-defunct neighborhood restaurant in Porter Square in Cambridge, nearly every weekend. They served wonderful braised red cabbage that I've never been able to duplicate. It had red wine, vinegar, and some sort of sugar to make it both sweet and sour. I'd love to find a recipe like this one.

Maple-Walnut Cookies
Melissa Hohler, Kettering, Ohio

Many years ago there was a restaurant in Yellow Springs, Ohio, called Carol's Kitchen. They made many things, but if you ask me, the best by far was their maple-walnut cookies. They were big, thick, and chewy, with a bit of a crunch on the outside and lots of walnuts. The walnut flavor was really strong but not artificial-tasting. I have searched out and tried many different recipes, but none has come close. I would love to find a recipe that truly replicates these cookies. Thanks.

Aunt Set's Albany Cakes
Cathleen Luce, Clifton, Va.

I'm looking for a recipe for a cookie that my great-great-aunt Emmie passed down to my grandmother. We called them Aunt Set's Albany Cakes. They were very large, soft, molasses-type cookies, but they were not spicy. They were rolled in sugar and then pressed with the bottom of a glass. My mother has lost the recipe, and I can't find one like it anywhere.

Pastita
Margaret DePaulo, Haverhill, Mass.

I'm trying to duplicate a recipe for something I had at a friend's house called pastita. It's a spaghetti pie (served at room temperature), with egg, ricotta, and fresh parsley. There may be some other cheeses in there as well. I'm wondering if anyone has a good recipe.

Deviled Ham Spread
Lola Wilson, Fort Wayne, Ind.

When I was a kid, I brought lunch to school every day, and one of my favorite sandwiches was made from Underwood Deviled Ham Spread. I know the company still makes it, but I'd prefer to create a better (and healthier) version of it myself. Does anyone have a good recipe for deviled ham that you're willing to share?

Kielbasa-Rice Casserole
Bari Sullivan, Glendive, Mont.

My best friend's mom used to make the most delicious supper in her electric skillet. This was back in the 1950s, when cream soups were all the rage. The recipe included browned kielbasa, rice, and vegetables (frozen, I think), and it had a wonderful creamy texture. It was topped with cheese (of course!). Maybe it was a promotional recipe for the electric skillet or cream soups? I'd love to find it.

Crab Rangoon
Laura Giesecke, Whitefish Bay, Wis.

When I'm eating out, I often order crab rangoon; it's one of my favorite appetizers. But often they seem to be made primarily of cream cheese, with very little crab meat inside. I'd love to find a crab rangoon recipe that actually tastes like crab.

Glazed Chocolate Doughnuts
Janice Koenig, Louisville, Ky.

My kids love chocolate dough-nuts. The ones I bought at a school bake sale recently were way better than those I usually buy from a nearby doughnut chain. They were soft and tender and actually tasted like choco-late, with a light, vanilla-flavored glaze. I'd like to try making them myself. Can you tell me how?

FIND THE ROOSTER!

A tiny version of this rooster has been hidden in the pages of this issue. Write to us with its location and we'll enter you in a random drawing. The first correct entry drawn will win our top-rated grill pan (see page 30), and each of the next five will receive a free one-year sub-scription to *Cook's Country*. To enter, visit **CooksCountry. com/rooster** by November 30, 2012, or write to Rooster, *Cook's Country*, P.O. Box 470739, Brookline, MA 02447. Include your name and address. Claire Ketch of Woodbridge, Va., found the rooster in the June/July 2012 issue on page 10 and won our winning innovative cutting board.

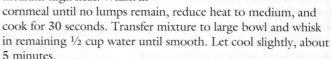

HOT WATER CORNBREAD Makes about 20 fritters
Use medium- or finely ground cornmeal. Serve with honey butter.

- 1½ cups water
- ¾ teaspoon salt
- 1 cup cornmeal
- 1 tablespoon all-purpose flour
- ½ teaspoon baking powder
- 1 large egg
- 1 cup peanut or vegetable oil

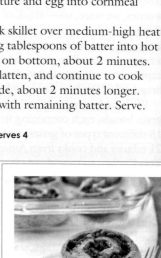

1. Set wire rack inside rimmed baking sheet. Bring 1 cup water and salt to boil in medium saucepan over medium-high heat. Whisk in cornmeal until no lumps remain, reduce heat to medium, and cook for 30 seconds. Transfer mixture to large bowl and whisk in remaining ½ cup water until smooth. Let cool slightly, about 5 minutes.

2. Whisk flour and baking powder together in small bowl until combined. Whisk flour mixture and egg into cornmeal mixture until smooth.

3. Heat oil in 12-inch nonstick skillet over medium-high heat to 350 degrees. Drop 10 heaping tablespoons of batter into hot oil and cook until golden brown on bottom, about 2 minutes. Flip each fritter, press lightly to flatten, and continue to cook until golden brown on second side, about 2 minutes longer. Transfer to wire rack and repeat with remaining batter. Serve.

HAMBURGER PINWHEELS Serves 4

- 1 teaspoon vegetable oil
- 1 pound 90 percent lean ground beef
- ½ teaspoon salt
- ½ teaspoon pepper
- 1 onion, chopped fine
- 3 tablespoons ketchup
- 1 tablespoon Worcestershire sauce
- 1 tablespoon spicy brown mustard
- 8 ounces sharp cheddar cheese, shredded (2 cups)
- 2¾ cups Bisquick baking mix
- ¼ teaspoon cayenne pepper
- ⅔ cup whole milk

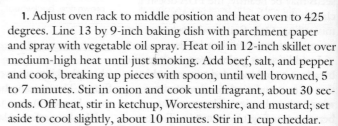

1. Adjust oven rack to middle position and heat oven to 425 degrees. Line 13 by 9-inch baking dish with parchment paper and spray with vegetable oil spray. Heat oil in 12-inch skillet over medium-high heat until just smoking. Add beef, salt, and pepper and cook, breaking up pieces with spoon, until well browned, 5 to 7 minutes. Stir in onion and cook until fragrant, about 30 sec-onds. Off heat, stir in ketchup, Worcestershire, and mustard; set aside to cool slightly, about 10 minutes. Stir in 1 cup cheddar.

2. Combine Bisquick, remaining 1 cup cheddar, and cayenne in large bowl. Stir in milk until incorporated. Form dough into ball and transfer to lightly floured counter. Roll dough into 14 by 9-inch rectangle, with long sides parallel to edge of counter. Spread hamburger mixture evenly over dough, leaving ½-inch border on long sides. Roll into tight log, slice into 8 equal pieces, and place cut side down in prepared baking dish. Press each pinwheel to 1-inch thickness. Bake until golden brown, about 20 minutes. Cool for 10 minutes, then separate pinwheels. Serve.

These garlick[...]

A*s I dis[...] a rece[...] Minn[...] Rang[...]* sandwiches are as [...] as burgers in that [...] country. These sa[...] all about the mea[...] shredded pork sea[...] fennel, garlic, sal[...] pepper and served [...] rolls. They are a s[...] take on Italian "[...] which was brough[...] Range by Italian [...] around the turn [...] century. Every res[...] and sandwich sho[...] on the menu. It's [...] parties and lunch[...] schools. The grocer[...] even sell seasoned [...] premixed spice pa[...] dish. In short, it's [...] But outside the re[...] sandwich becomes [...] It's much too good[...] unknown.

So I set out to deve[...] sion. Recipes for porke[...] between—apparently, i[...] Iron Range, your mom[...] to make it (and if you d[...] well, you've probably n[...] And the recipes I did tr[...] often no more than list[...] (pork roast, garlic, fenn[...] pepper—period) with n[...] preparation tips, or coo[...] In the Iron Range you [...] see porketta made with [...] (turketta), or beef (bee[...] no tofuetta yet.) But ac[...] porketta experts at two [...]

Maple-Pumpkin Stack Cake

Why stop at two? Spice up your holiday table
this year with four layers of moist, tender pumpkin cake
sandwiched with maple cream.

To make this cake you will need:

1½ cups (7½ ounces) all-purpose flour
2 teaspoons pumpkin pie spice
1 teaspoon baking powder
1 teaspoon baking soda
1 teaspoon salt
1¼ cups (8¾ ounces) sugar
8 tablespoons unsalted butter,
    melted and cooled
3 large eggs
1 (15-ounce) can unsweetened pumpkin
    puree
1½ cups heavy cream, chilled
¼ cup maple syrup
¼ cup pecans, toasted and chopped

FOR THE CAKE: Adjust oven rack to middle position and heat oven to 350 degrees. Grease two 8-inch round cake pans, line with parchment paper, grease parchment, then flour pans. Whisk flour, pumpkin pie spice, baking powder, baking soda, and salt together in bowl. Using stand mixer fitted with paddle, beat sugar, butter, and eggs on medium-high speed until pale and fluffy, about 3 minutes. Reduce speed to low, add pumpkin, and mix until incorporated. Slowly add flour mixture and mix until only few small flour streaks remain, about 30 seconds. Spread one-fourth of batter (about 1 cup) in even layer in each prepared pan. Bake until toothpick inserted in center

comes out clean, 12 to 14 minutes. Let cool on wire rack for 10 minutes. Invert each cake onto large plate, peel off parchment, and reinvert onto lightly greased rack. Cool completely. Reprep pans and repeat with remaining batter.

TO ASSEMBLE: Using dry, clean bowl and whisk attachment, whip cream and maple syrup together on medium speed until stiff peaks form, about 3 minutes. Place 1 cake layer on cake plate or pedestal, then spread one fourth of whipped cream (scant cup) evenly over top. Repeat with remaining cake layers and whipped cream. Sprinkle pecans on top and serve.

Dear Country Cook,

A few years ago, my daughter Caroline went out and harvested a small evergreen not too far from the farmhouse and put it up in the living room. When it was decorated, it looked like a sad Charlie Brown Christmas tree, with gaps between the branches and festooned with a haphazard shower of icicles. But it was homegrown and lovingly decorated and had a certain charm—infinitely more heartwarming than the perfect specimen we usually pick up at the local landscaper.

When I was a kid, nobody ever told me about the pursuit of domestic perfection. Martha Stewart was still in junior high, Thursday was spaghetti with jarred meat sauce night, and in the summer we lived in a tiny cabin in the mountains and dined at a picnic table covered with a blue-checkered plastic tablecloth. Ignorance was bliss.

I recently came across a large cardboard box from my mother that contained our family Christmas decorations: walnut-size colored lights and the standard repertoire of ornaments, from ruby-cheeked Santa orbs and birch Scandinavian wooden sleighs to the odd crescent-shaped man in the moon and a handful of seraphic angels. It reminded me that there was a happy time before good taste, before we knew how to look in the mirror.

I picked out a few of the more garish ornaments and decided to hang them on the tree this year. It was a small gesture, I admit, but I am beginning to think that good taste is about how something makes you feel rather than how it makes you look.

[signature]

Christopher Kimball
Founder and Editor, Cook's Country

Two boys chopping down a Christmas tree, circa 1950s.

Cook's Country

Founder and Editor Christopher Kimball
Editorial Director Jack Bishop
Editorial Director, Magazines John Willoughby
Executive Editor Peggy Grodinsky
Managing Editor Scott Kathan
Senior Editors Lisa McManus, Bryan Roof, Diane Unger
Test Kitchen Director Erin McMurrer
Associate Editors Chris Dudley, Amy Graves, Rebeccah Marsters, Sarah Wilson
Test Cooks Sarah Gabriel, Nick Iverson, Carolynn Purpura MacKay, Cristin Walsh
Assistant Editors Hannah Crowley, Shannon Friedmann Hatch, Taizeth Sierra
Copy Editors Nell Beram, Megan Chromik
Executive Assistant Christine Gordon
Assistant Test Kitchen Director Gina Nistico
Test Kitchen Manager Leah Rovner
Senior Kitchen Assistant Meryl MacCormack
Kitchen Assistants Maria Elena Delgado, Ena Gudiel, Andrew Straaberg Finfrock
Executive Producer Melissa Baldino
Associate Producer Stephanie Stender
Production Assistant Kaitlin Hammond

Contributing Editors Erika Bruce, Eva Katz, Jeremy Sauer
Consulting Editors Anne Mendelson, Meg Ragland
Science Editor Guy Crosby, Ph.D.
Executive Food Editor, TV, Radio & Media Bridget Lancaster

Managing Editor, Web Christine Liu
Associate Editors, Web Eric Grzymkowski, Mari Levine, Roger Metcalf
Senior Video Editor Nick Dakoulas

Design Director Amy Klee
Art Director Julie Cote
Deputy Art Director Susan Levin
Associate Art Director Lindsey Timko
Staff Photographer Daniel J. van Ackere
Color Food Photography Keller + Keller
Styling Catrine Kelty
Designer, Marketing/Web Mariah Tarvainen
Photo Editor Steve Klise

Vice President, Marketing David Mack
Circulation Director Doug Wicinski
Circulation & Fulfillment Manager Carrie Fethe
Partnership Marketing Manager Pamela Putprush
Marketing Assistant Joyce Liao
Customer Service Manager Jacqueline Valerio
Customer Service Representatives Jessica Haskin, Morgan Hamner

Chief Operating Officer David Dinnage
Production Director Guy Rochford
Senior Project Manager Alice Carpenter
Workflow & Digital Asset Manager Andrew Mannone
Production & Traffic Coordinator Brittany Allen
Production & Imaging Specialists Judy Blomquist, Heather Dube, Lauren Pettapiece
Systems Administrator Marcus Walser
Helpdesk Support Technician Brianna Brothers
Senior Business Analyst Wendy Tseng
Web Developer Chris Candelora
Human Resources Manager Adele Shapiro

VP New Media Product Development Barry Kelly
Social Media Manager Steph Yiu
Assistant Editor, New Media Amy Scheuerman
Chief Financial Officer Sharyn Chabot
Director of Sponsorship Sales Anne Traficante
Retail Sales & Marketing Manager Emily Logan
Client Service Associate Kate May
Publicity Deborah Broide

ON THE COVER:
Magic Chocolate Flan Cake
Keller + Keller, Catrine Kelty
ILLUSTRATION: Greg Stevenson

Follow us on **Twitter**
twitter.com/TestKitchen

Find us on **Facebook**
facebook.com/CooksCountry

Cook's Country magazine (ISSN 1552-1990), number 48, is published bimonthly by Boston Common Press Limited Partnership, 17 Station St., Brookline, MA 02445. Copyright 2012 Boston Common Press Limited Partnership. Periodicals postage paid at Boston, MA, and additional mailing offices. USPS #023453. Publications Mail Agreement No. 40020778. Return undeliverable Canadian addresses to P.O. Box 875, Station A, Windsor, ON N9A 6P2. POSTMASTER: Send address changes to Cook's Country, PO Box 6018, Harlan, IA 51593-1518. For subscription and gift subscription orders, subscription inquiries, or change of address notices, visit AmericasTestKitchen.com/customerservice, call 800-526-8447 in the U.S., or 515-248-7684 from outside the U.S., or write us at Cook's Country, P.O. Box 6018, Harlan, IA 51593-1518. PRINTED IN THE USA

DECEMBER/JANUARY 2013

Contents

HOLIDAY STRIP ROAST, 4

SHRIMP COCKTAIL, 7

CHOCOLATE SURPRISE COOKIES, 22

Features

In Every Issue

The Country gets (more) wired
Download our new *Cook's Country* app for iPad and start a free trial subscription or purchase a single issue of *Cook's Country* magazine. Each issue is enhanced with full-color step-by-step "cooking mode" slide shows and expanded reviews and ratings charts. Go to **CooksCountry.com/iPad**.

America's TEST KITCHEN
RECIPES THAT WORK®

America's Test Kitchen is a very real 2,500 square-foot kitchen located just outside of Boston. It is the home of Cook's Country and Cook's Illustrated magazines and is the workday destination for more than three dozen test cooks, editors, and cookware specialists. Our mission is to test recipes over and over again until we understand how and why they work and until we arrive at the best version. We also test kitchen equipment and supermarket ingredients in search of brands that offer the best value and performance. You can watch us work by tuning in to Cook's Country from America's Test Kitchen (CooksCountryTV.com) and America's Test Kitchen (AmericasTestKitchenTV.com) on public television.

Getting to Know Chocolate

All chocolate starts with the cacao bean. From there, different processing, flavorings, ingredients, and percentages of cocoa solids and cocoa butter can produce chocolate of all sorts. Here's a sampler. BY REBECCAH MARSTERS

Unsweetened Chocolate
BAKER'S BAR

The aptly named James Baker started manufacturing unsweetened chocolate in Massachusetts in 1765; his Baker's Unsweetened Chocolate is still sold today. Hershey's followed about a century later, and it's our favorite for its "intense" chocolate flavor and "caramel" and "cinnamon" nuances. For every ounce of unsweetened chocolate called for in a recipe, you can substitute 1½ ounces of bittersweet or semisweet chocolate and subtract 1 tablespoon of sugar.

Milk Chocolate
DAIRY QUEEN

Milk chocolate must contain at least 12 percent milk solids, says the U.S. Food and Drug Administration (FDA). It's usually sweeter than dark chocolate, too, although manufacturers today are making deeper, darker milk chocolates. Dove Silky Smooth Milk Chocolate is our favorite brand. Store all chocolate in a cool, dry place to prevent "bloom," a harmless but unsightly gray coating. Try our chocolate pound cake: **CooksCountry.com/chocolatepoundcake**.

Dark Chocolate
ALL GROWN UP

Dark chocolate has a higher cocoa percentage and less sugar than milk chocolate, thus deeper, more complex flavor. Labels may say either "bittersweet" or "semisweet," but the FDA doesn't distinguish between them, so look for the cocoa content: Dark chocolate must contain at least 35 percent. We like much more than that—60 percent—for baking. For fast melting, microwave chopped dark (or any) chocolate in 30-second intervals, stirring between intervals.

White Chocolate
THE PRETENDER

Because it contains no cocoa, white chocolate is not actually chocolate. It's made from cocoa butter (the fat from the bean), sugar, vanilla, and milk solids. Our favorite brand, Guittard Choc-au-Lait White Chips, replaces much of the cocoa butter with hydrogenated palm kernel oil (so the chips hold their shape better). We use white chocolate to add creaminess and structure in some surprising places, such as vanilla ice cream (**CooksCountry.com/magicvanillaicecream**).

Chocolate Chips
COOKIE CLASSIC

In the 1930s, the innkeeper at the Toll House Inn in Whitman, Massachusetts, chopped up a chocolate bar to mix into ordinary butter cookies and made cookie history. Some time later, she struck a deal with Nestlé. First, it printed her recipe on its bar chocolate package. Soon the company was manufacturing chips. These chips have less cocoa butter than bar chocolate, so they retain their shape in baked goods. For creamy recipes, like mousse, use bar chocolate, which melts without getting grainy.

Cacao Nibs
IN THE RAW

These cracked bits of roasted cacao beans—the raw material for bar chocolate and cocoa powder—are unsweetened, giving them a bitter but not unpleasant flavor; tasters found them "woodsy," "leathery," and "earthy." Cacao nibs add intense flavor and crunch to granola and many baked goods, such as chocolate cookies or pavlovas. Find them in natural foods stores and in some supermarkets.

Gianduia (zhan-DOO-yah)
ITALIAN CHARMER

You may know the flavor of *gianduia* from Nutella, a popular hazelnut and chocolate spread. Gianduia also comes in bars for baking and as candies called *gianduiotti*, which are popular in Torino, Italy—gianduia's birthplace. Hazelnut paste gives this (milk or dark) chocolate its nutty flavor and soft, fudgy texture. Make your own spread to top toast, fill crêpes, or sandwich together cookies: **CooksCountry.com/chocohazelnutspread**.

Couverture (koo-vehr-TYOOR)
PRO'S CHOICE

Serious bakers use this chocolate for coating candy or making chocolate decorations. Extra cocoa butter (between 32 and 39 percent) helps it form a thin shell, and tempering (a process of melting and cooling chocolate) gives it good snap and high gloss. Couverture is usually sold by the pound in pellets, or "callets," for even melting. You can buy it online and in some baking supply stores, but we usually leave couverture to pastry chefs and chocolatiers.

Chocolate Extract
FLAVOR BOOSTER

Vanilla extract is a staple in every baker's pantry, so why not chocolate extract? Like vanilla, chocolate extract uses alcohol to draw out the bean's flavor. Chocolate extract gave our favorite brownie batter richer, more complex chocolate flavor. Try substituting chocolate extract for half of the vanilla in recipes for chocolate cake or brownies. It costs about as much as vanilla.

Mexican Chocolate
TRUE GRIT

Much Mexican chocolate is stone-ground in the traditional manner, which accounts for its gritty texture. (Other chocolate is conched, a process invented in the late 19th century to smooth and refine it.) Sweetened Mexican chocolate (which is often ground with cinnamon) tastes of molasses, dried fruit, and/or coffee, our tasters found. In the United States, look for Taza, Abuelita, or Ibarra brands.

Natural Cocoa Powder
WINTER WARMER

Cocoa powder, made from partially defatted, ground, and dried cocoa solids, is our go-to ingredient when we want chocolate flavor without added sugar or fat (or when we make hot chocolate). We like Hershey's Natural Cocoa, because it's "intense," "complex," "bright," and affordable. For many recipes, we "bloom" cocoa powder in hot water, which makes the chocolate taste fuller and richer.

Dutch-Processed Cocoa Powder
DUTCH TREAT

Dutching, a process invented in the 19th century (by a Dutchman), neutralizes naturally acidic cocoa powder. Despite that, we've found that Dutch-processed cocoa is usually interchangeable with natural cocoa. The exception is when you want the reddish tinge that comes from the reaction of baking soda and natural cocoa powder—for instance, when baking devil's food or red velvet cakes.

EASY CHICKEN AND SALSA TACOS

THAI COCONUT-CHICKEN SOUP

SKILLET TERIYAKI BEEF AND VEGETABLES

**PAN-SEARED CHICKEN WITH
MUSHROOM-SAGE SAUCE**

THAI COCONUT-CHICKEN SOUP

Serves 4

WHY THIS RECIPE WORKS: Quickly frying scallion whites, cilantro, and red curry paste is a fast route to potent Southeast Asian flavor.

- 2 teaspoons vegetable oil
- 3 scallions, white parts minced, green parts sliced thin
- 6 tablespoons minced fresh cilantro
- 2 tablespoons red curry paste
- 4 teaspoons fish sauce
- 4 cups low-sodium chicken broth
- 3½ cups coconut milk
- 1 pound boneless, skinless chicken breasts, trimmed, halved lengthwise, and cut into ¼-inch slices
- 1 sweet potato, peeled, quartered, and sliced thin
- 3 tablespoons lime juice (2 limes)

1. Heat oil in large saucepan over medium heat until shimmering. Add scallion whites, 3 tablespoons cilantro, and curry paste and cook until fragrant, about 1 minute. Stir in 2 teaspoons fish sauce, broth, and coconut milk and bring to boil over high heat. Cover, reduce heat to low, and simmer for 5 minutes.

2. Increase heat to medium-high, add chicken and sweet potato, and cook until chicken is no longer pink and potato is tender, about 5 minutes. Remove soup from heat and stir in lime juice and remaining 2 teaspoons fish sauce. Portion soup into serving bowls and sprinkle with scallion greens and remaining 3 tablespoons cilantro. Serve.

TEST KITCHEN NOTE: You will need 2 cans of coconut milk. The soup will separate as it sits. If reheating, whisk well to recombine before serving.

EASY CHICKEN AND SALSA TACOS

Serves 4

WHY THIS RECIPE WORKS: By using rotisserie chicken and jarred salsa, you can put this satisfying supper together in minutes.

- 12 taco shells
- 1 (2½-pound) rotisserie chicken, skin and bones discarded, meat shredded into bite-size pieces (3 cups)
- 2 cups mild salsa
- ¼ cup minced fresh cilantro
- 2 tablespoons lime juice
- ¾ teaspoon chipotle chile powder
- ½ cup sour cream
- 1 cup shredded iceberg lettuce
- 4 ounces cheddar cheese, shredded (1 cup)

1. Adjust oven rack to middle position and heat oven to 375 degrees. Arrange taco shells on rimmed baking sheet and bake until warmed through, about 3 minutes.

2. Combine chicken and salsa in large saucepan over medium heat and cook, stirring occasionally, until chicken is hot, about 5 minutes. Off heat, stir in 3 tablespoons cilantro, 1 tablespoon lime juice, and chile powder.

3. Combine sour cream, remaining 1 tablespoon cilantro, and remaining 1 tablespoon lime juice in bowl. Divide chicken mixture among taco shells. Top with sour cream mixture, lettuce, and cheddar. Serve.

TEST KITCHEN NOTE: If you prefer soft tacos, skip the taco shells and wrap a stack of 12 corn tortillas in a clean dish towel. Microwave for 2 minutes to soften. You can use regular chili powder in place of the chipotle chile powder.

PAN-SEARED CHICKEN WITH MUSHROOM-SAGE SAUCE

Serves 4

WHY THIS RECIPE WORKS: Cooking the chicken skin side down for the entire time ensures well-rendered, brown skin.

- 4 (12-ounce) bone-in split chicken breasts, trimmed and halved crosswise
  Salt and pepper
- 1 tablespoon vegetable oil
- 8 ounces cremini mushrooms, trimmed and sliced thin
- ¼ cup chopped fresh sage
- 1 shallot, minced
- ¼ cup white wine
- ¾ cup heavy cream
- ½ cup low-sodium chicken broth

1. Pat chicken dry with paper towels and season with salt and pepper. Heat oil in 12-inch skillet over medium-high heat until just smoking. Cook chicken, skin side down, until well browned, about 5 minutes. Reduce heat to medium, cover, and cook until chicken registers 160 degrees, about 15 minutes. Transfer to plate and tent loosely with aluminum foil.

2. Return now-empty skillet to medium-high heat. Add mushrooms, sage, shallot, ¼ teaspoon salt, and ⅛ teaspoon pepper and cook, stirring occasionally, until any mushroom juice has evaporated, about 5 minutes. Add wine and cook until reduced by half, about 2 minutes. Add cream and broth and cook until slightly thickened, about 3 minutes. Season with salt and pepper to taste. Pour sauce over chicken. Serve.

TEST KITCHEN NOTE: You can use white button mushrooms in place of cremini mushrooms. Serve with noodles or rice.

SKILLET TERIYAKI BEEF AND VEGETABLES

Serves 4

WHY THIS RECIPE WORKS: Our easy stir-fry makes an all-in-one meal. No need for vegetables on the side.

- ½ cup teriyaki sauce
- ½ cup water
- 2 tablespoons rice vinegar
- 2 teaspoons cornstarch
- 1 (1½-pound) flank steak, trimmed
  Salt and pepper
- 2 tablespoons vegetable oil
- 3 carrots, peeled and sliced ⅛ inch thick on bias
- 8 ounces snow peas, strings removed
- 1 garlic clove, minced

1. Whisk teriyaki sauce, water, vinegar, and cornstarch in bowl. Pat steak dry with paper towels and season with salt and pepper. Heat 1 tablespoon oil in 12-inch nonstick skillet over medium-high heat until just smoking. Cook steak until well browned and meat registers 125 degrees (for medium-rare), about 5 minutes per side. Transfer to large plate and tent loosely with aluminum foil.

2. Heat remaining 1 tablespoon oil over medium-high heat in now-empty skillet until shimmering. Add carrots and snow peas and cook until lightly browned, about 3 minutes. Add garlic and cook until fragrant, about 30 seconds. Transfer vegetables to platter.

3. Add teriyaki mixture and any accumulated meat juice to now-empty skillet and simmer until thickened, about 3 minutes. Slice steak thin on bias against grain and transfer to platter with vegetables. Spoon teriyaki sauce over top. Serve.

TEST KITCHEN NOTE: Annie Chun's All Natural Teriyaki Sauce is our taste-test winner. Serve with rice.

MEATBALLS FLORENTINE

**HONEY-ROSEMARY PORK MEDALLIONS
WITH FENNEL SALAD**

**FILET MIGNON WITH SMASHED POTATOES
AND HORSERADISH SAUCE**

MAPLE-DIJON CHICKEN WITH BACON COUSCOUS

HONEY-ROSEMARY PORK MEDALLIONS WITH FENNEL SALAD Serves 4

WHY THIS RECIPE WORKS: Preparing the salad before cooking the pork allows the salad's flavors to meld.

- ¼ cup lemon juice (2 lemons)
- 1 teaspoon Dijon mustard
  Salt and pepper
- 3 tablespoons olive oil
- 1 fennel bulb, stalks discarded, bulb halved, cored, and sliced thin
- 1 Gala apple, cored, halved, and sliced thin
- ¼ cup honey
- 1 teaspoon minced fresh rosemary
- 2 (12- to 16-ounce) pork tenderloins, trimmed and cut crosswise into 1½-inch-thick medallions

1. Combine 2 tablespoons lemon juice, mustard, ½ teaspoon salt, and ¼ teaspoon pepper in large bowl. Slowly whisk in 1 tablespoon oil until incorporated. Add fennel and apple and toss to combine; set aside. Whisk honey, remaining 2 tablespoons lemon juice, rosemary, and ¼ teaspoon pepper in bowl; set aside.

2. Pat pork dry with paper towels and season with salt and pepper. Heat remaining 2 tablespoons oil in 12-inch nonstick skillet over medium-high heat until just smoking. Cook pork until well browned all over, about 10 minutes. Add honey mixture to skillet, turning pork to coat, and continue cooking until glaze has thickened and pork registers 145 degrees, about 5 minutes. Transfer pork to platter, tent loosely with aluminum foil, and let rest for 5 minutes. Serve pork with fennel salad.

TEST KITCHEN NOTE: Use a mandoline (or V-slicer) to make quick work of slicing the fennel and apple. You can use any sweet apple in place of the Gala.

MEATBALLS FLORENTINE
Serves 4

WHY THIS RECIPE WORKS: We streamline the cooking (and cleaning) by cooking the meatballs, sauce, and pasta in the same pan.

- 1 pound meatloaf mix
- 3 ounces (3 cups) baby spinach, chopped
- ⅓ cup panko bread crumbs
- 1 large egg, lightly beaten
- 5 garlic cloves, minced
  Salt and pepper
- 1 tablespoon olive oil
- 1 (28-ounce) can crushed tomatoes
- 2 cups water
- 8 ounces spaghetti, broken in half
- ¼ cup chopped fresh basil

1. Combine meatloaf mix, 1 cup spinach, panko, egg, half of garlic, and 1 teaspoon salt in bowl and knead gently until incorporated. Form mixture into 3 dozen 1-inch meatballs. Heat oil in 12-inch nonstick skillet over medium-high heat until just smoking. Cook meatballs until well browned all over, about 5 minutes; transfer to plate.

2. Add remaining garlic to now-empty skillet and cook until fragrant, about 30 seconds. Stir in tomatoes, water, spaghetti, and ½ teaspoon salt and bring to boil. Cover, reduce heat to medium-low, and cook, stirring often, until spaghetti begins to soften, about 7 minutes. Add meatballs and continue to simmer, covered, until meatballs are cooked through and spaghetti is al dente, about 5 minutes. Off heat, stir in remaining 2 cups spinach and basil. Season with salt and pepper to taste. Serve.

TEST KITCHEN NOTE: You can substitute equal parts ground beef and ground pork for the meatloaf mix. Serve with grated Parmesan.

MAPLE-DIJON CHICKEN WITH BACON COUSCOUS
Serves 4

WHY THIS RECIPE WORKS: Bacon, parsley, and vinegar add depth and brightness to quick-cooking couscous.

- ¼ cup Dijon mustard
- ¼ cup maple syrup
  Salt and pepper
- 4 slices bacon, chopped
- 4 (6-ounce) boneless, skinless chicken breasts, trimmed
- 1 shallot, minced
- 1¼ cups low-sodium chicken broth
- 1 cup couscous
- 1 tablespoon chopped fresh parsley
- 2 teaspoons cider vinegar

1. Whisk mustard, maple syrup, ½ teaspoon salt, and ¼ teaspoon pepper together in bowl; set aside. Cook bacon in 12-inch nonstick skillet over medium heat until crisp, 6 to 8 minutes. Using slotted spoon, transfer bacon to paper towel–lined plate.

2. Pour off all but 2 tablespoons fat from skillet and return pan to medium-high heat until fat shimmers. Pat chicken dry with paper towels and season with salt and pepper. Cook chicken until golden brown and meat registers 160 degrees, about 6 minutes per side. Transfer to platter, brush with mustard mixture, and tent loosely with aluminum foil.

3. Add shallot to now-empty skillet and cook over medium heat until softened, about 3 minutes. Add broth and bring to simmer. Stir in couscous, cover, remove from heat, and let stand for 5 minutes. Stir cooked bacon, parsley, and vinegar into couscous. Season with salt and pepper to taste. Serve couscous with chicken.

TEST KITCHEN NOTE: If you don't have 2 tablespoons of fat in the skillet after frying the bacon, supplement with vegetable oil.

FILET MIGNON WITH SMASHED POTATOES AND HORSERADISH SAUCE Serves 4

WHY THIS RECIPE WORKS: Sour cream and heavy cream do double duty in the smashed potatoes and the horseradish sauce.

- 2 pounds red potatoes, unpeeled, cut into 1-inch pieces
- ¼ cup vegetable oil
- 1 cup sour cream
- ½ cup heavy cream
  Salt and pepper
- 4 (6- to 8-ounce) center cut filets mignons, 2 inches thick, trimmed
- ¼ cup prepared horseradish, drained
- 2 teaspoons Dijon mustard
- ¼ teaspoon sugar

1. Combine potatoes and 2 tablespoons oil in large bowl, cover, and microwave until tender, 10 to 12 minutes, stirring once halfway through cooking. Add ½ cup sour cream and ¼ cup cream and mash with potato masher until combined. Season with salt and pepper to taste. Cover and keep warm.

2. Pat steaks dry with paper towels and season with salt and pepper. Heat remaining 2 tablespoons oil in 12-inch skillet over medium-high heat until just smoking. Cook steaks until well browned and meat registers 125 degrees (for medium-rare), 3 to 5 minutes per side. Transfer to plate and tent loosely with aluminum foil.

3. Combine remaining ½ cup sour cream, remaining ¼ cup cream, horseradish, mustard, and sugar in bowl. Season with salt and pepper to taste. Serve steaks with potatoes and sauce.

TEST KITCHEN NOTE: We prefer brined (not creamy) horseradish. Buy refrigerated prepared horseradish, not the shelf-stable kind, which contains preservatives and additives.

Chicken Véronique

This classic French combo of wine, cream sauce, grapes, and (in this case) chicken should be understated and elegant. But misguided modern cooks have made it a messy patchwork. BY SARAH WILSON WITH CHRIS DUDLEY

Grapes might seem odd here, but they add brightness to the wine-flavored cream sauce.

CHICKEN VÉRONIQUE IS the landlocked spin-off of the classic French dish sole Véronique, which features sole poached in white wine, enhanced with cream sauce, finished with tarragon, and garnished with grapes. The delicious combination of flavors suits chicken, too: The fresh, bright grapes invigorate mild chicken breast and the cream enriches it. At its best, chicken Véronique is easy and fast yet effortlessly chic—a recipe that embodies "less is more."

Unfortunately, recipe writers don't seem to share my point of view. They think that overwrought equals elegant. To the classic ingredients, recipes variously called for adding garlic, mushrooms, orange segments, marmalade, balsamic vinegar, oil, and sugar or honey. I tried these recipes, and given how they read on the page, I can't say I was surprised at how they cooked in the kitchen. Tasters described them as "bland," "busy," "ungapatchka," "stodgy," and "crazy sweet." I pulled together a recipe as a starting point, nixing all the extras, and got my own development under way. I pictured a pared-down chicken Véronique that got its taste from good flavor, not needless add-ins.

I settled on boneless, skinless breasts because they were fast and easy. (Also, the recipe with skin-on chicken parts produced rubbery skin.) To ensure even cooking, I pounded the breasts to uniform thickness. Then I tested the two cooking techniques I'd come across: One, sear the raw breasts in butter or oil and then poach them in broth and wine. Two, plop the raw breasts straight into the simmering liquid to poach. Searing the breasts (in butter, *mais oui*) took only a couple of minutes per side, and the chicken definitely had more flavor. Also, I knew that the browned bits left in the skillet after the sear would intensify the taste of the cream sauce I was about to build.

I removed the seared chicken from the skillet. Then I deglazed the pan with wine, stirred up those browned bits, poured in the chicken broth, added back the breasts, covered the skillet, and poached the chicken for less than 10 minutes, until it was cooked through. I set aside the cooked chicken as I transformed the poaching liquid into a sauce. To do so, I'd need cream and a thickener. Thickening with flour made the sauce pasty. So I tried cornstarch,

mixing it with a little chicken broth first (what's known as a slurry) so it would distribute evenly. Now the sauce was delicate and silken.

But my chicken Véronique still underwhelmed us. I wanted subtle flavor, not insufficient flavor. It occurred to me that the recipe had no onions. No wonder it was bland. I made the chicken again, this time softening chopped shallot in the skillet after the breasts had browned. An onion, and a classic French onion at that, didn't violate my principle of simplicity. At last, the sauce had quiet but definite savory flavor.

Classic versions of chicken Véronique call for skinning the grapes. If I had a sous chef, so would I. But I was alone at the stove, so I left the skins on. Most recipes simply scatter the raw grapes over the finished dish. Hoping to imbue the sauce with their fruity sweetness, I halved them and stirred them in with

the tarragon at the very end, letting everything meld for just 1 minute. A bit of lemon juice brightened the sauce, as well as the faces of my tasters, who pronounced my Chicken Véronique a rousing success. I'd transformed boring poached chicken into an effortlessly elegant weeknight meal.

CHICKEN VÉRONIQUE Serves 4

- 4 (6-ounce) boneless, skinless chicken breasts, trimmed
  Salt and pepper
- ¾ cup plus 1 tablespoon low-sodium chicken broth
- 1 teaspoon cornstarch
- 2 tablespoons unsalted butter
- 1 shallot, minced
- ¾ cup dry white wine
- ⅓ cup heavy cream
- 4½ ounces seedless green grapes, halved lengthwise (¾ cup)
- 1 tablespoon chopped fresh tarragon
- ½ teaspoon lemon juice

1. Place chicken between 2 sheets of plastic wrap and pound to ½-inch thickness. Season with salt and pepper. Whisk 1 tablespoon broth and cornstarch together in small bowl to make slurry; set aside. Melt butter in 12-inch nonstick skillet over medium heat. Add chicken and cook until very lightly browned, about 2 minutes per side. Transfer chicken to plate.

2. Add shallot to now-empty skillet and cook until softened, about 1 minute. Add wine and cook until reduced to ½ cup, about 3 minutes. Add remaining ¾ cup broth, chicken, and any accumulated juice; reduce heat to medium-low; cover; and simmer until chicken registers 160 degrees, 5 to 7 minutes.

3. Transfer chicken to serving platter and tent loosely with aluminum foil. Increase heat to medium-high, add cream and cornstarch slurry to skillet, and cook until reduced to ¾ cup, 5 to 7 minutes. Stir grapes, tarragon, lemon juice, and any accumulated juice from chicken into sauce until heated through, about 1 minute. Season with salt and pepper to taste. Pour sauce over chicken. Serve.

Origin Myth: Who Was Véronique?

Culinary historians are still arguing about this. According to one account, French chef Auguste Escoffier created sole Véronique around 1904, naming the dish in honor of the composer André Messager, whose comic opera *Véronique* was then playing at the Apollo Theatre in London, just a few blocks from Escoffier's kitchen at the Carlton Hotel. Another story credits the dish to Émile Malley, chef de cuisine at the London Ritz: One evening, a line cook was preparing fish in white-wine sauce with grapes for a special dinner. When Malley checked on its progress, he discovered that the cook was overcome with emotion and unable to poach. Apparently, the fellow's wife had just delivered a baby girl—Véronique. The dish, says this version of events, was named for the newborn.

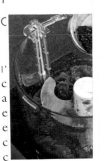

1. BLEND TOMA AND CHIPOTLE
of diced tomato
teaspoons of chi
in adobo sauce
processor.
WHY? Processir
ensures its even

5. BROWN IN
Sear the meat in
in bacon fat.
WHY? Beef plu
adds up to extr
Brown the meat
ensure a good s
sear equals goc

9. SIMMER C
Reduce the hea
simmer, covered
WHY? A nice
allows the flavo
Keeping the lid
evaporation to
for now.

Equipment Review Moderately Priced 12-Inch Skillets

We wanted a sturdy, well-designed skillet, but we didn't want to break the bank. BY TAIZETH SIERRA

A 12-INCH SKILLET is a kitchen workhorse, and a well-made one should last a lifetime. Still, our longtime favorite, the All-Clad 12-Inch Stainless Fry Pan, sells for $155, leading us to wonder if we really need to spend so much to guarantee great performance and durability.

We bought seven 12-inch skillets (see the full chart at **CooksCountry.com/jan13**), all for less than $100 and none nonstick. Six share our favorite pan's fully clad, tri-ply construction, meaning three layers, with stainless steel sandwiching aluminum. Fully clad pans usually transmit heat more gently and evenly across the cooking surface because the aluminum core conducts heat quickly while the slower stainless steel layers hold heat and reduce temperature fluctuation. The only pan in our lineup not constructed this way had a disk bottom: The three layers of metal are confined to the base of the pan, where a stainless steel–covered disk of metal is attached to the stainless steel skillet. We haven't liked disk-bottom skillets in the past, but this pan has a copper core, the best heat conductor in cookware, so it sounded promising.

We seared steaks, made pan sauces, pan-roasted chicken parts, and sautéed onions, tracking the pans' heating patterns with an infrared camera. All completed each task without catastrophe, but some made us work harder for good results. A few gave steaks a nice sear and cooked them to a perfect medium, while others ran hot, threatening to burn the meat's exterior before the interior was done. As we pan-fried chicken pieces, we encountered hot spots, so some pieces were pale yellow and others dark brown. We got similar uneven results when we browned onions. These pans required adjusting the heat more often or extra stirring. As for the disk-bottom pan, cooking was mostly even, but oil scorched around the perimeter, where the disk doesn't protect it.

Weeks of cooking and moving multiple skillets of hot chicken from burner to oven made us appreciate pans that were lighter, thus easier to handle. The weight range was 2.75 pounds (same as the All-Clad) to 4.15 pounds. We need both hands to move the heavier pans, making us grateful for helper handles. Pans with short handles (less than 8 inches) had less leverage, which made lifting hefty full skillets awkward. And while larger pans offered more space to maneuver pieces of food, the extra space often came with extra weight.

After putting the skillets through their paces on the stovetop, we tested their sturdiness. While manufacturers recommend that you never heat a pan dry or plunge a hot pan into cold water, what panicked cook has never stuck a smoking pan in a sink to avoid a fire? This "thermal shock" can warp metal and weaken the rivets and disk-bottom bond, problems that are exacerbated with impact. To see if thermal shock or impact would hurt our skillets, we heated each one to 550 degrees and then plunged each into an ice bath; we then banged it with moderate force against the sidewalk three times. While no disk or rivets came loose, some of the pans got dinged up, and thermal shock caused one to warp. The top performers came out virtually unscathed.

In the end, none of these pans matched the performance of the All-Clad pan, but one came remarkably close. At just $40, the Tramontina pan provided steady, controlled heat (it browned steak slightly unevenly) and survived our abuse testing. Because it weighs over a pound more than the All-Clad, it's somewhat harder to maneuver. Still, its performance, design, sturdy construction, and price make it an excellent choice. It's our new Best Buy.

KEY Good ★★★ Fair ★★ Poor ★

RECOMMENDED

	CRITERIA		TESTERS' NOTES

TRAMONTINA 12-Inch Tri-Ply Clad Sauté Pan
Model: 80116/509 **Price:** $39.97
Source: walmart.com
Weight: 3.9 lb
Cooking Surface Diameter: 9½ in
Handle Length: 8½ in
Material: Fully clad, stainless with aluminum core

Cooking ★★★
Handling ★★
Durability ★★★

BEST BUY

In performance, design, and construction, this skillet resembled our favorite high-end All-Clad skillet. It's big enough to pan-roast eight pieces of chicken without crowding and offers steady heat for good browning; a long handle for good leverage; and low, flaring sides to encourage evaporation. Our abuse testing left barely visible dents. Our only gripe: its weight—it's considerably heavier than the All-Clad pan.

EMERIL Pro-Clad Stainless Steel Tri-Ply 12-Inch Fry Pan
Model: E9830764 **Price:** $59.99
Source: cutleryandmore.com
Weight: 2.75 lb
Cooking Surface Diameter: 9 in
Handle Length: 7½ in
Material: Fully clad, stainless with aluminum core

Cooking ★★½
Handling ★★
Durability ★★

This pan weighed 2.75 pounds, the same as our high-end favorite pan by All-Clad. It cooked fairly well, heating just slightly faster than our winner, with food getting darker more quickly. The pan was mostly comfortable to use, but the short handle made it awkward to move a loaded pan into the oven. The pan suffered a few dings during durability testing.

CUISINART 12-Inch MultiClad Pro Skillet
Model: MCP22-30H **Price:** $69.95
Source: cuisinart.com
Weight: 3.7 lb
Cooking Surface Diameter: 10½ in
Handle Length: 8½ in
Material: Fully clad, stainless with aluminum core

Cooking ★★½
Handling ★★
Durability ★★

Fitting eight pieces of chicken in this spacious skillet was no problem, and the helper handle eased moving this somewhat hefty pan in and out of the oven. Inconsistent heating was a minor problem: The onions cooked slowly and evenly at the start, but later on hot spots appeared. Still, overall, the pan performed adequately in all of our tests.

RECOMMENDED WITH RESERVATIONS

COOL KITCHEN Integral 3 by Josef Strauss
Model: CKZ30SK **Price:** $99
Weight: 4.15 lb
Cooking Surface Diameter: 9¾ in
Handle Length: 9¾ in
Material: Fully clad, stainless with aluminum core

Cooking ★★
Handling ★
Durability ★★★

At more than 4 pounds, this was the heaviest skillet we tested. Its helper handle made it easier—but still not easy—to maneuver. It heated a little slower than other skillets we tested and slightly unevenly. The pan sailed through the durability tests unscathed.

CALPHALON Tri-Ply Stainless Steel 12-Inch Omelette Pan
Model: 1767730 **Price:** $94.95
Weight: 3.2 lb
Cooking Surface Diameter: 9¾ in
Handle Length: 8¼ in
Material: Fully clad, stainless with aluminum core

Cooking ★★
Handling ★★
Durability ★★

This pan was acceptable in every test but never impressive. It heats a little fast, requiring extra vigilance to avoid overbrowning or burning. In the durability testing it got a little dinged up. (Although the manufacturer labels it an "omelette pan," it's meant to be used as an ordinary skillet, not merely for omelets.)

T-FAL Ultimate Stainless Steel Copper Skillet
Model: C8360764 **Price:** $36.52
Weight: 3.3 lb
Cooking Surface Diameter: 10 in
Handle Length: 6¼ in
Material: Disk bottom; stainless steel pan with copper and stainless steel disk

Cooking ★
Handling ★
Durability ★

We hoped the copper disk would make this pan a star performer. Oh well. While it heated slowly and for the most part evenly, there were hot spots where the disk ended. Also, grease that splashed onto the thin, stainless steel sides scorched on in an instant. The short handle flexed and was too hot to hold.

When Price Is No Object
The All-Clad 12-Inch Stainless Fry Pan, which sells for about $155, is our top-rated traditional skillet. It weighs 2.75 pounds, with a cooking surface that measures 9¾ inches.

THE GOLD STANDARD
Worth every penny.

CHILI C
Serves 6 to
If the ba
spoons o
vegetab
corn mu
cornbrea
to serve
cubed a
wedges,

1 (14
2 te
ch
4 sli
1 (3
ch
se
cu
Sa
1 on
1 jal
an
3 tal
4 ga
1½ te
½ te
4 cu
1 tal
2 tal

1. Pr
juice an

Taste Test Ready-Made Pie Crusts

Many store-bought pie crust options are grim: dense and doughy or greasy
and cracker-crisp. Could we find a crust that's closer to homemade? BY HANNAH CROWLEY

HANDS DOWN, HOMEMADE pie crust is worth the effort, but we don't always have the time. Enter premade crust—it may not be Grandma's, but it's fast and easy. When we last tasted commercially made crusts, we could recommend only one product, and with reservations at that. Since then, more have entered the market. Could we find one that is convenient *and* delicious?

We put eight products to the test, choosing a mix of frozen and refrigerated doughs, including three sold in sheets and five ready in aluminum pie plates (we discounted box mixes; if we have to bring out the mixing bowl, we'll just make it ourselves). All the packages make two single-crust pies or one double-crust pie. We ate the shells baked plain, in single-crust pumpkin pies, and in double-crust apple pies, evaluating them on flavor, texture, capacity, and handling. Our benchmark was homemade crust: buttery, tender, and flaky.

A premade crust should be easy to use—after all, convenience is the point. That's the appeal of crusts sold in throwaway pie plates: Just fill and bake. Unfortunately, they were too small for our pumpkin pie recipe; one-third of the filling didn't fit. A standard pie plate is 9 inches in diameter. These pans claim to be the same, but when we measured them, they were 8½ to 8¾ inches—a significant disadvantage.

Another drawback? How could we make double-crust pies from crusts already shaped to fit pie plates? The instructions recommend flipping a second preshaped shell on top of a filled bottom crust. For every brand but one, sealing the already-molded edges was awkward. Worse, the top crusts were too small to stretch over the filling and seal with bottom crusts. In addition, because heat penetrates faster through flimsy aluminum pans, the crusts burned in spots; standard recipe baking times were inaccurate. To solve some of these problems, we attempted to transfer the dough from the aluminum pie plates they came in to our favorite Pyrex pie plate. They were too small to fit. We tried to roll them out more, but the dough was finicky and difficult to enlarge. For all of these reasons, we don't recommend pan-style crusts for double-crust pies, and even for single-crust pies we can recommend them only with reservations.

How did the other styles of premade crust handle? Two of the roll (or tinless) crusts were refrigerated; one was frozen. The refrigerated versions unrolled effortlessly, without tearing, and were easy to shape, forming perfect flutes and producing windowsill-worthy pies. The frozen roll must be defrosted for 3 hours (it can then be refrigerated for up to three days), and it sometimes took a little coaxing to unroll without tearing.

Convenience, of course, isn't the only factor. Taste and texture are also decisive. Manufacturers use different types of fat in premade crusts: shortening, margarine, lard, palm or canola oil, or a combination. Each fat has a different melting point and crystalline structure, which affect the taste and texture of the crust. A product using all shortening had a "delightfully light and flaky" crust but also, no surprise, the bland, fatty taste of shortening. Two products blended shortening and margarine to glean the flaky benefits of the former with the wannabe butter flavor of the latter; unfortunately, these were dense and tasted "processed." Two used lard, which has a neutral taste and makes for very flaky crust; alas, one added too much sugar, the other too much salt. The two crusts we preferred used palm oil for a tender, flaky texture; they were neither too savory nor too sweet, and they didn't taste artificial.

In the end, we concluded that options have definitely improved. We found one product we could recommend and six we could recommend with reservations. Our two top picks were from the same company—Wholly Wholesome. We preferred the taste and texture of Wholly Wholesome Organic Traditional 9" Pie Shells ($3.59), but the product suffered from all the pan-style disadvantages described earlier. We can recommend it for single crust pies only and with a major reservation: You will likely throw away some filling.

Our top pick overall is Wholly Wholesome 9" Certified Organic Traditional Bake at Home Rolled Pie Dough ($5.99—it costs more than the pan version because the production process is less mechanized). This pie dough is "tender" and "subtly sweet," and it holds an entire batch of filling. Plus, we could use our own pie plate and depend on recipe baking times.

RECOMMENDED	CRITERIA		TESTERS' NOTES
WHOLLY WHOLESOME 9" Certified Organic Traditional Bake at Home Rolled Pie Dough **Price:** $5.99 **Style:** Roll **Fat:** Palm oil 	Flavor Texture Capacity Handling	★★★ ★★ ★★★ ★★	Slightly less flaky than the pan version from the same maker, this dough was "subtly sweet, rich," and "tender." It fluted well but takes a little care to unroll (sold frozen, it requires 3 hours of defrosting). It's an acceptable substitute if you don't have time to make a homemade crust.
RECOMMENDED WITH RESERVATIONS			
WHOLLY WHOLESOME Organic Traditional 9" Pie Shells **Price:** $3.59 **Style:** Pan **Fat:** Palm oil 	Flavor Texture Capacity Handling	★★★ ★★★ ★ ★★	In texture and taste, this crust was our favorite—"light and flaky," "crispy but yielding," with a "toasty," "buttery" flavor. But the shell was too small to hold fillings for standard 9-inch pie crust recipes. It was also slightly too dry to flute when we made a double-crust pie.
PILLSBURY Pie Crusts **Price:** $3.49 **Style:** Roll **Fat:** Partially hydrogenated lard	Flavor Texture Capacity Handling	★ ★ ★★★ ★★★	Our previous favorite, formerly known as Pillsbury Just Unroll!, excelled at handling, producing perfect-looking pies that were dead easy to shape but baked up "thin," "brittle," and "cracker-like." Some found the dough "too salty" and disliked the "oily" finish.
MARIE CALLENDER'S 2 Deep Dish Pie Shells **Price:** $2.99 **Style:** Pan **Fat:** Vegetable shortening	Flavor Texture Capacity Handling	★ ★★ ★★ ★★★	These crusts were "delightfully light," but were "devoid of flavor." Said one taster: "Tastes like shortening," which was, in fact, the second ingredient. They handled the best of all pan-style crusts during our double-crust pie testing.
PET-RITZ Pie Crusts by Pillsbury **Price:** $3.69 **Style:** Pan **Fat:** Partially hydrogenated lard	Flavor Texture Capacity Handling	★★ ★★ ★★ ★	These "light" yet "firm" crusts had the "sandy," "crisp" crumble of "shortbread," with a "sweet, cookie-like flavor." Yet they became "mushy" when filled with pumpkin pie filling.
MRS. SMITH'S Deep Dish Pie Crusts **Price:** $2.99 **Style:** Pan **Fat:** Vegetable shortening, margarine	Flavor Texture Capacity Handling	★★ ★★ ★ ★★	These tightly packed crusts were "dense" and "short," with a "nice fatty crumble," but they turned mushy under pumpkin pie filling. The flavor was lackluster: "inoffensive" but "neutral." They baked without shrinking or tearing.
ORONOQUE ORCHARDS 9" Deep Dish Pie Crusts **Price:** $3.59 **Style:** Pan **Fat:** Vegetable shortening, margarine	Flavor Texture Capacity Handling	★★ ★★ ★ ★★	Tasters found this crust virtually indistinguishable from Mrs. Smith's, which makes both products (the company said there are slight ingredient differences), with similarly "short" and "dense" crusts that were "basic," if somewhat "bland." Pumpkin pie filling turned the crust soggy.
NOT RECOMMENDED			
IMMACULATE BAKING CO. Ready-to-Bake Pie Crusts **Price:** $3.99 **Style:** Roll **Fat:** Palm fruit and canola oils	Flavor Texture Capacity Handling	½ ½ ★★★ ★★★	This dough handled well but had a strong "sour" flavor: One taster called it a "deadly aftertaste"; another wrote "rancid." Cultured whey is added, which could produce a sour, fermented flavor.

Looking for a Recipe

Baked Orange-Ginger Chicken

Becky Sorenson, Concord, Mass.

Back in the early 1980s, I used to shop at Goodies to Go, a gourmet food shop in Lexington, Massachusetts, that sold prepared foods and bakery items. My favorite thing was the orange-ginger chicken. An employee told me that the chicken was marinated for a couple of days in a puree of fresh oranges, brown sugar, soy sauce, and fresh ginger. The chicken was fall-off-the-bone tender. If anyone else remembers this chicken and has a recipe, please share.

Matrimonial Cake

Gilles Marchand, Halifax, Nova Scotia

I'd love to learn how to make a treat popular in Western Canada called matrimonial cake. It's actually a date-and-oat bar (not sure why it's called "cake" or what the matrimonial part is). Anyway, the bars are great for an afternoon snack with coffee. Does anyone have a good recipe?

Avocado Pie

Ronnie Fishman, New York, N.Y.

A college roommate of mine from California used to make a wonderful pie out of avocado and sweetened condensed milk. It was rich, creamy, and just sweet enough. We all thought it was weird back then, but it really is an ingenious way to eat a healthy dessert. I'm hoping a fellow reader will have a recipe.

Pineapple Cream Pie

Toni Marino, Minneapolis, Minn.

When I was younger, my mom would take us to the Woolworth store in downtown Minneapolis, where we'd have lunch in the cafeteria. I always ordered the pineapple cream pie. It was so good and so refreshing. I haven't seen or heard of it since. Thank you in advance for anything you can find out for me about this pie.

Curried Fruit Bake

Andrea Mooney, Quincy, Mass.

Back in the 1950s, my mom used to make a delicious dish she called curried fruit bake. It had canned peaches, pineapple, and maraschino cherries and was baked with brown sugar, butter, maple syrup, and curry powder. It was considered quite exotic at the time. She always served it with ham steaks. Does anyone have a recipe?

FIND THE ROOSTER!

A tiny version of this rooster has been hidden in the pages of this issue. Write to us with its location and we'll enter you in a random drawing. The first correct entry drawn will win our top-rated moderately priced 12-inch skillet (see page 30), and each of the next five will receive a free one-year subscription to *Cook's Country*. To enter, visit **CooksCountry.com/rooster** by January 31, 2013, or write to Rooster, *Cook's Country*, P.O. Box 470739, Brookline, MA 02447. Include your name and address. Lisa Herren of Franklin, Va., found the rooster in the August/September 2012 issue on page 25 and won our winning rolling pin.

U.S. POSTAL SERVICE STATEMENT OF OWNERSHIP, MANAGEMENT AND CIRCULATION

1. Publication Title: Cook's Country; 2. Publication No. 1552-1990; 3. Filing Date: 9/15/12; 4. Issue Frequency: Dec/Jan, Feb/Mar, Apr/May, Jun/Jul, Aug/Sep, Oct/Nov; 5. No. of Issues Published Annually: 6; 6. Annual Subscription Price: $29.70; 7. Complete Mailing Address of Known Office of Publication: 17 Station Street, Brookline, MA 02445; 8. Complete Mailing Address of Headquarters or General Business Office of Publisher: 17 Station Street, Brookline, MA 02445; 9. Full Names and Complete Mailing Address of Publisher, Editor and Managing Editor: Publisher: Christopher Kimball, 17 Station Street, Brookline, MA 02445; Editor: Jack Bishop, 17 Station Street, Brookline, MA 02445; Managing Editor: Scott Kathan, 17 Station Street, Brookline, MA 02445; 10. Owner: Boston Common Press Limited Partnership, Christopher Kimball, 17 Station Street, Brookline, MA 02445; 11. Known Bondholders, Mortgagees, and Other Securities: None; 12. Tax Status: Has Not Changed During Preceding 12 Months; 13. Publication Title: Cook's Country; 14. Issue Date for Circulation Data Below: August/September 2012; 15a. Total Number of Copies: 368,387 (Aug/Sep 2012: 366,553); b. Paid Circulation: (1) Mailed Outside-County Paid Subscriptions Stated on PS Form 3541: 267,794 (Aug/Sep 2012: 259,996); (2) Mailed In-County Paid Subscriptions Stated on PS Form 3541: 0 (Aug/Sep 2012: 0); (3) Paid Distribution Outside the Mails Including Sales Through Dealers and Carriers, Street Vendors, Counter Sales, and Other Paid Distribution Outside the USPS: 28,125 (Aug/Sep 2012: 28,716); (4) Paid Distribution by Other Classes of Mail through the USPS: 0 (Aug/Sep 2012: 0); c. Total Paid Distribution: 295,919 (Aug/Sep 2012: 288,712); d. Free or Nominal Rate Distribution: (1) Free or Nominal Rate Outside-County Copies Included on PS Form 3541: 1,775 (Aug/Sep 2012: 1,626); (2) Free or Nominal Rate In-County Copies Included on Form PS 3541: 0 (Aug/Sep 2012: 0); (3) Free or Nominal Rate Copies Mailed at Other Classes Through the USPS: 0 (Aug/Sep 2012: 0); (4) Free or Nominal Rate Distribution Outside the Mail: 515 (Aug/Sep 2012: 515); e. Total Free or Nominal Rate Distribution: 2,290 (Aug/Sep 2012: 2,141); f. Total Distribution: 298,209 (Aug/Sep 2012: 290,853); g. Copies Not Distributed: 70,178 (Aug/Sep 2012: 75,700); h. Total: 368,387 (Aug/Sep 2012: 366,553); i. Percent Paid: 99.23% (Aug/Sep 2012: 99.26%).

STEAK FINGERS Serves 8 as an appetizer

Jerry Little, Nampa, Idaho

- 1 (20-ounce) jar dill pickles
- ½ teaspoon baking soda
- ¼ cup steak sauce, plus extra for serving
- 2 tablespoons paprika
- 1 tablespoon Worcestershire sauce
- 2 teaspoons garlic powder
- 2 pounds beef flap meat, trimmed and cut against grain into 4 by ½-inch strips
- 2 cups all-purpose flour
- 1 tablespoon pepper
- 3 quarts peanut or vegetable oil

1. Set wire rack inside rimmed baking sheet. Line platter with triple layer of paper towels. Drain pickles, reserving 1½ cups juice; reserve pickles. Combine pickle juice and baking soda in large bowl. When foaming subsides, whisk in steak sauce, 1 tablespoon paprika, Worcestershire, and 1 teaspoon garlic powder. Add beef and toss to combine. Cover and refrigerate for 30 minutes.

2. Combine flour, pepper, remaining 1 tablespoon paprika, and remaining 1 teaspoon garlic powder in large bowl. Remove beef from marinade (discard marinade) and pat dry with paper towels. Toss beef in flour mixture to coat thoroughly, transfer to prepared rack, and let sit for 10 minutes. Return beef to flour mixture, toss to coat, and return to wire rack.

3. Add oil to large Dutch oven until it measures 2 inches deep and heat over medium-high heat to 375 degrees. Add half of beef to oil and fry, stirring occasionally, until golden brown and crispy, about 2 minutes. Transfer to prepared platter. Return oil to 375 degrees and repeat. Serve with pickles, passing extra steak sauce separately.

SCRAPPLE Serves 4 to 6

Molly Hayes, Scranton, Pa.

- 3 tablespoons unsalted butter
- 1 small onion, chopped fine
- 1 pound bulk breakfast sausage
- 1 teaspoon ground sage
- ½ teaspoon ground fennel
- 3 cups water
- 1 cup yellow cornmeal
- 1¼ teaspoons salt
- 1 teaspoon pepper
- 2 tablespoons vegetable oil

1. Grease 8½ by 4½-inch loaf pan. Melt 1 tablespoon butter in Dutch oven over medium-high heat. Add onion and cook until lightly browned, about 5 minutes. Add sausage, sage, and fennel and cook, breaking sausage into small pieces with spoon, until no longer pink, about 5 minutes.

2. Add water. Whisk in cornmeal, salt, and pepper. Bring to boil, reduce heat to medium-low, and simmer, stirring constantly, until thickened and mixture pulls away from sides of pot, about 3 minutes. Off heat, stir in remaining 2 tablespoons butter. Scrape mixture into prepared pan. Smooth top and tap firmly on counter. Let cool completely, then cover with plastic wrap and refrigerate until firm, at least 3 hours.

3. To serve, turn out scrapple onto cutting board and slice into 12 equal pieces. Heat oil in 12-inch nonstick skillet over medium-high heat until just smoking. Add 6 scrapple slices and cook until well browned, about 3 minutes per side. Repeat with remaining scrapple. Serve.

White Fruitcake

Our White Fruitcake is citrusy, vibrant, and light—plus it doesn't require months of advance planning for the traditional brandy soak.

To make this cake you will need:

- ½ **cup orange juice**
- 2 **pounds glacéed fruit (4 cups)**
- 1½ **cups (6¾ ounces) slivered almonds**
- 1 **cup (3 ounces) sweetened shredded coconut**
- 2 **cups (10 ounces) all-purpose flour**
- 1 **teaspoon baking powder**
- 1 **teaspoon salt**
- 12 **tablespoons unsalted butter, softened**
- 1 **cup (7 ounces) granulated sugar**
- 4 **large eggs, room temperature**
  Confectioners' sugar

Adjust oven rack to lower-middle position and heat oven to 275 degrees. Generously grease 12-cup tube pan and line bottom with parchment paper. Microwave orange juice in medium bowl until hot, about 30 seconds. Add glacéed fruit and stir to coat completely. Let cool completely, about 15 minutes, stirring occasionally. Process 1 cup almonds, coconut, and ¼ cup flour in food processor until finely ground, about 1 minute. Transfer to second medium bowl and whisk in remaining 1¾ cups flour, baking powder, and salt. Using stand mixer fitted with paddle, beat butter and granulated sugar on medium-high speed until pale and fluffy, about 3 minutes. Add eggs, one at a time, and beat until combined. Reduce speed to low and add flour mixture in 3 additions, alternating with glacéed fruit in 2 additions, scraping down bowl as needed. Give batter final stir by hand. Pour batter into prepared pan and smooth top. Sprinkle evenly with remaining ½ cup almonds. Bake until skewer inserted in center comes out clean, about 2 hours, rotating pan halfway through baking. Let cake cool in pan on wire rack for 30 minutes. Remove cake from pan, discarding parchment and reinverting so almonds are on top, and let cool completely, about 3 hours. Dust lightly with confectioners' sugar. Serve.

Recipe Index